PAINT SHOP PRO 6
POWER!

WRITTEN BY
LORI J. DAVIS

Paint Shop Pro 6 Power!

Library of Congress Catalog Number: 99-068119

ISBN: 0-9662889-2-0

5   4   3   2   1

Educational facilities, companies, and organizations interested in multiple copies or licensing of this book should contact the publisher for quantity discount information. Training manuals, CD-ROMs, and portions of this book are also available individually or can be tailored for specific needs.

MUSKA&LIPMAN

Muska & Lipman Publishing
2645 Erie Avenue, Suite 41
Cincinnati, Ohio 45208
www.muskalipman.com
publisher@muskalipman.com

This book is composed in Melior, Columbia, Helvetica, and Courier typefaces using QuarkXpress 4.0.4, Adobe PhotoShop 5.0.2, and Adobe Illustrator 8.0. Created in Cincinnati, Ohio, in the United States of America

About the Author

Lori Davis

Lori Davis, a former college teacher and former software manual writer, makes her living writing. She discovered Paint Shop Pro a few years ago, when she was designing a personal Web page on gardening. PSP soon took center stage, and the gardening site was just about abandoned in favor of a PSP site.

Lori is one of the PSP instructors at ZDU and is also one of the contributing authors of Andy Shafran's award-winning book, *Creating Paint Shop Pro Web Graphics* (Muska & Lipman).

When Lori isn't writing or experimenting with PSP, she enjoys photography, knitting, and (yes) gardening. She lives with her husband, Larry, and their two cats in a very small house on a very small lot near a very big ocean.

Dedication

To my creative spouse and siblings—Larry, Mark, Sher, and John Paul—who work in words, wood, fabric, and photons.

Acknowledgments

There are so many wonderful people I've met in the online PSP community that I'd be afraid of accidentally leaving someone out if I tried to list them all. Even though I won't mention you all by name, please know that I appreciate both your creativity and your friendship.

Thanks to Todd Matzke of Jasc Software for his comments and suggestions and for answering my questions quickly and going out of his way to research some points.

Special thanks to the book's technical editor, Sarah Arnott, and to the PSP staff at ZDU, particularly my fellow instructors Pat Kalbaugh and Nancy Dixon, and one of my earliest and dearest PSP partners in work and play, Barb Jarjoura. A hearty round of applause, too, for my fellow contributing authors for *Creating Paint Shop Pro Web Graphics*: Brad Castle and Robin Kirkey, as well as Pat Kalbaugh.

The editorial folks at Muska & Lipman have been a joy to work with. Thanks to Elizabeth Bruns for holding everything together. An extra special thanks to Ben Milstead, who worked on an earlier version of this book, and to Julie MacLean. Great working with you, Julie!

Finally, thanks to Andy Shafran for helping to get me excited about PSP in the first place. (Audrey helped on that score, too.)

Credits

Publisher
Andy Shafran

Editorial Services Manager
Elizabeth A. Bruns

Managing Editor
Hope Stephan

Development & Copy Editor
Julie MacLean

Technical Editor
Sarah Arnott

Proofreader
Audrey Grant

Cover Designers
Dave Abney &
Michael Williams

Production Manager
Cathie Tibbetts

Production Team
DOV Graphics
Michelle Frey
Stephanie Japs
Tammy Norton

Printer
C.J. Krehbiel Co.

Contents

Introduction

Welcome to *Paint Shop Pro 6 Power!* This book explores the tools that you, an experienced PSP user, can use to create exciting graphics for computer display or printing.

This introduction briefly outlines what you'll find in the various chapters and describes conventions that will be used throughout the book.

What You'll Find in This Book

This book will provide you with an in-depth look at how to use Paint Shop Pro. Some of the basics will be mentioned at least briefly, but most of the content goes beyond the basics. In many cases, you'll look not only at *how* things work, but *why* they work the way they do.

Who This Book Is For

This book is for graphics professionals and experienced nonprofessionals who are interested in using PSP for computer graphics and/or printed graphics. It assumes that you are already at least somewhat familiar with PSP or a similar graphics program. If you are not yet familiar with PSP or a similar program, you might want to start out instead with a more basic book on PSP, such as Muska & Lipman's *Creating Paint Shop Pro Web Graphics*.

How This Book is Organized

This book includes twelve chapters:

▶ Chapter 1, "Basic Drawing and Painting Tools." Investigate the subtleties of PSP's most basic tools.

▶ Chapter 2, "Advanced Painting Tools." Master PSP's powerful editing tools to produce special effects, retouch photorealistic images, and clone figures.

▶ Chapter 3, "Being Selective." Get acquainted with PSP's versatile selection tools to restrict editing to only part of your image or to isolate a figure for use in another image.

▶ Chapter 4, "Mastering Layers and Blend Modes." Discover how easy it is to achieve complex effects with layers.

▶ Chapter 5, "Working with Vectors." Find out how vector graphics enable you to create both simple and complex drawings with a minimum of effort.

▶ Chapter 6, "PSP Effects." Experiment with PSP's various effects to add depth and interest to your images.

▶ Chapter 7, "PSP Deformations." Utilize PSP's Deformation operations and the Deform tool to add perspective and other effects to your images.

▶ Chapter 8, "Filters." Examine PSP's built-in filters and third-party plugin filters, and take a first look at User Defined Filters.

▶ Chapter 9, "Making Adjustments." Explore PSP's tools for correcting the color, brightness, and contrast in your digital photos and other digital art.

▶ Chapter 10, "Selections, Masks, and Channels." Learn how advanced selection techniques, masking, and channel operations can help you to create effects that would otherwise be difficult or close to impossible to achieve.

▶ Chapter 11, "Adding to Your Toolkit." Create your own PSP tools, including paper textures, custom brushes, Picture Tubes, and User Defined Filters.

▶ Chapter 12, "Animation Shop." Try out Animation Shop, Jasc Software's GIF animation program that comes bundled with PSP.

Conventions Used in This Book

The following conventions are used in this book:

▶ For convenience, I'll usually refer to operations involving the primary mouse button with phrases such as "the left mouse button" and "left-clicking." For operations involving the secondary mouse button, I'll usually use phrases such as "the right mouse button" and "right-clicking." Please keep this in mind if you have your mouse set up as a left-hand mouse.

▶ A single-layered image with an opaque background will be referred to as "a flat image," and a multilayered image will be referred to as either "a multilayered image," "an image that has layers," or "a layered image." The opaque Background present in all flat images and in some layered images will be referred to as either "the Background layer" or "the Background" (with a capital *B*). Other layers—layers that allow transparency—will be referred to as "real layers" or simply as "layers."

▶ All URLs mentioned in the book appear in **boldface**.

▶ Hotkeys for menu items are indicated in boldface when you're specifically being instructed to choose menu commands.

Besides these terminological and typographic conventions, the book also features the following special displays for different types of important text:

TIP
Text formatted like this provides a helpful tip relevant to the topic being discussed in the main text.

CAUTION
Warnings about actions or operations that could make irreversible changes to your image or might lead to consequences that are potentially confusing are displayed as a "CAUTION." Be sure to read Caution text—it can help you avoid some very troublesome pitfalls!

NOTE
Notes highlight other interesting or useful information that relates to the topic under discussion in the main text.

Keeping the Book's Content Current

For updates, corrections, and other information related to the content of the book, head out to **http://www.psppower.com/**.

Images Used in This Book

All photographs in the book are my own copyrighted photos, taken either with my trusty 20-year-old Pentax K1000 SLR or my equally trusty 1-year-old Kodak DC120 digital camera. Slides, negatives, and prints were scanned on a Microtek X6EL.

Other images are my own drawings and simple text graphics. Many of these images include Jasc Software's Picture Tubes, as well as tubes that I've made myself. The rose-tube bouquet in Chapter 2, "Advanced Painting Tools," also features the roseleaf tube by scullycj (**http://www.geocities.com/Heartland/Plains/6524/tubes.html**).

Paint Shop Pro Quick Start

This section of the book provides a quick introduction to PSP's interface and a brief summary of what's new in PSP6. If you're unfamiliar with PSP, this section will help you get started. And even if you're experienced with PSP version 5 or earlier, you'll probably want to at least skim this section, since PSP's interface has changed a bit between versions 5 and 6.

The PSP Workspace and Interface

PSP's workspace, the large solid-colored area in which you do your image editing work, is surrounded by PSP's major palettes and menu (see Figure QS.1): the Tool Palette, Color Palette, the toolbar, and the menubar. At the bottom of the workspace is PSP's status bar.

Fig. QS.1
The PSP workspace, major palettes, and the status bar.

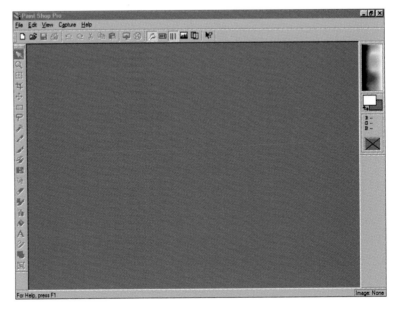

The Tool Palette

The Tool Palette, which appears by default along the left edge of the workspace, contains all of PSP's image editing and selection tools. Figure QS.2 shows the Tool Palette displayed horizontally.

Fig. QS.2
The Tool Palette.

To select a tool, click its icon on the Tool Palette. The individual tools are discussed in various chapters of this book.

The Color Palette

The Color Palette, which by default appears on the right edge of the workspace, enables you to select the active colors for drawing and painting (see Figure QS.3).

Fig. QS.3
The Color Palette.

The Color Palette has three panes: the Available Colors panel at the top, the Active Colors panel in the middle, and the Color at the bottom:

▶ **Available Colors panel**—Position the cursor over this multicolored panel, and the cursor changes to the Dropper tool. Click with the Dropper to set the foreground color (the color used when you click or drag with a drawing or painting tool). Right-click with the Dropper to set the background color (the color used when you right-click or right-drag with a drawing or painting tool).

▶ **Active Colors panel**—This panel contains the Foreground Color swatch (on the panel's upper left), the Background Color swatch (on the panel's lower right), and the Color Switcher (the double-headed bent arrow pointing to the two swatches).

Change the foreground color by clicking the Foreground Color swatch, which opens the Select Color from Palette dialog box (for images with 256 colors or less) or the Color dialog box (for images with color depth greater than 8 bit), where you can select a new color.

Change the background color similarly, by clicking the Background Color swatch.

Switch the foreground and background colors with each other by clicking the Color Switcher.

TIP

You can also change colors by right-clicking on the Foreground Color or Background Color swatch, opening the Recent Colors dialog box. In this dialog box, you can choose from both a set of standard colors and the most recently used colors.

The Recent Colors dialog box is available not only on the Color Palette, but also in any dialog box that includes a color swatch control.

▶ **Current Color panel**—This panel displays information about whatever color the Dropper tool is currently positioned over. Depending on PSP's current preference settings, either the color's RGB (Red/Green/Blue) or HSL (Highlight/Saturation/Lightness) values are displayed. Below these values, a color swatch containing the color is displayed.

When the Dropper tool is not in use or is not positioned over a color, the color swatch is grey with an X through it, and the RGB or HSL values are blank.

The Toolbar

The toolbar, which by default appears toward the top of the workspace, enables you to access the most commonly used PSP commands and palettes (see Figure QS.4).

Fig. QS.4
The toolbar.

TIP

You can customize the toolbar, adding or removing icons for the various operations and palettes. To customize the toolbar, choose **F**ile, Preferences, Customize Toolbar.

PAINT SHOP PRO QUICK START

Floatable Palettes

Each of these palettes—the Tool Palette, the Color Palette, and the toolbar—is floatable and dockable. To float the Tool Palette or toolbar, drag the handle on the palette's left or top. (The handle appears on the left when the palette is currently docked and horizontal. The handle appears on the top when the palette is currently docked and vertical.) To float the Color Palette, drag on an empty grey area of the palette.

You can reposition a floating palette on the workspace by dragging its title bar. To redock one of these floating palettes, just drag it to one of the side edges or top of the workspace.

TIP

You also can float a floatable palette by double-clicking the palette in any area that is empty. To redock the palette, double-click an empty area on the palette again.

The Menubar

The menubar, which appears at the very top of the workspace, contains menus for accessing PSP commands and operations. As Figure QS.5 shows, the menubar includes menus labeled **F**ile, **E**dit, **V**iew, **I**mage, **C**olors, **L**ayers, **S**elections, **M**asks, **C**apture, **W**indow, and **H**elp.

Fig. QS.5
The menubar.

You will explore most of these menus throughout this book.

TIP

You can access PSP's tools and palettes, along with most of the commands and operations available on the menubar, with keyboard shortcuts. See Appendix E, "PSP Keyboard Shortcuts" for listings.

The Status Bar

At the very bottom of the PSP workspace is the status bar, which displays a variety of information:

▶ When you mouse-over a tool's icon on the Tool Palette, a description of the tool is displayed.

▶ When you mouse-over an icon on the toolbar, a description of the relevant PSP command or operation is displayed.

▶ When you mouse-over areas of the Color Palette, the status bar indicates what the various parts of the palette are for.

▶ When you position the mouse cursor in an image canvas, the status bar displays the coordinates of the cursor, the dimensions of the image, and the amount of memory being used to edit the image. Other useful information might also be displayed, depending on which one of PSP's tools is active.

Using the Tool Options Palette

One of the most important palettes to understand and master is the Tool Options palette: the palette you use to set options for PSP's tools. Each tool on the Tool Palette has its own version of the Tool Options palette. Depending on the tool, you'll find either two or three tabs on the Tool Options palette. The leftmost tab is the tool's main tab. Figure QS.6 shows the Tool tab for the Selection tool. Notice that this tab is labeled with the tool's icon as it appears on the Tool Palette.

Fig. QS.6
An example of the Tool tab on the Tool Options palette.

TIP

When you have an image open and the Tool Options palette is not displayed, just press the letter O key on your keyboard or click the Tool Options palette icon on the toolbar.

To toggle the Tool Options palette off, press O or click the palette's icon on the toolbar again.

PAINT SHOP PRO QUICK START

The Tool Options Tab

For tools that have more controls than can fit on a single tab, there's also a Tool Options tab. Figure QS.7 shows the Tool Options tab for the Flood Fill tool.

Fig. QS.7
An example of the Tool Options tab on the Tool Options palette.

NOTE

The Tool Options tab is not active when the Fill Style of the Flood Fill tool is set to Solid Color on the Tool Options palette's main tab. This is because all of the controls needed for Solid Color are present on the palette's main tab.

For all other Fill Styles, the Tool Options tab is active.

Numeric Edit Controls

Some settings on the Tool Options palette of some tools are made with numeric edit controls, like the one shown in Figure QS.8.

Fig. QS.8
A numeric edit control.

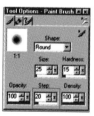

A numeric edit control provides you with several ways to set a numeric value:

▶ Type a value in the Number Box textbox.

▶ Click or drag in the Meter Box (directly below the Number Box).

▶ Click one of the spin controls (to the right of the Number Box).

▶ Click the Slider button (to the right of the spin controls), and then drag the slider on the resulting pop-up slider bar.

Numeric edit controls appear in several PSP dialog boxes, in addition to the Tool Options palette.

The Cursor and Tablet Tab

All tools have a Cursor and Tablet tab, shown in Figure QS.9.

Fig. QS.9
The Cursor and Tablet tab on the Tool Options palette.

This tab contains controls for setting options for the cursor and for pressure-sensitive tablets (the tablet controls are active only if you have a pressure-sensitive tablet). If you make a change to the options on this tab, the settings remain in effect—even if you switch to a different tool—until you change the settings again.

The Tool Selection Button

Something else that's available on any Tool Options palette is the Tool Selection button, on the upper right of the main tab. Click this button to access a drop-down menu of all the tools available on the Tool Palette. This handy feature makes it possible to access the tools even if you have the Tool Palette turned off (by choosing **V**iew, **T**ool Bars). When you want to select a tool, just click the Tool Selection button and make your selection. Figure QS.10 shows the menu that opens when you click the Tool Selection button.

Fig. QS.10
The Tool Selection menu, accessible from the Tool Options palette.

Auto Rollup

Besides being able to toggle the Tool Options palette on and off, you can enable Auto Rollup by clicking the rollup lock button at the right of the palette's title bar (just to the left of the palette window's Close button). Click this button again to disable Auto Rollup.

With Auto Rollup on, the palette will automatically minimize to its title bar when you move the cursor away from the palette and start working in another window, such as an image canvas or another palette.

NOTE

Auto Rollup is also available for the Histogram window (discussed in Chapter 9, "Making Adjustments") and for the Layer Palette (discussed in Chapter 4, "Mastering Layers and Blend Modes").

What's New in PSP6

Besides changes to the interface, here are some of the most important new features of PSP6:

▶ Editable text and text on a path (discussed in Chapter 5, "Working with Vectors").

▶ Editable gradients for the Flood Fill tool (discussed in Chapter 2, "Advanced Painting Tools").

▶ Vector layers and objects (discussed in Chapter 5, "Working with Vectors").

▶ New effects (discussed in Chapter 6, "PSP Effects") and deformations (discussed in Chapter 7, "PSP Deformations").

▶ Adjustment layers (discussed in Chapter 9, "Making Adjustments").

▶ The Picture Frame Wizard (discussed in Chapter 11, "Adding to Your Toolkit").

▶ Better integration of PSP and Animation Shop (discussed in Chapter 12, "Animation Shop").

▶ Built-in support for more brands and models of digital cameras (discussed in Appendix A, "Acquiring Images into PSP").

▶ Transparent GIF Export facility and JPEG Optimization facility (discussed in Appendix C, "Web Graphics").

▶ Digital watermarking (not discussed in this book but can be found in the *PSP User's Guide* included with the PSP software).

▶ Multiple image printing (not discussed in this book but can be found in the *PSP User's Guide*).

1

Basic Drawing and Painting Tools

The first tools that you're likely to use in Paint Shop Pro (PSP) are the basic drawing and painting tools, such as the Paintbrush, Airbrush, Preset Shapes, the Draw tool, and the Text tool. In this chapter, you'll explore these simple drawing and painting tools by looking at both the basic functions and the more advanced features of each one. For now, you'll examine painting and drawing only on raster layers. In Chapter 5, "Working with Vectors," you'll examine vector drawing.

Throughout this chapter, keep in mind that most of the drawing and painting tools behave differently, depending on whether you use them with the left mouse button or the right mouse button. If you draw or paint with the left mouse button depressed, the current foreground color is used. If you draw or paint with the right mouse button depressed, however, the current background color is used. (Refer to the Quick Start section of this book or to the PSP documentation if you're unsure how to select the foreground and background colors.)

Here's what you'll be exploring in this chapter:

▶ Using brushes and paper textures
▶ Drawing lines and shapes
▶ Adding text to images

The Paintbrush and Airbrush

The Paintbrush and Airbrush are the most basic painting tools. They differ from each other only in the way they apply "paint" to an image. The Paintbrush applies paint in dabs—keeping the mouse in one place while continuously holding down either mouse button, which is no different than simply single-clicking the mouse button. The Airbrush, on the other hand, applies paint like an aerosol spraycan—if you keep the mouse in one place and hold down one of the mouse buttons, paint is applied until you release the mouse button. In other respects, however, these two tools are very similar. With either one of these tools selected, open the Tool Options palette by pressing O (if the palette isn't already visible) to see the controls shown in Figure 1.1.

Fig. 1.1
The Tool Options palette for the Paintbrush. The same set of controls is also present in the Tool Options palette of the Airbrush.

When using either of these tools, you can control the brush shape and size, the opacity of the paint, the density and hardness of the brush or spray, and the "steps" between the dabs or spray bursts painted when you drag the mouse. To see the effect that these settings have on your brush, keep an eye on the preview window in the upper-left corner of the Paintbrush tab of the Tool Options palette. The brush image in this window changes as you change the following brush settings:

▶ **Shape**—Available brush shapes are Square, Round, Left Slash, Right Slash, Horizontal, and Vertical.

▶ **Size**—Available brush sizes range from 1 to 200 pixels.

▶ **Opacity**—Controls the opacity of the paint applied, and ranges from 1 (least opaque) to 100 (most opaque).

▶ **Density**—Controls how solid the brush is, and also ranges from 1 (least dense) to 100 (completely solid).

▶ **Hardness**—Controls how hard or how diffuse the edges of the brush are, and ranges from 0 (most diffuse) to 100 (completely hard).

▶ **Step**—Controls how the brush shape is repeated as you drag the mouse while you're painting. The lower the Step value, the smoother and more continuous the line that's drawn with the brush. As the Step value increases, the repeated brushstrokes or spray bursts that form the line become more pronounced individually and less continuous as a line, as demonstrated in Figure 1.2.

Fig. 1.2
Step set to 1, 25, 50, 75, 100 (from left to right).

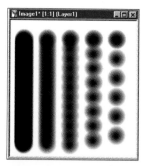

CHAPTER 1

In addition to the individual brush controls, the main tool tab of the Tool Options palette includes a button that opens a menu of pre-defined brush types—the Brush Options menu. These brush types include Normal (which defaults to the last settings that you used); Custom, which enables you to create your own brushes (explored in Chapter 11, "Adding to Your Toolkit"); and a series of brushes that simulate artist's tools: Paintbrush, Pen, Pencil, Marker, Crayon, Chalk, and Charcoal. Figure 1.3 shows the Brush Options menu.

Fig. 1.3
Tool Options palette with Brush Options menu open.

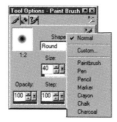

To see what happens when you work with one of the brush options, choose Charcoal. The Size and Step settings remain as they were, but all the other settings will change, as follows:

Charcoal Setting

    Shape: Square

    Opacity: 100

    Density: 33

    Hardness: 90

Each of the other brush options has its own characteristic settings, too.

Figure 1.4 illustrates some of the different effects that you can create with the different brush options, and Table 1.1 lists the settings for each brush option.

Fig. 1.4
Paintbrush, Pencil, Crayon, and Chalk brush options (from left to right).

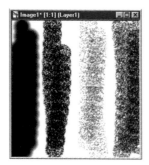

Table 1.1.
Settings for the
Paintbrush, Pencil,
Crayon, and Chalk
Brush Options

	Paintbrush	Pencil	Crayon	Chalk
Shape	(current shape)	Round	Round	Round
Opacity	100	100	50	80
Density	100	50	11	33
Hardness	50	90	100	90

Brush characteristics aren't all that you can change to create different effects with the Paintbrush and Airbrush tools. Choose the Options tab on the Tool Options palette to see a list labeled Paper texture. The default Paper texture is None, but if you choose any of the other Paper textures from the list, the Paintbrush or Airbrush reacts as though paint is being applied on a surface that has the texture that you've selected. Figure 1.5 shows the result of painting with the Chalk brush alone (left) and selecting Medium Bricks (right).

Fig. 1.5
Chalk brush with Paper
texture None (left) and
with Medium Bricks
(right).

CAUTION
Paint Shop Pro (PSP) "remembers" the last Paper texture you selected, even if you leave PSP and restart it later. Suppose, for example, that you select Lava for the Paper texture with the Paintbrush and then select Woodgrain for the Airbrush. The next time you choose the Paintbrush, the Paper texture will be Woodgrain, not Lava.

CHAPTER 1

NOTE

The Paintbrush has another control on the Options tab of its Tool Options palette: Build Up Brush.

With Build Up Brush checked, paint will build up when you paint over an area that already has paint, even during a single mouse drag. This is similar to using an artist's brush and watercolor wash.

With Build Up Brush unchecked, repainting an area has no effect during a single mouse drag. When you release the mouse button and then begin painting again, however, areas that were painted during previous mouse drags will be built up with paint if they're not already fully opaque.

Although you usually will be doing freehand painting when you use the Paintbrush or Airbrush tool, you also can use these tools to draw straight lines. To draw a straight line, click where you want to begin the line. Hold down the Shift key and click where you want the line to end—left-click to produce a line in the foreground color, or right-click to produce a line in the background color. As explained a bit later in this chapter, you also can use the Draw tool, with somewhat different effects, to create straight lines.

The Preset Shapes Tool

With the Preset Shapes tool, you can draw simple, regular shapes precisely. The available shapes, which you choose from the Tool Options palette when the Preset Shapes tool is active, are Square, Rounded Square, Rectangle, Rounded Rectangle, Circle, Ellipse, Pentagon, Hexagon, Octagon, a five-pointed star, a six-pointed star, and three different arrows, as shown in Figure 1.6.

Fig. 1.6
The various shapes available with the Preset Shapes tool.

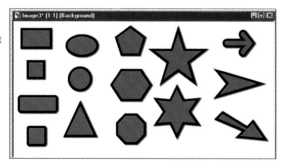

On the Preset Shapes Tool Options palette (see Figure 1.7), you also can set the Style of your shape:

▶ **Filled**—Produces a shape with a solid color.

▶ **Stroked**—Produces an outlined shape with a "hollow" interior. The width of the outline is determined by the setting for Width. The current foreground color is used when you drag with the left mouse button depressed; the current background color is used when you drag with the right mouse button depressed.

▶ **Filled & Stroked**—Produces an outline shape with a filled interior. The width of the outline is determined by the setting for Width. When you drag with the left mouse button depressed, the Fill is drawn with the current background color and the Stroke is drawn with the current foreground color; when you drag with the right mouse button depressed, the Fill is the foreground color and the Stroke is the background color.

Fig. 1.7
The Tool Options palette for the Preset Shapes tool.

Another option that you can set for the Preset Shapes tool is whether or not the shape is antialiased. *Aliasing* is the stepped effect produced when a line is drawn on a computer screen. *Antialiasing* is a method of smoothing this jagged effect by adding pixels along the edge of the line, in colors that are intermediate between the color of the line and the background color.

CAUTION
Antialiasing is available only with 256-greyscale images and with 24-bit color images (that is, color images with a color depth of 16 million colors).

Figure 1.8 shows a zoomed-in view of a Filled & Stroked circle created without antialiasing in effect. Figure 1.9 shows a zoomed-in view of a Filled & Stroked circle created with antialiasing. As you can see, the jagged edges of the non-antialiased circle appear to be much smoother in the antialiased version.

CHAPTER 1

Fig. 1.8
A circle without
antialiasing.

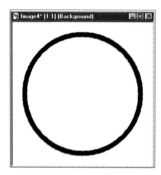

Fig. 1.9
A circle with
antialiasing.

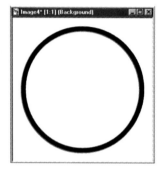

CAUTION

Antialiasing does a great job smoothing lines, but you have to be careful when you manipulate antialiased elements. If you paste an antialiased figure into an image or Flood Fill around an antialiased figure, "ghosting" will occur around the figure's edges where the blended pixels are located. You'll see examples of ghosting in the section on cutting and pasting in Chapter 3, "Being Selective."

There's also a checkbox labeled *Create as vector* in the Preset Shapes Tool Options palette. For now, leave that box unchecked. We'll look at vectors in depth in Chapter 5, "Working with Vectors."

Before leaving the topic of the Preset Shapes tool, you should note that not all shapes are drawn in the same way. Rectangles and squares are drawn from one corner to the diagonally opposite corner. Circles and ellipses are drawn from the center and grow or contract as you drag away from or back toward the center.

TIP

As you draw a shape, look on the left of the PSP status bar. You'll see several sets of numbers in the following form:

(n1, n2) -> (n3, n4) = (n5, n6) [n7]

Although it might not be clear to you at first, the numbers on the left of the equals sign are coordinates:

(Left, Top) -> (Right, Bottom) = (Width, Height) [Aspect Ratio]

Imagine that a rectangle is drawn around your shape, touching its leftmost, top, rightmost, and bottom points. The coordinates displayed are the coordinates of this imaginary rectangle. These coordinates can help you to draw your shape with a particular size or a particular *aspect ratio* (the ratio of width to height).

You can constrain your shape to a 1:1 aspect ratio by holding down the Shift key as you drag to draw your shape.

The Draw Tool

The Draw tool is the tool of choice when you want to create either straight lines or smooth curves. You can select any of four line types in the Tool Options palette when the Draw tool is active: Single line, Bézier curve, Freehand line, or Point to Point line. Single lines are simply straight lines. Freehand lines are curves you draw by hand, simply by dragging the mouse. Bézier curves and Point to Point lines are complex, smooth curves that you will explore later in this section.

Four other settings are available on the main tab of the Tool Options palette for the Draw tool: Width, which sets the width of the line; Antialias, which determines whether or not antialiasing is in effect; Create as vector, for creating vector lines rather than raster lines; and Close path, for ensuring that a shape that you draw by hand is completely closed. (See the previous section, "The Preset Shapes Tool," for a discussion of antialiasing. See Chapter 5, "Working with Vectors," for a discussion of vector lines. For now, keep Create as vector unchecked when you draw a line.)

To draw a straight line, in the Tool Options palette choose Single Line as the Type, choose the Width you'd like, and check Antialias if you want antialiasing to be in effect. Then, in the image canvas, click the mouse button at the spot where you want the line to begin. Click the mouse button again where you want the line to end. If you click the left mouse button, the line will be drawn in the current foreground color. If you click the right mouse button, the line will be drawn in the current background color. Figure 1.10 shows a line being drawn.

Fig. 1.10
Drawing a line with the
Draw tool.

When you want to restrict your line drawing to horizontal lines, vertical lines, and other lines at 45-degree increments, hold down the Shift key while you drag to draw your line.

You can get a little bit fancier by modifying the Cap on the Options tab of the Draw tool's Tool Options palette. You can make the ends of your line rounded instead of square by choosing the rounded cap option.

To draw freehand instead of drawing a straight line or a set of straight lines, choose Freehand as the Style. Be sure to set Curve tracking, too, on the second tab of the Tool Options palette. Freehand lines are made from a continuous set of line segments, and Curve Tracking determines the length of each segment. The smaller the value for Curve Tracking, the shorter the line segments.

Understanding Bézier Curves

Bézier curves, as implemented in PSP, are curved lines that are defined by two endpoints and two other control points. With Type set to Bézier in the Tool Options palette, you can draw curves almost as easily as you can draw a straight line with the Single Line option. To draw a Bézier curve, follow these steps:

1. Choose Bézier as the Type in the Tool Options palette.

2. Click within your image canvas at the point where you want the line to begin and drag to where you want the line to end (see Figure 1.11a).

3. Click away from the line in the direction toward which you'd like the curve to be warped. You'll see a line that begins at the first endpoint of your line segment and extends to the control point that you just defined. The line segment is warped along this line and curves back toward the second endpoint, halfway between the first endpoint and the control point. You can drag the control point to adjust the warping of the now curved segment (see Figure 1.11b).

If you want to create an elbow-like curve, click to define your second control point at the same position as you did the first control point. When you release the mouse button, your line will be drawn. If you want a line that resembles an S-curve instead, click somewhere else away from the line—where you'd like the warping for the second part of the curve to occur—and drag to adjust the shape of the curve (see Figure 1.11c). When you release the mouse button, your line will be drawn (see Figure 1.11d).

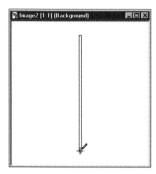

Fig. 1.11a
Defining the endpoints of a Bézier curve.

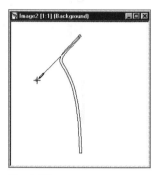

Fig. 1.11b
Setting the first control point.

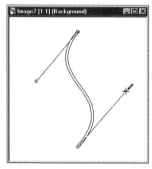

Fig. 1.11c
Setting the second control point.

Fig. 1.11d
The completed Bézier curve.

Creating Complex Lines with Bézier Curves

After you read the brief discussion of Bézier curves in the PSP User's Guide, you might think that you can make only S-curves and semicircles with Type set to Bézier. Actually, Bézier curves can be used to make quite complex curved lines.

First, look more closely at the simple case of an S-curve. Figure 1.12 shows the endpoints (labeled A and B) and control points (labeled C and C') for creating an S-curve.

Fig. 1.12
An S-curve.

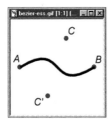

Figures 1.13a and 1.13b illustrate two other simple cases: a semicircle and a parabola. Notice that the only difference between the two is the distance of the control points from the line's endpoints.

Fig. 1.13a
A semicircle.

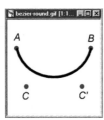

Fig. 1.13b
A parabola.

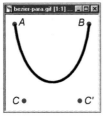

More complex curves are just as easy to create—you simply need to place the control points differently. To create a loop like the one shown in Figure 1.14, position the control points so that they define an imaginary line that is perpendicular to the line defined by the endpoints.

Fig. 1.14
A simple open loop.

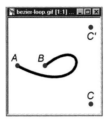

The cursive-L-shaped loop in Figure 1.15 has its first control point above and to the right of the second endpoint, with the second control point just to the left of the first endpoint.

Fig. 1.15
A cursive-L-shaped loop.

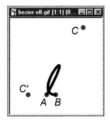

You also can create some pretty neat curves by using either a single position for both endpoints (see Figure 1.16), a single position for both control points (see Figure 1.17), or a single position for one of the endpoints and one of the control points (see Figure 1.18).

Fig. 1.16
A closed loop.

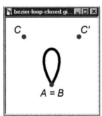

Fig. 1.17
An elbow.

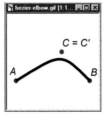

Fig. 1.18
A sharp curve.

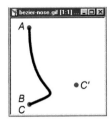

After you discover these and other possibilities, you can use multiple
Bézier curves to create quite interesting drawings. Figure 1.19 shows a
simple example.

Fig. 1.19
A drawing made with
Bézier curves, the Preset
Shapes tool, and Flood
Fill.

Some of the complex curves in this example were made by drawing one
Bézier curve, beginning another at one of the endpoints of the first curve,
and so on. Other sets of curves, such as the sets of petals for the flower
heads, were created from one curve that was copied, pasted, mirrored,
and rotated (operations discussed in Chapter 9, "Making Adjustments").

Point to Point Lines

Point to Point lines provide a lot of control when drawing vector lines
and shapes. This Draw method also gives you some of the power of
vectors without actually using vectors: With Point to Point lines, you
draw straight line segments and curves by defining nodes, and you can
utilize Node Editing with either vectors or raster curves/lines.

You will explore Node Editing in detail in the section on vectors in Chapter 5, "Working with Vectors," but for now take a look at a simple raster example of a Point to Point line. To draw a curve or shape made up of a series of straight line segments, set Type to Point to Point lines in the Tool Options palette and then simply click at the endpoints of each segment, as shown in Figure 1.20.

Fig. 1.20
A shape created with straight line segments by using Point to Point lines.

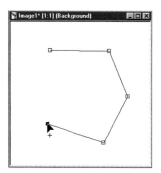

To create curves, click to define the first node (the start point) and then click to define the second node and drag. As you drag away from the node, you'll see an arrow-shaped control. Dragging away from the node in the direction of the arrow, with the cursor on either the head or tail of the arrow, increases the length of the arrow and adds to the length of the segment between the nodes. Swiveling the arrow changes the curvature of the segment at the node. Add more nodes by clicking and dragging. Figure 1.21 shows a curved path being drawn in this way.

Fig. 1.21
A shape created with curved segments by using Point to Point lines.

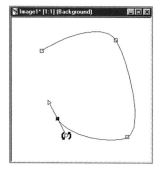

If you want to close the curve, right-click anywhere in the image canvas. This brings up the Node Edit menu. Choose Close. When you want the line/shape to be drawn, click anywhere outside of the image canvas. The end result for the example in Figure 1.20 is shown in Figure 1.22, with Style set to Stroked & Filled and Width set to 5.

Fig. 1.22
A shape made with
Point to Point lines,
with Style set to Stroked
& Filled and Width set
to 5.

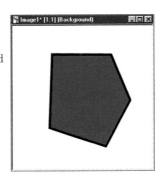

The Text Tool

To use the Text tool, choose the tool from the menubar and click within
your image at the point where you want your text block to appear. The
Text Entry dialog box will then open. You adjust the settings for the Text
tool in this dialog box rather than in the Tool Options palette.

NOTE

The only control active in the Tool Options palette when the Text tool is
selected is the Zoom drop-down list, which you can use to zoom in or zoom
out on the view of your image.

The Text Entry dialog box is divided into several sections, each of which
contains a set of controls (see Figure 1.23).

Fig. 1.23
Text Entry dialog box.

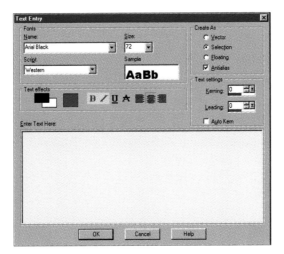

The upper-left portion of the Text Entry dialog box, labeled Fonts, has controls related to font selection:

▶ **Name**—A scroll list in which you select the font face for your text.

▶ **Size**—A scroll list in which you select the point size for your text. Alternatively, you can enter the point size in the textbox above this list, which enables you to select a point size that isn't included in the list. For example, although 100 isn't included in the scroll list, you can set the font size to 100 points by entering 100 in this textbox.

▶ **Script**—A scroll list for selecting the script type. For most PSP users, this will normally be kept as Western.

The upper-left portion of the Text Entry dialog box has several Create As options:

▶ **Vector**—Select this radio button if you want to create text on a vector layer rather than on a raster layer. You'll explore vector text in Chapter 5, "Working with Vectors."

▶ **Selection**—Select this radio button if you want an empty text selection. This gives you a standard (nonfloating) selection in the shape of the text you specify. Essentially, it acts like a "cookie cutter" pressed into the active layer.

For text selections created on raster layers, when you click inside a text selection and drag with the Text tool, you'll drag both the text selection marquee and the part of the layer that it contains. On a background layer, the displaced pixels will be replaced with the current background color specified on the Color Palette (see Figure 1.24). On a real layer, the displaced pixels will be replaced with transparency.

Fig. 1.24
Moving a standard text selection. When you stop dragging a standard text selection, it will automatically become a floating selection.

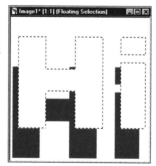

TIP

To move just the marquee of a standard selection without moving the selection's contents, choose the Mover tool and right-drag within the selection.

▶ **Floating**—Select this radio button to create your text as a floating selection. The text will "float" above the active layer and will be filled with whatever color you select in the Text effects section of the Text Entry dialog box.

If you drag a floating text selection with the Text tool, the colored text will move and the pixels of the layer beneath the selection will remain untouched.

▶ **Antialias**—Antialiasing works with text as it does with shapes and lines. If you select Antialias, the jagged edges of your text will be made smooth by blending the text color with the background color. Keep in mind that checking this box has an effect only if your image is a 256-greyscale image or a 24-bit color image.

To anchor your text in place, click the right mouse button while using the Text tool. The selection marquee will disappear and your text will no longer be movable.

TIP

If you anchor your text and then notice that it isn't quite where you want it, you can get the text selection back by clicking the Undo button, by pressing Ctrl+Z, or by choosing **Edit, Undo**.

Below the Fonts section of the Text Entry dialog box is the section labeled Text effects, where you select the color of your text, any special attributes, and the alignment:

▶ **Color swatches**—Click the foreground color swatch to set the text color to the current foreground color as set in the Color Palette. Click the background swatch to set the color to the current background color.

To set the text color to some other color, click the swatch that's just to the right of the foreground/background swatches. This will bring up the Color Picker, where you can select whatever color you like. You can also right-click the color swatch to bring up the Recent Colors dialog box.

▶ **Attribute buttons**—To the right of the color swatches are attribute buttons for bold, italics, underline, and strikethrough. You can select any combinations of these attributes or none at all. Only attributes available for the chosen font will be active.

▶ **Alignment buttons**—To the right of the attribute buttons are the
alignment buttons: Align Left, Center, and Right Align. These buttons
determine where your text is placed and how multiple lines of text
are aligned relative to one another.

Align Left—All text is left-aligned. The block of text is placed in your
image so that the left edge of the first line of the text is placed at the
point you clicked on when you activated the Text tool.

Center—All text is centered. The block of text is placed so that the
first line of the text is centered horizontally around the point you
clicked on when you activated the Text tool.

Right Align—All text is right-aligned. The block of text is placed so
that the right edge of the first line of text is placed at the point you
clicked on when the Text tool was activated.

Figure 1.25 illustrates the different alignments.

Fig. 1.25
Examples of Align Left
(top), Center (middle),
and Right Align
(bottom).

NOTE
Although you can set the horizontal alignment for text, vertical alignment
cannot be set. The baseline of the first line of text is placed at the point you
clicked on with the Text tool.

To the right of the Text effects section in the Text Entry dialog box are the
Text settings controls:

▶ **Kerning**—This affects the spacing between adjacent characters. The
Kerning control is active only if the cursor is placed in the text entry
box between two characters (or in front of or after a single character)
or if a string of text is selected.

Positive values for kerning increase the amount of spacing, and negative values decrease the spacing. Set the kerning by clicking between two characters (or before or after a single character) or by selecting text by dragging across the text. Then adjust the Kerning control.

▶ **Leading**—The Leading control affects the amount of space between lines of text. Enter positive values to increase the spacing, and enter negative values to decrease the spacing. Set the leading by clicking at the end of a line and adjusting the Leading control.

▶ **Auto Kern**—Automatically sets the kerning appropriately for the font.

The lower half of the Text Entry dialog box is where you enter your text. You have all sorts of options here! You can simply enter text of a single color and font size, but you can also do a lot more. For example, suppose you start out by entering the text shown in Figure 1.26a, with Trebuchet MS as the font, 36 as the point size, and the color set to blue.

Fig. 1.26a
Entering blue 36pt Trebuchet MS text in the Text Entry dialog box.

You can change the properties of any portion of the text by highlighting that portion and then adjusting the appropriate settings. For instance, in this example, you can change the font, font size, and color of just the word "World."

1. Highlight the word by dragging across it.

2. Set the font and size.

3.   Click the color swatch and choose a new color in the Color Picker. Figure 1.26b shows the new settings, and Figure 1.26c shows the resulting text.

Fig. 1.26b
Changing the word "World" to maroon 48 pt Verdana text.

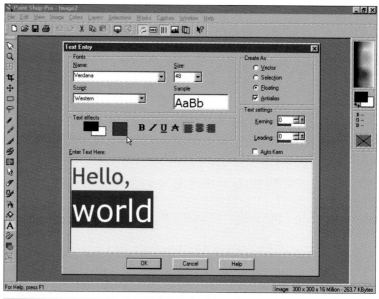

Fig. 1.26c
The resulting text.

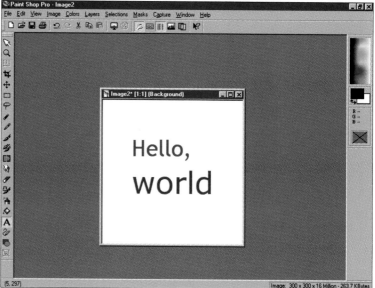

Those are the basics for adding text to your images. In Chapter 5, "Working with Vectors," you'll explore advanced text manipulation techniques using vectors, such as making text conform to a curved path and modifying the shape of characters.

2

More Painting Tools

In this chapter, you will explore the remaining painting tools. These include the editing tools, which people who are new to PSP sometimes miss—the Eraser tool, the Color Replacer tool, and the very versatile Clone Brush and Retouch tools, which you can use to remove a blemish, eliminate an intrusive object, brighten an overly dark area, sharpen blurred areas, and more. And don't forget the Picture Tube tool—a handy tool that you can use to create multiple copies of a single figure or a family of figures.

Here's what you'll be exploring in this chapter:

▶ Using the Eraser and Color Replacer tools

▶ Mastering the Clone Brush and Retouch tools

▶ Painting with the Picture Tube tool

▶ Flood filling with colors, patterns, and gradients

The Eraser

The first editing tool that you should get to know well is the Eraser, which is much more versatile than a pencil eraser.

In unlayered images, the Eraser acts like the Paintbrush in reverse: If you paint with the left mouse button depressed, the pixels that you paint over become the current background color; if you paint with the right mouse button depressed, the pixels become the current foreground color.

In layered images (discussed in Chapter 4, "Mastering Layers and Blend Modes"), the Eraser has a more interesting use. On any layer except for the Background, painting with the Eraser makes the pixels transparent, and using the Eraser with the right mouse button depressed reapplies any paint that was previously removed.

The Tool Options palette for the Eraser has the same controls and settings as the Paintbrush. So, for example, you can set the Opacity of the Eraser to 50 to tint an image with the current background color.

NOTE

If you right-drag the Eraser on a layer, the paint that you reapply might look somewhat different than it looked originally. The settings for Opacity, Density, Hardness, or Paper texture for the Eraser can produce different effects from the original.

Figure 2.1 shows one way that you can use the Eraser settings to create a special effect.

Fig. 2.1
Painting a border with the Eraser.

To create the effect in Figure 2.1, use the following settings:

Eraser Shape: Round
Size: 120
Opacity: 13
Density: 43
Hardness: 27
Step: 22

Drag the Eraser around the edge of the image, and the background color (white in this case) forms a soft, snow-like border. You can produce a similar effect with the Paintbrush or Airbrush, except that those tools paint with the foreground color.

Now, take a look at an Eraser effect that you can't produce with the Paintbrush or Airbrush. In Figure 2.2, fully opaque paint surrounding a butterfly on one layer of a layered image was erased completely, revealing solid-white paint on the layer below. The paint on the butterfly layer was then reapplied by right-dragging with the Eraser, this time with the settings for Hardness and Opacity reduced and the Paper texture set to Woodgrain.

Fig. 2.2
A textured edge made with the Eraser.

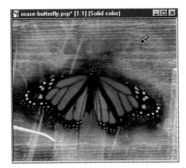

Using white paint and the Woodgrain Paper texture might create an effect that resembles what you can produce with the Paintbrush; however, there's an important difference. By using the Eraser, you introduce transparency on the upper layer. You can then easily modify the background color that shows through simply by flood filling the lower layer with another color, as was done in Figure 2.3.

Fig. 2.3
Modifying the background color that shows through the upper layer.

The Color Replacer

You use the Color Replacer to replace an existing color in your image with another color—either by changing the current background color to the current foreground color, or vice versa, depending on whether you use the tool with the left mouse button or the right mouse button.

The main tab of the Color Replacer's Tool Options palette is just like the one for the Paintbrush. The Options tab for the Color Replacer is a bit different, though: Again there's a drop-down list for Paper textures, but instead of a Build Up Brush control, there's a Tolerance control. If you set Tolerance to 0, the pixels to be replaced must match the specified color exactly. Setting the Tolerance to a higher number tells PSP to also change pixels that closely match the specified color. With a Tolerance setting of 200, all the pixels are changed.

Compare Figures 2.4 and 2.5. In Figure 2.4, the foreground color is set to white, and the background color is set to a brownish color found in the original coins image, with Tolerance set to 0. In Figure 2.5, the foreground and background colors are the same, but this time Tolerance is set to 40.

Fig. 2.4
Color Replacer with
Tolerance set to 0.

Fig. 2.5
Color Replacer with
Tolerance set to 40.

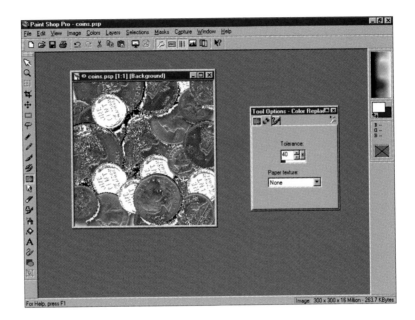

TIP

Painting with the Color Replacer is convenient when you want to replace a color in only certain parts of your image. But if you want to replace *all* instances of a certain color in your image, you can take a shortcut.

To change all instances of the current background color to the current foreground color, double-click your image with the left mouse button. To change all instances of the current background color with the current foreground color, double-click your image with the right mouse button.

You can create some interesting effects by using the Color Replacer with a high Tolerance setting to replace a color; after you've replaced the color, use the Color Replacer again, but this time with a low Tolerance and with the foreground and background colors switched to change the altered pixels *back* to the original source color. Figure 2.6 shows the result of changing the white areas of Figure 2.5 to dark brown, with Tolerance set to 0.

Fig. 2.6
Coins image with new
white areas changed to
brown.

By increasing the areas of brown, you've given the coins a somewhat tarnished look. The effect isn't all that refined in this particular example, but this gives you an idea of what you might achieve.

The Clone Brush

The Clone Brush is a particularly handy tool, especially if you need to modify a photorealistic image. You use the Clone Brush to apply portions of an image as "paint." The source image can be either the image that you're modifying or some other image. The Clone Brush works only with 256-greyscale images and 16-million color images. If you use separate images for your source and your target, make sure that both are 256 greyscale or that both have a color depth of 16 million colors.

The main tab of the Tool Options palette for the Clone Brush is the same as for the Paintbrush, and all the controls can be set just as they can be for the Paintbrush. The Options tab has four controls: a Clone mode drop-down list; a Paper texture drop-down list; a Sample Merged checkbox; and a Build Up Brush checkbox. (You won't explore Sample Merged here, but you will return to it in Chapter 4, "Mastering Layers and Blend Modes." As for Build Up Brush, it works just as it does with the Paintbrush.)

The Clone mode, which you can set to either Aligned or Non-Aligned, controls where the Clone Brush begins to pick up paint from your source each time you begin to paint with the Clone Brush.

▶ **Non-Aligned**—The Clone Brush returns to the source point each time that you stop painting and then restart (unless you first choose a new starting point).

▶ **Aligned**—The starting point of your cloning shifts to the point at which you start painting again, relative to your original starting point (again, unless you first choose a new starting point).

To begin painting with the Clone Brush, right-click in the source image at the point where you want to begin picking up paint. How the Clone Brush then behaves depends on whether you've selected Non-Aligned or Aligned as the Clone mode.

Aligned Clone Mode

Here's an example with Clone mode set to Aligned. Suppose that you want to clone the image in Figure 2.7 so that part of the image is opaque on a smooth surface and the rest of the image is semitransparent and textured.

Fig. 2.7
Source image to be cloned.

1. Open both the original image and a new image with the same dimensions and with a white background.

2. In the Tool Options palette, set the Brush size to a moderately large size (about 30 to 50) and the Shape to Round. Set Opacity to 100; Density to 100; and Hardness to 0. This produces a solid, round brush with diffuse edges. On the Options tab, make sure that the Paper texture is set to None and the Clone mode is set to Aligned.

3. Now, right-click the area in the source image where you want to begin picking up the paint. When you then start painting in the target image, you'll see a crosshair in the source image that shows where the paint is being picked up, as shown in Figure 2.8.

Fig. 2.8
The cloned image in
progress.

NOTE

When you right-click with the Clone Brush, you'll hear a click from your PC's speaker. This click is to alert you that you've changed the start point for the cloning.

4. When the solid area in the target image is the way you like it, go back to the Tool Options palette and change the setting for Opacity to about 50 and choose a Paper texture. (Coarse Canvas is used in this example.)

5. Start painting around the edge of your completely opaque area in the target, and click around the edges of this new textured area, creating a gradual fade to the edge of the image. Notice that, because the Clone mode is Aligned, your paint in the source starts out in an area aligned with where you restart in your target. The results are shown in Figure 2.9.

Fig. 2.9
The completed clone
image.

Here's another example of how to use the Clone Brush with Clone mode set to Aligned. Suppose that you have a photorealistic image that has an imperfection or an object that's obstructing the main figure of your image. The Clone Brush can be used to paint out the imperfection or the obstructing object.

Figure 2.10 shows a photorealistic image of lilies. Very pretty, isn't it? Too bad a big ugly fly is sitting on one of the lily petals! Fortunately, you can remove the fly with the Clone Brush.

Fig. 2.10
A marred image.

1. This time, open just the marred photo image. Choose the Clone Brush tool and set the brush Shape to Round or Square; the Size to about 2 or 3; and the Step fairly low.

2. Set all the other Brush Tip controls to their maximums. For the Clone mode on the Options tab, choose Aligned and set the Paper texture to None.

3. Right-click several pixels to the right of the fly and carefully start painting over the fly. If you make a mistake, click the Undo button on the PSP toolbar or press Ctrl+Z. Because you're in Aligned mode, you'll pick up your paint in the right place when you start to paint again. Figure 2.11 shows the repair of the lily image in progress.

CHAPTER 2

Fig. 2.11
Painting out the
imperfection.

4. Continue in this way until the whole obstruction is painted out. If
    you need to adjust the source point at any time in the process, just
    right-click again at the point where you want to start picking up
    paint next. The finished product is shown in Figure 2.12.

Fig. 2.12
The corrected image.

This method is useful not only for painting out intrusive objects, such
as the fly in our lilies example, but also for correcting imperfections in
a photo, such as dust spots or scratches. It can even be used to make
cool fantasy images (for example, by cloning an animal's head onto a
human body).

Non-Aligned Clone Mode

Setting Clone mode to Non-Aligned is most useful when you want to add multiple copies of a single object or pattern, perhaps overlapping the copies with one another. For instance, clone a single horse to get a whole herd of horses, or clone a tree to create a forest.

Figure 2.13 shows a simple example of this mode.

Fig. 2.13
Cloning with the Non-Aligned Clone mode set.

NOTE
The grey-and-white checkerboard pattern in the sphere image isn't actually part of the image. It's the default pattern that PSP uses to indicate transparency in an image with a transparent background. You'll sometimes want to use an image with a transparent background as the source for cloning because an image with an opaque background might accidentally pick up the background color as well as the areas that you want to clone.

The Retouch Tool

The Retouch tool is often overlooked, but it has two handy functions: touching up photorealistic images and digital painting. For example, when you want to darken an overly light area of a photo, you can use Retouch in either its Burn mode or Darken RGB mode. To soften the edge of a pasted-in selection, you can use Soften mode. For digital painting, use the Smudge and Push modes.

The Tool Options palette for the Retouch tool is much like the Tool Options palette for the other painting tools. In fact, the main tab of the Tool Options palette is exactly the same as for the Paintbrush and Airbrush. And on the Options tab for the Retouch tool there's a control for Paper texture, just as there is for the Paintbrush and Airbrush. The Retouch tool, however, also has a unique control: Retouch mode (see Figure 2.14).

Fig. 2.14
Tool Options palette of Retouch tool, showing the Options tab.

Nineteen Retouch modes are available. And, as the name of the tool suggests, most of these modes—including Dodge, Burn, and all the Color, Hue, Lightness, and Saturation adjustment modes—are useful for retouching photorealistic images. The other modes—Soften, Sharpen, Emboss, Smudge, and Push—are good not only for retouching photorealistic images, but also for creating interesting effects in digital drawings and paintings. Figure 2.15 shows just one example, in which Emboss mode is used to add a tarnished-metal effect to the edge of some text.

Fig. 2.15
Retouch's Emboss mode used to enhance some text.

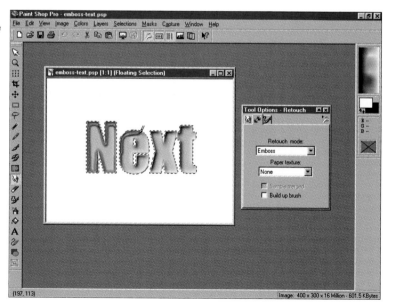

You also can heighten the metallic effect by going over the embossed edge with the Retouch mode set to Sharpen.

> **TIP**
>
> You can use the Soften Retouch mode to blend aliased edges of a pasted-in figure into the background, to approximate an antialiased effect.
>
> Use the Smudge and Push modes to convert a photorealistic image into a painting, or to create your own freehand paintings.

As an example of what can be done with the Retouch tool, take a look at the digital photo in Figure 2.16. This image isn't meant to be a work of art, but even as a snapshot, it has a very major flaw—you can see the photographer's shadow in the lower-right corner.

Fig. 2.16
A snapshot in need of retouching.

You can bleach out the dark shadow and reveal the details in that area of the photo by using the Dodge Retouch mode. Before starting out with the Retouch tool, though, you probably should select the area that needs retouching so that other areas of the image aren't affected. Figure 2.17 shows the selection made by using the Magic Wand and the Freehand tool.

> **NOTE**
> Chapter 3, "Being Selective," covers selection in detail.

Fig. 2.17
Selected area to be
retouched.

The image is now ready for retouching. With Retouch mode set to Dodge and Paper texture set to None, set the Brush Size quite large and the Opacity very low. By doing so, you can click the selection area a few times until you achieve the effect that you want. Figure 2.18 shows the retouched version—with no noticeable trace of the intruding shadow.

Fig. 2.18
The retouched snapshot.

TIP

When you're retouching a selected area as was done here, you might want to hide the selection marquee by choosing **S**elections, **H**ide Marquee. Just be sure to turn the marquee back on when you're finished, so that you don't inadvertently define a selection you can't see.

Take a look at another example. The photo shown in the upper-left area of Figure 2.19 is flat and overly dark. To give the image a feeling of depth, use Soften mode to blur the background. In the retouched version, in the lower-right area of Figure 2.19, Soften was used at 100% Opacity on the background and at about 20% on the fine fellow's left hand, to create a gradual fading of detail from the foreground to the background.

Fig. 2.19
Giving some depth and revealing some detail with Retouch.

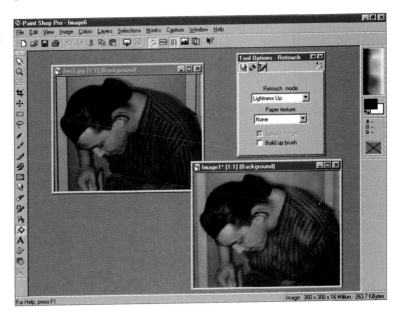

To lighten the dark areas in order to reveal details that are hidden in a shadow, you can use Dodge, as you did in the previous example, but for this particular photo, Dodge might exacerbate the oversaturation that is already a problem. A better choice in this case is Lighten RGB. After you take care of the lightening, you can tone down the oversaturated skin tones of the original with Saturation Down, giving the skin a more natural look. The result is shown in the retouched version.

The examples in this section give only a hint of what you can achieve with the Retouch tool. Figure 2.20 further illustrates some of the effects that you can produce with Retouch.

Fig. 2.20
Some Retouch effects.

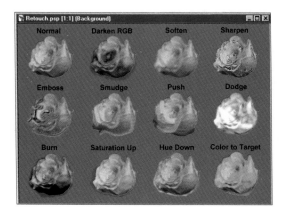

Picture Tubes

One of PSP's most popular features is Picture Tubes. A *tube file* is a collection of image elements, such as a series of flowers or other objects, that can be painted onto your image. A tube can have a single element or many elements, with four to six being about average.

Tubes are used to repeatedly apply an object or set of objects to your image. This can be useful for creating a matched set of buttons and icons for a Web site, as in Figure 2.21, or for creating bouquets, forests, crowds, or other massed figures in computer-displayed or print images, as in Figure 2.22.

Fig. 2.21
Matched Web elements made with tubes.

Fig. 2.22
A bouquet made with tubes.

The Tool Options palette for tubes has a preview thumbnail and seven controls: one for tube selection, five for the various tube options, and an Options button (see Figure 2.23).

Fig. 2.23
Tool Options palette for tubes.

The Scale control adjusts the size of the Picture Tube elements. You can set the Scale anywhere from 10% to 250%, with 100% being the default. You can also set the Placement Mode, Selection Mode, and Step.

In conjunction with Step Size, Placement Mode—which can be set to either Random or Continuous—determines how the tube elements are placed as you paint with the Picture Tube tool. Step (measured in pixels) determines either exactly how far apart the center of one tube element is from the next (if Placement Mode is set to Continuous) or what the maximum distance is between tube elements (if Placement Mode is set to Random). Selection Mode determines how the different elements in the tube are selected as you paint with the Picture Tube tool. The following are the settings available for Selection Mode:

▶ **Random**—Tube selection is (as you might suspect) random.

▶ **Incremental**—Each tube element is selected sequentially, and then the sequence is repeated.

▶ **Angular**—Tube selection is determined by the direction in which you drag the mouse as you paint.

▶ **Pressure**—This is effective only if you're painting with a pressure-sensitive graphics tablet and have PSP set up to recognize different pen pressures.

▶ **Velocity**—Tube selection is dependent on the speed of your mouse drag.

CHAPTER 2

For example, Jasc's Beetles tube has both Placement Mode and Selection Mode set to Random. Draw a line across an image canvas once with this tube, release the mouse button, and then draw again, and you'll see that the two lines are quite different, as shown in Figure 2.24.

Fig. 2.24
A tube that has both Placement Mode and Selection Mode set to Random.

Compare this with Jasc's Arachnophobia tube, in which Placement Mode is set to Continuous, and Selection Mode is set to Incremental. Draw one line with this tube and you produce a series of evenly spaced figures. Release the mouse button, draw another line, and you produce the same spacing and the same series of figures, as shown in Figure 2.25.

Fig. 2.25
A tube with Placement Mode set to Continuous and Selection Mode set to Incremental.

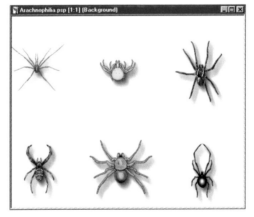

An example of a tube that has Angular as its Selection Mode is Jasc's Pointing Hands. Figure 2.26 shows the result of dragging with this tube up diagonally from left to right, and then down from left to right, and then across from right to left.

Fig. 2.26
A tube that has Selection Mode set to Angular.

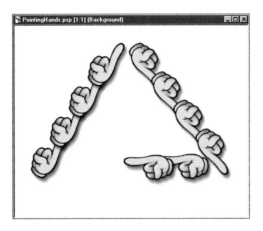

The last control on the Picture Tube Tool Options palette is the Options button.

Clicking the Options button opens up the Picture Tube Options dialog box, shown in Figure 2.27.

Fig. 2.27
Picture Tube Options dialog box.

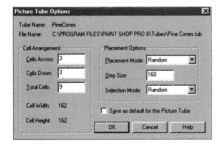

When you're using (as opposed to creating or installing) Picture Tubes, you should adjust only the *Placement Options* on the right of the Options dialog box. The *Cell Arrangement* textboxes on the left side of the Picture Tube Options dialog box should not be changed. You use these controls only to create your own tubes (as described in Chapter 11, "Adding to Your Toolkit") or to export an add-on tube file that you've acquired from a third party.

CHAPTER 2

TIP
You can find tubes for downloading from Jasc Software at
http://www.jasc.com/tubes/tubedl.html. The site also lists several other
sources of downloadable tubes.

You might wonder why you'd ever want to use the Options button, since
the controls you'd normally use in the Picture Tube Options dialog box
are the same as those available on the Tool Options palette itself. The
difference is that you can adjust the default settings for the tube when
using the Picture Tube Options dialog box. To make your adjusted
settings the new defaults, check the box labeled *Save as default for this
Picture Tube*.

Setting Up Third-Party Tubes

People who are accustomed to adding tubes in PSP 5 will undoubtedly
be happy to find that new third-party tubes are much easier to install
in PSP 6.

To use third-party tubes that were created in PSP 6, all you need to do is
put the TUB file in PSP's Tubes subfolder. The next time you access the
Tube drop-down list in the Picture Tube Tool Options palette, you'll find
the name of your new tube included in the list.

TIP
If PSP is open and the Picture Tube tool active when you add a new tube, you
may need to select another tool and then reselect the Picture Tube tool before
the new tube shows up in the Tool Options palette.

One thing you need to keep in mind, though, if you're adding tubes
created in PSP 5, is that the format of tube files created in PSP 5 is not
the same as the format for PSP 6 tubes. Old PSP 5 tubes that you want to
use in PSP 6 need to be converted. To make PSP 5 tubes available in PSP
6, you'll need to do one of two things:

▶ Run PSP 6's Tube Converter, TubeConverter.exe (run either from the
　PSP Installation program or as a standalone program).

▶ Open the tube image and then export the image as a tube.

To export a TUB file as a PSP 6 tube, follow these steps:

1. Place your new TUB file in the PSP Tubes subfolder, and select **F**ile, **B**rowse from the PSP menubar. Thumbnails of each of the TUB files will be displayed.

2. Double-click on the thumbnail of the new tube. The file will open up in an image window, showing the tube elements on a transparent layer, with the elements arranged in columns and rows, as in Figure 2.28.

Fig. 2.28
Jasc's Champagne
Picture Tube file opened
in PSP.

3. Choose **F**ile, **E**xpor**t**, **P**icture Tube to open the Picture Tube Options dialog box. Fill in the number of rows and columns for the tube file. The total number of tubes will then be calculated automatically. Set the Placement Options as you'd like them, and enter the name of the tube as you'd like it to appear in the Tubes drop-down list. Click OK. The next time you use the Picture Tube tool, your new tube will be available for you to use.

Here's a summary of the Picture Tube Options:

▶ **Placement Mode**—Determines how tube elements are spaced when you drag with the Picture Tube tool. With ***Random*** spacing, tube elements are spaced randomly, anywhere from 0 pixels up to the number of pixels set with Step Size. With ***Continuous*** spacing, the tube elements always have the spacing set with Step Size.

▶ **Step Size**—Determines the number of pixels for the brush step for your tube. Setting Step Size in the Export Picture Tube dialog box sets the default brush step. You can modify the Step Size in the Picture Tube Options dialog box.

▶ **Selection Mode**—Determines how the different tube elements are selected when you drag with the Tube tool.

Random—Selects the elements randomly. This, the default, is probably the most commonly used Selection Mode.

Incremental—Selects the elements in a fixed order, from left to right and from top to bottom, in the tube cell arrangement. After all the tube elements have been selected, selection begins again with the first tube element.

Angular—Selects the tube elements based on the direction of the drag.

Pressure—Relevant only if you're using a pressure-sensitive tablet. Selection here is based on stylus pressure as you draw with the Picture Tube tool.

Velocity—Selects the elements based on the speed of your drag.

For now, don't worry too much about the details of the Picture Tube settings. If you decide to create your own tubes, though, you'll want to return to this summary to consider what options you have available for placing and selecting the elements of your tubes. You'll see how to create your own tubes in Chapter 11, "Adding to Your Toolkit."

Flood Fill

The Flood Fill tool, in its simplest form, is like a paint bucket from which you can pour paint onto your image. And, by using different settings for Fill Style, Blend Mode, Paper Texture, Match Mode, and Tolerance in the Tool Options palette, you can create more complex effects.

Figure 2.29 shows the main tab of the Tool Options palette for the Flood Fill tool, and Figures 2.30a-c show a few of the effects that you can produce with the various Flood Fill settings.

Fig. 2.29
Tool Options palette for the Flood Fill tool.

Fig. 2.30a
Grey-shaded text filled with a pattern (Fill Style: Pattern; Match Mode: None; Opacity: 75; Blend Mode: Overlay).

Fig. 2.30b
Solid-colored gradient applied with a Paper Texture on grey, beveled text (Fill Style: Solid Color; Match Mode: None; Opacity: 100; Blend Mode:Screen, Paper Texture: Granite2).

Fig. 2.30c
Jasc Software's Sunset gradient applied to the image in Fig. 2.30b (Fill Style: Sunburst Gradient; Match Mode: None; Opacity: 30; Blend Mode: Normal).

The Fill Styles

The Fill Styles available are Solid Color, Pattern, Linear Gradient, Rectangular Gradient, Sunburst Gradient, and Radial Gradient. Except for Solid Color, each of these styles has a special set of options, accessed via the Options tab of the Flood Fill Tool Options palette. Figures 2.31a-f show examples of each of the Fill Styles.

CHAPTER 2

Fig. 2.31a
Solid Color Fill Style
(Paper Texture: Woodgrain).

Fig. 2.31b
Pattern Fill Style.

Fig. 2.31c
Linear Gradient Fill Style,
Repeats set to 0.

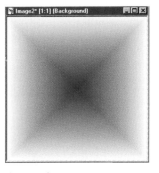

Fig. 2.31d
Rectangular Gradient Fill Style,
Repeats set to 0.

Fig. 2.31e
Sunburst Gradient Fill Style,
Repeats set to 0.

Fig. 2.31f
Radial Gradient Fill Style,
Repeats set to 1.

With the Solid Color Fill Style, either the foreground or background color is used as the fill color, depending on whether you click the left or the right mouse button, respectively, in the image canvas. You can alter the effect of the fill by adjusting Tolerance, Opacity, Paper Texture, Blend Mode, and Match Mode. Blend Mode, which you will explore in Chapter 4, "Mastering Layers and Blend Modes," controls how the pixels of your fill are blended in with the pixels that the fill covers. Used with Match Mode set to None and/or with Opacity set to less than 100, the various Blend Modes can produce some very interesting effects.

The Pattern Fill Style enables you to use the contents of an image as your fill pattern. For example, open an image to use as the source of your pattern. Then, on the Options tab of the Tool Options palette, select that file from the New pattern source drop-down list; the pattern will then appear in the palette's Preview window. After selecting your pattern, click in your target image to fill it with the pattern.

You can adjust the Linear Gradient Fill Style to create a linear gradient that transitions in various ways and that is set at any angle. You select a gradient transition in the Gradient drop-down list, located on the Options tab of the Tool Options palette. You adjust the angle either by dragging the pointer in the Direction dial or by entering the angle number directly in the Angle textbox above the dial. To fill your target image with the gradient, click within the image.

TIP

You can reverse the direction of the gradient transition by right-clicking inside the target instead of left-clicking.

The last three Gradient Fill Styles (Rectangular, Sunburst, and Radial) all have the same controls on the Options tab of their Tool Options palettes. Select a gradient and choose the number of Repeats (the number of additional times that the gradient pattern is repeated in the fill). Set the Vertical and Horizontal coordinates of the gradient's center either by dragging the sliders or by entering the coordinates directly into the textboxes. Figures 2.32a-c show a few examples of a Rectangular Gradient Fill used with different settings for Repeats, Vertical, and Horizontal.

CHAPTER 2

Fig. 2.32a
Rectangular Gradient
Fill with Repeats set to
0; Vertical set to 30; and
Horizontal set to 20.

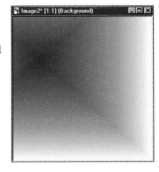

Fig. 2.32b
Rectangular Gradient
Fill with Repeats set to
2; Vertical set to 30; and
Horizontal set 20.

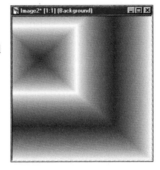

Fig. 2.32c
Rectangular Gradient
Fill with Repeats set to
5; Vertical set to 50; and
Horizontal set to 50.

That's just the beginning of the Flood Fill settings. Now that you've looked at the Fill Style Options, take a look at the other settings available in the Tool Options palette when Flood Fill is active.

Flood Fill Settings

When you click with the Flood Fill tool in your image, pixels surrounding the spot where you click will fill according to the current Match Mode. Match Mode has four different options:

▶ **RGB Value**—Surrounding pixels matching the Red-Green-Blue color value of the target pixel will be filled.

▶ **Hue**—Pixels that are filled match the Hue value (for example, where 0 is red, 90 is green, 180 is blue, 225 is red-violet, and 255 is red again).

▶ **Brightness**—Pixels are filled according to their level of brightness.

▶ **None**—All areas are filled, regardless of what the characteristics are of the pixel that you click.

Figures 2.33a and b illustrate how the Match Modes affect the behavior of Flood Fill. Figure 2.33a shows the original image. Figure 2.33b shows the result of clicking the center pixel with the Flood Fill tool, with the following settings:

Fill Style: Solid Color

Match Mode: RGB Value

Tolerance: 50

Opacity: 100

Figure 2.33c shows the result of clicking the same pixel with the same settings, except that Match Mode is set to Hue. Figure 2.33d shows the result of clicking on the same pixel with the same settings except that Match Mode is set to Brightness.

CHAPTER 2

Fig. 2.33a
Original image.

Fig. 2.33b
Match Mode set to RGB Value.

Fig. 2.33c
Match Mode set to Hue.

Fig. 2.33d
Match Mode set to Brightness.

With Match Mode set to None, the entire image canvas is filled, no matter where you click inside the image.

Tolerance, which can be set from 0 to 200, determines how similar to the target pixel surrounding pixels must be in order to be filled. With Tolerance set to 0, only pixels that exactly match the target pixel (according to the Match Mode) are filled. The higher the Tolerance settings, the less closely the pixels need to match the target pixel to be among those that are filled.

TIP

If you try to fill the seemingly solid center of an antialiased outlined shape, you might find a fuzzy fringe of pixels between the edge of your fill and the inside edge of the outline. To fill the entire center of the outlined shape, increase the Tolerance for the fill so that the antialiasing pixels are also included as target pixels of the fill.

Opacity can be set from 0 to 100 (percent). A setting of 100 makes the fill completely opaque. Lower values make the fill less opaque (that is, more transparent), letting some of the original color show through.

The *Sample Merged* checkbox is relevant only for layered images. With *Sample Merged* unchecked, only pixels on the current layer determine what areas are to be filled. With *Sample Merged* checked, the pixels of all layers are examined to see what areas are to be filled, just as if the layers were merged. Only areas on the current layer are actually affected, however. You will explore this in more detail in Chapter 4, "Mastering Layers and Blend Modes."

Gradient Editing

One of the new features of PSP6 is a facility for creating and editing multicolored gradients. To create a new gradient, choose the Flood Fill tool and select one of the gradient Fill Styles. Then press the Edit button on the Options tab of the Tool Options palette to open the Gradient Editor dialog box, as shown in Figure 2.34.

Fig. 2.34
Gradient Editor
dialog box.

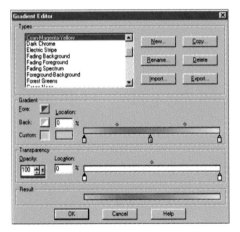

When you want to create a whole new gradient from scratch, click the New button. When you'd rather start by editing an existing gradient, highlight the existing gradient's name in the scroll list and then click the Copy button. In either case, you'll be presented with a dialog box— the New Gradient dialog box or the Copy Gradient dialog box— in which you can enter the name of your new gradient. Then you're ready for the actual editing.

CAUTION

When you edit a gradient and then click OK to close the Gradient Editor, the gradient will be permanently changed. So remember to edit a *copy* of any existing gradient rather than the original gradient itself, unless you really do want to lose the original gradient!

To use an existing gradient as the basis of a new gradient, be sure to copy the gradient and name the new copy *before* beginning to edit.

Notice that there are three bars in the Gradient Editor: the Gradient bar, the Transparency bar, and the Result bar. You use the controls for the Gradient bar to set the colors and color blending for your gradient. On the Transparency bar, you set the transparency/opacity of the gradient. The Result bar gives you a preview of your gradient as you edit it.

Try creating a new gradient step-by-step:

1.   Click the New button and name your gradient; the Gradient Editor will look something like Figure 2.35.

Fig. 2.35
Gradient Editor with
Gradient thumbs at
0 and 100.

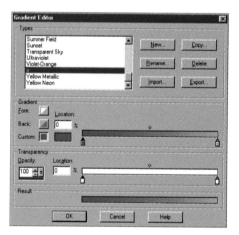

Notice that below the Gradient bar there are two pencil-point shaped controls, called "thumbs." You use the thumb on the right to set the color for that end of the gradient pattern. You use the thumb on the left to set the color for that end of the gradient pattern.

Above the Gradient bar is a diamond-shaped control, called a "midpoint." Between any two thumbs, there's a midpoint. A midpoint controls the blending of the two colors of the gradient between two thumbs. Drag a midpoint to the left, and the colors blend at 50/50 at a location closer to the left thumb. Drag a midpoint to the right, and the colors blend at 50/50 closer to the right thumb.

2. To add a thumb to the gradient, click beneath the Gradient bar anywhere where there currently is no thumb (see Figure 2.36).

Fig. 2.36
Adding a Gradient thumb.

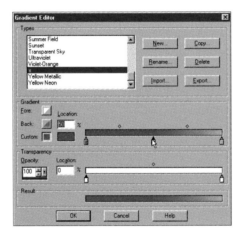

3. To change the color of a thumb (thus altering the color of the gradient at the thumb's location), click the thumb to activate it and then click one of the color buttons: Fore, Back, or Custom. Choosing Fore sets the color to whatever the foreground color in the Color Palette is when the gradient is applied, while Back sets the color to whatever the background color is when the gradient is applied. To choose a fixed color, click the Custom button. Then, to select a new Custom color, click the color swatch to the right of the Custom button to bring up the Color dialog box. In this example, activate the new thumb and change its color to a lighter shade. Then drag the midpoints to adjust the blending as you like (see Figure 2.37). At this point, the Results bar will look something like Figure 2.38:

Fig. 2.37
Changing the thumb color and adjusting the midpoints.

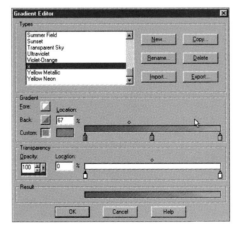

Fig. 2.38
Preview of the gradient
so far, shown on the
Result bar.

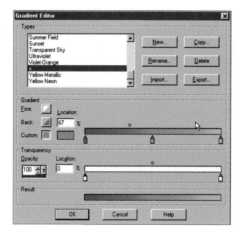

4. Adjust the opacity/transparency of the new gradient by using the
    Transparency bar, which has thumbs and midpoints just like the
    Gradient bar. By default, all areas of a new gradient are opaque.
    To make an area of the gradient transparent or semitransparent, you
    first activate a thumb at the point where you want the adjustment
    to be made.

    Next, set the opacity/transparency in the Opacity box to the far left of
    the Transparency bar. An Opacity of 100 is fully opaque, and Opacity
    of 0 is fully transparent, with intermediate values producing various
    levels of semitransparency. Figure 2.39 shows the right thumb with
    Opacity set to 75 percent.

Fig. 2.39
Adjusting the gradient's
transparency.

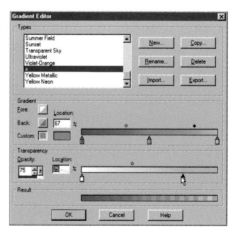

5. As with the Gradient bar, you can adjust a midpoint between two
    thumbs on the Transparency bar. This adjusts the blending of the
    opacity/transparency as set by the thumbs surrounding that
    midpoint. For this example, drag the midpoint so that Location is set
    to 60 percent.

You also can adjust the position of the thumbs on the Transparency bar. Figure 2.40 shows the left thumb dragged to Location 35%. This gives all the area to the left of the thumb 100 percent Opacity, just like the thumb itself. (And if you drag the right thumb away from Location 100%, everything to the right of that thumb will have 75% Opacity, just like the thumb itself.)

Fig. 2.40
Adjusting a thumb on the Transparency bar.

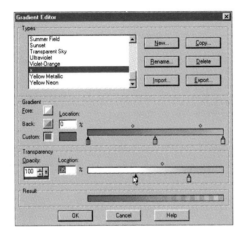

Figure 2.41 shows the finished gradient applied as a Linear gradient to a textured image with the following settings:

Blend Mode: Normal

Paper Texture: None

Match Mode: None

Opacity 100: Repeats 0

Angle: 90

Fig. 2.41
New gradient applied to a textured image.

CHAPTER 2

Before leaving the topic of the Gradient Editor, take a look at the buttons in addition to New and Copy:

▶ **Delete**—To delete a gradient, highlight the gradient's name and then click the Delete button.

▶ **Rename**—To rename a gradient, highlight its name, click Rename, and then enter the new name.

▶ **Import**—The Import button enables you to import Adobe Photoshop gradients for use in PSP.

▶ **Export**—The Export button enables you to export a PSP gradient for use in Photoshop.

One final thing to note is that gradients you create are stored on disk and can be shared with other PSP users. New gradients are stored in PSP's Gradients folder, with an extension of JGD. You also can use Adobe Photoshop gradient files (with an extension of GRD); just place these files in your Gradients folder. On the Web, you can find many sources of downloadable PSP and Photoshop gradients.

3

Being Selective

It's time to look at the basic tools and techniques for making and using selections. Also included in this chapter are directions on how to use some of the most important operations available on the Edit menu—operations for isolating an area of your image so that you can alter it, move it, place it in a new image, or eliminate it entirely.

Here's what you'll be exploring in this chapter:

▶ Using the selection tools
▶ Making standard selections and floating selections
▶ Using the Edit operations to alter or create images
▶ Using Clear to flood a selection or image with color or transparency

Making Selections

You can restrict image editing to a part of your image by making a *selection*. Some selection functions are performed with the Selections menu, which is shown in Figure 3.1, and you also can make a selection from a mask; you will make most selections, however, by using one of the selection tools.

> **NOTE**
> *Masks* are similar to selections. They isolate areas of your image and can be saved and loaded like selections. You'll be looking at masks in detail in Chapter 10, "Selections, Masks, and Channels."

Fig. 3.1
The Selections menu.

The following are the three tools that you can use to make selections:

▶ **Selection tool**—Use this tool to define a regularly shaped selection by dragging the cursor.

▶ **Freehand tool**—Use this tool to define an irregularly shaped selection by dragging the cursor. This is good for isolating a figure in an image.

▶ **Magic Wand**—Use this tool to define a selection based on color or brightness. Excellent for selecting a solid-colored area, such as a background in a drawing.

The edges of a selection are marked with a *marquee*, a flashing line of dashes popularly referred to as "marching ants." Notice the selection marquee in Figure 3.2, which shows a circular selection on a solid-colored image.

Fig. 3.2
A selection marquee
(aka "marching ants").

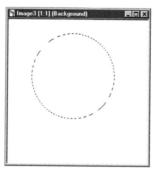

The edge of a selection can be sharp or soft. To soften the edges of a selection, you can *feather* the selection. Feathering fades the color of the pixels within the selection, blending the selection with the background. To set the feather, either use the Tool Options palette of a selection tool or choose **S**elections, **M**odify, **F**eather from the menubar.

Figure 3.3a shows an example of a nonfeathered selection cut from one image and pasted onto a solid background. Figure 3.3b shows the same selection, but with some feathering added. The zoom factor in both of these examples is set to 2 so that you can see the difference better. Notice how the edges of the feathered version are softer than the edges of the nonfeathered version.

Fig. 3.3a
A nonfeathered selection pasted onto a solid background.

Fig. 3.3b
A feathered version of the same selection pasted onto the same background.

CHAPTER 3

NOTE

Another way to soften the edges of a selection is to check Antialias in the Tool Options palette of a selection tool. Antialiasing works much like feathering, but the transition between the selection and the background is smoother with antialiasing. Both feathering and antialiasing are covered in more depth later in this chapter, along with cutting and pasting.

You can move selections by clicking inside them and dragging with either a selection tool or the Mover tool. Whether the content of the image moves along with the selection depends on whether the selection is a *standard selection* or a *floating selection*.

▶ **Standard selection**—A standard selection is like a cookie cutter pressed into your image; move a standard selection, and the image's contents also move.

▶ **Floating selection**—As its name suggests, a floating selection "floats" above your image. Move a floating selection that has no contents of its own, and only the marquee moves. Move a floating selection that contains pixels of its own, however, and both the marquee and the selection's contents move, but the pixels below the selection remain unaffected.

Figures 3.4a and 3.4b illustrate the difference between standard and floating selections.

Fig. 3.4a
Moving a standard selection.

Fig. 3.4b
Moving a floating
selection.

Figure 3.4a shows a standard selection that has been moved up and to the right. Notice how the pixels of the original image have also been moved, and the area from which the selection was moved is filled with the current background color.

Figure 3.4b shows a floating selection filled with blue pixels; this selection has also been moved up and to the right. Here, the floating selection and its contents have moved, but the pixels of the original image are unaffected.

NOTE

After you move a standard selection, it automatically becomes a floating selection.

CAUTION

If you try to move a standard selection that contains only transparency, you'll receive the error message, "This operation could not be completed because the current layer does not contain any active data within the current selection area."

To reposition the marquee of such a selection, choose the Mover tool, right-click inside the selection area, and drag with the right mouse button depressed.

To turn off a selection, right-click with a selection tool anywhere on the image canvas, press Ctrl+D, or choose **S**elections, Select **N**one.

What you've seen so far applies to all selections. Now, it's time to explore each of the selection tools and take a closer look at the Selections menu. In a few places, some things about layers and selections are mentioned. If you don't yet know much about layers, just skip over those remarks for now. You will return to selections in multilayered images in Chapter 10, "Selections, Masks, and Channels."

CHAPTER 3

The Selection Tool

The easiest selection tool to use is, in fact, called the Selection tool (see Figure 3.5). You use this tool to define a selection that has any one of these four shapes: rectangle, square, ellipse, or circle. As with the Shape tool, a rectangle or a square is drawn from one corner to the diagonally opposite corner, whereas an ellipse or circle is drawn from the center outward.

Fig. 3.5
Defining a selection
with the Selection tool.

You use the Tool Options palette to set the Selection Type (that is, the shape of the selection) and whether the selection is feathered or antialiased.

The Freehand Tool

You won't always want a regularly shaped selection. To make irregularly shaped selections, use the Freehand tool (also called the "lasso").

When the Freehand tool is active in the Tool Options palette, the following three Selection Types are available:

Fig. 3.6
Defining a selection with the Freehand Selection Type.

▶ **Freehand**—Enables you to drag the mouse to draw a freeform selection (see Figure 3.6).

Fig. 3.7
Defining a selection with the Point to Point Selection Type.

▶ **Point to Point**—Enables you to click various points, usually around the edges of a figure, to define the edges of your selection (see Figure 3.7). This has the effect of "roping off" a figure or other area of your image.

Fig. 3.8
Defining a selection with the Smart Edge Selection Type.

▶ **Smart Edge**—Enables you to click along the edge of a figure, and PSP defines the selection edge based on differences in contrast (see Figure 3.8). This is best used to isolate a figure on a background.

NOTE

To undo the last selection point that you set with either Point to Point or Smart Edge, just press the Delete key.

TIP

If you make your own Picture Tubes, you might find that Smart Edge is especially useful for creating tube elements from scanned images. Make sure that the background you use during the scan contrasts with the objects that you're scanning. (You might, for example, cover the objects with a light-colored cloth if the scanner cover provides a background that's too dark.) Then, use the Freehand tool with Smart Edge to isolate the scanned objects. You might need to adjust the selection a bit, but Smart Edge will do most of the work.

(To make your own Picture Tubes, see Chapter 11, "Adding to Your Toolkit.")

CHAPTER 3

In addition to controls for setting feathering and antialiasing, the Tool Options palette for the Freehand tool has a control labeled Sample Merged. This control is meaningful only for multilayered images. When this control is checked, the selection is made as if all visible layers in the image were merged into a single layer. When this control is *not* checked, the selection is made based only on the pixels on the currently active layer.

NOTE

When you have a layer that includes transparency, and you make a selection around a figure on that layer, the selection marquee snaps to the edges of the figure if you move the selection.

The Magic Wand

One of the handiest PSP tools—the Magic Wand—can truly be magical. The Magic Wand enables you to make selections based on the color or brightness of a target pixel that you click on in your image. The pixels that are selected will either match the target pixel exactly or fall within a tolerance range, depending on the settings you select.

The Tool Options palette for the Magic Wand has four controls: Match Mode, Tolerance, Feather, and Sample Merged (see Figure 3.9).

Fig. 3.9
Tool Options palette for the Magic Wand.

Match Mode

Match Mode determines what the Magic Wand uses as the basis for selection. The following lists the available Match Mode settings, along with a description of how each setting affects the Magic Wand's selection criteria:

▶ **RGB Value**—The pixels selected match the Red-Green-Blue color value of the target pixel. This is the mode you undoubtedly will use most often.

▶ **Hue**—The pixels selected match the Hue value of the target pixel (for example, 0 is red, 85 is green, and 170 is blue). This enables you to make a selection without regard to the pixel's saturation or brightness.

▶ **Brightness**—The pixels selected match the target pixel's brightness rather than its color. This might be useful, for example, if you want to select a dark figure on a light background.

▶ **All Pixels**—The selection includes all pixels in nontransparent areas.

Tolerance

Tolerance determines how closely pixels must match the target pixel. A Tolerance setting of 0 restricts the selection to pixels that match the target exactly. A Tolerance of 200, the maximum, makes your selection match all pixels in your image. Different intermediate Tolerance values match more or less closely to the target. Figures 3.10a-c show examples of the selections made with Tolerance settings of 10, 40, and 80, respectively.

Fig. 3.10a
Tolerance set to 10.

Fig. 3.10b
Tolerance set to 40.

Fig. 3.10c
Tolerance set to 80.

CAUTION

Keep in mind that Tolerance and Match Mode can influence each other. When Tolerance is set to 200, all pixels are matched regardless of the Match Mode setting. When Match Mode is set to All Pixels, all pixels are matched regardless of the Tolerance setting.

Feathering works just as it does with the other selection tools, and *Sample Merged* works just as it does with the Freehand tool. Feather settings greater than 1 soften the edges of the selection, blending them in with the background. Sample Merged treats all visible layers of a multilayered image as if the layers were merged together as a single layer, operating on the pixels on all the visible layers.

Adding to and Subtracting from a Selection

When you make a complex selection, you normally start with a simple selection and then edit that selection by adding to it or subtracting from it. PSP provides an easy way to add to and subtract from a selection. With any of the selection tools, hold down the Shift key and click or drag to add to a selection. Unless you've set up PSP to use a precise cursor, a "+" will appear near the cursor to remind you that you're adding to the selection. To subtract from a selection, hold down the Ctrl key and click or drag. A "–" will appear near the cursor to remind you that you're subtracting from a selection.

Suppose that you start with an image such as the one in Figure 3.11a, and you want to select the two lower spheres but not the sphere in the upper–right corner.

Fig. 3.11a
An image that contains figures you want to select.

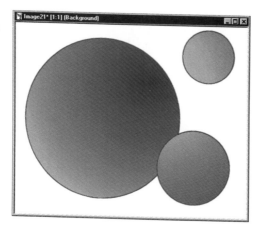

To start, you can choose the Magic Wand, set it to a fairly high Tolerance setting, and then click one of the lower spheres. The result might look something like Figure 3.11b.

Fig. 3.11b
Beginning the selection.

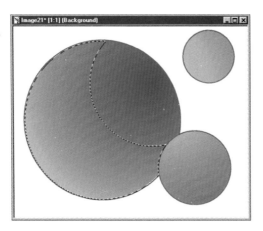

That didn't quite do the trick. What you could do, then, is click the Undo button and try again at a higher Tolerance setting, but that really isn't necessary. Instead, just Shift+click with the Magic Wand in one of the unselected areas that you want to be included in the selection. Continue in this way until you have the entire area that you want selected.

Figure 3.11c shows an intermediate step in adding to the selection, and Figure 3.11d shows the complete selection.

Fig. 3.11c
Adding to the selection.

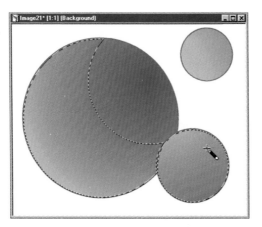

Fig. 3.11d
The complete selection.

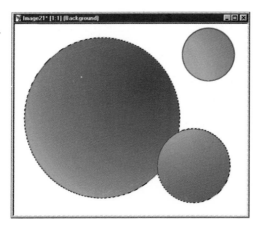

Another approach that you can take with the image in Figure 3.11a is to start by selecting the white background and then inverting the selection. This produces the selection in Figure 3.12a.

Fig. 3.12a
Select the figures by selecting the background and inverting the selection.

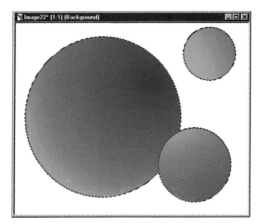

Now you want to eliminate the upper sphere from the selection. An easy way to do this is to choose the Freehand tool and set it to Freehand mode. Then, Ctrl+drag around the area that you want to remove from the selection. Figure 3.12b shows this step in progress, with the end result being the same as you saw in Figure 3.11d.

Fig. 3.12b
Subtracting from the
selection.

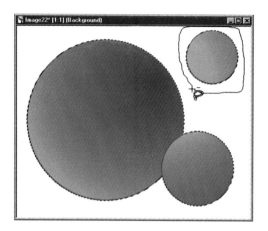

The Selections Menu

The Selections menu enables you to alter a selection, make a selection
from a mask, create a seamless tile from a selection, "promote" a selection
to a layer, save a selection to disk or to an alpha channel, and load a
selection from disk or from an alpha channel.

Many of the items on the Selections menu, such as From Mask, are
examined in Chapter 10, "Selections, Masks, and Channels," but for now,
take a look at the items that enable you to alter a selection and create a
seamless tile.

Select All and Select None

The first two items on the Selections menu are Select All and Select
None, which do exactly as their names suggest. Choosing Select All
selects all pixels in an image (or, in a multilayered image, all pixels on a
layer). Choosing Select None turns off a selection and is equivalent to
right-clicking your image with a selection tool.

NOTE

In most cases, using Selections, Select All is unnecessary. By default, most
PSP operations—including, for example, Edit, Copy—affect the entire flat
image or layer anyway.

Select All is most useful when you don't actually want the entire image or
layer selected. To get the selection you want, choose Selections, Modify. We'll
see an example of this later in this chapter.

CHAPTER 3

Invert

The fourth item on the Selections menu is Invert. This is a very handy operation, especially when used in combination with the Magic Wand. When using the Magic Wand, you'll often find that selecting what you *don't* want selected is easier than selecting what you *do* want selected. If you select the areas of your image that you don't want and then choose Selections, Invert, the selection is "inverted" and the resulting selection is the part of the image that you *did* want selected. An example of this is given in Figures 3.13a and 3.13b.

Fig. 3.13a
Original selection, made with the Magic Wand.

Fig. 3.13b
Inverted selection.

TIP
You can easily invert an existing selection by pressing Shift+Ctrl+I.

Matting

The next Selections menu item, Matting, has three subitems: Defringe, Remove Black Matte, and Remove White Matte. Each of these works only with floating selections (see the next section) and only with greyscale or 16-million color images.

NOTE
To use any of the Matting operations on a selection, you must have a floating selection. If you have a standard selection instead, choose **S**elections, **F**loat to change your selection to a floating selection.

Defringe, Remove Black Matte, and Remove White Matte are used to remove pixels that are blended into the edge of a selection as a result of feathering or antialiasing. Remove Black Matte and Remove White Matte are for removing black and white fringe, respectively. Defringe is for removing any other background color fringe.

The Matting operations can produce mixed results. For fringed selections on solid backgrounds or on their own separate layers, you might prefer to do defringing by hand. To remove fringe by hand, you use a few operations under the next item in the Selections menu—Modify—as follows:

1. With your antialiased/feathered selection selected, choose **S**elections, **M**odify, **C**ontract and set the number of pixels to 1 (or to whatever number of pixels you want to bleed out).

2. Invert the selection with **S**elections, **I**nvert (or press Shift+Ctrl+I).

3. Feather this inverted selection by choosing **S**elections, **M**odify, **F**eather, and set the number of pixels to 1 (or to whatever number of pixels you used in Step 1).

4. For a selection on a solid-colored background, set the background color in the Color Palette to the color of the solid background. (For a selection on its own layer, the setting for the current background color doesn't matter; just make sure that the layer containing the selection is the active layer.)

5. Press the Delete key a few times. The more you hit the Delete key, the more the fringe bleeds out.

6. Turn off the selection, either by choosing **S**elections, Select **N**one, by pressing Ctrl+D, or by right-clicking the image canvas.

Voilà! Your selection is defringed—and without too much trouble.

Modify

The Modify menu selection can be used for all sorts of things, not just defringing by hand. The operations included under Modify are Contract, Expand, Feather, Grow Selection, Select Similar, and Transparent Color. Contract, Expand, and Feather are all pretty much self-explanatory—use these to make a selection smaller by a number of pixels, larger by a number of pixels, or feathered by a number of pixels. The other operations are explained here:

▶ **Grow Selection**—Expands the selection. However, whereas Expand maintains the selection's basic shape while expanding the selection based on a given number of pixels from the current selection's edge, Grow Selection expands the selection based on the color of pixels in the current selection, within the current Tolerance setting of the Magic Wand, which oftentimes markedly changes the basic shape of the selection.

▶ **Select Similar**—Also expands the selection based on the color of pixels in the current selection, within the current Tolerance setting of the Magic Wand. The difference is that Grow Selection selects only pixels that are adjacent to the current selection, whereas Select Similar selects all matching pixels in the image or layer.

CHAPTER 3

Figures 3.14a-c illustrate this difference. Figure 3.14a shows the original selection, Figure 3.14b shows the results of applying Grow Selection with Tolerance set to 20, and Figure 3.14c shows the result of applying Select Similar with the same Tolerance setting of 20.

Fig. 3.14a
Original selection.

Fig. 3.14b
Grow Selection applied.

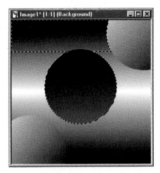

Fig. 3.14c
Select Similar applied.

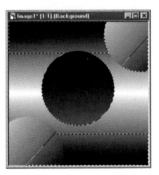

▶ **Transparent Color**—Enables you to subtract pixels of a particular color from the current selection. When you choose Selections, Modify, Transparent Color, the dialog box that appears lets you set the color that you want to have eliminated from the selection— Foreground, Background, Black, White, Red, Green, or Blue—and the Tolerance level for matching that color.

Here's one of the times that choosing Select All can come in handy.
Suppose that you have a multicolored figure with black outlines, as in
Figure 3.15, and you want to select everything but the outlines.

Fig. 3.15
Original image with
black outlines.

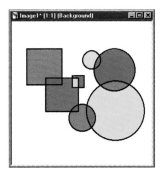

You can choose Selections, Select All, followed by Selections, Modify,
Transparent Color with the transparent color set to Black. The result is
shown in Figure 3.16.

Fig. 3.16
Selections, Modify,
Transparent Color
applied after Selections,
Select All.

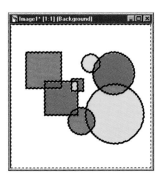

This is a good way to isolate either the content of an outlined image or (if
followed with Selections, Invert) the outline itself. Isolating an outline is
just what you want if you're trying to add a metallic texture to a hand-
drawn stained-glass window, for example.

Be careful when you use the Transparent Color method, however. All
instances of the color that you choose as the transparent color will be
eliminated from the selection. This might go too far, eliminating areas of
the selection that you want to include in the selection.

CHAPTER 3

Hide Marquee

The next item in the Selections menu, Hide Marquee, can be quite useful. In fact, setting Hide Marquee would have been a good idea when you were defringing by hand; that way, the effect on the edge would have been clear during the editing, because the marquee wouldn't be covering the edge. Hide Marquee makes the selection marquee invisible until you uncheck Hide Marquee again. The selection border is still there—you just can't see it. Use Hide Marquee whenever you need to see what's happening at the edge of your selection.

CAUTION

After you check Hide Marquee, it's easy to forget that you have a selection! If you're trying to paint in your image and nothing seems to happen, or if your paint is applied only in part of your image, check whether the selection marquee is hidden. You might have a selection set and not know it.

Convert to Seamless Pattern

The last item from the Selections menu that you'll look at in this chapter is Convert to Seamless Pattern, which can help you make your own seamless background tiles/textures. A *seamless pattern* is a pattern that can be tiled in a large area without showing any "seam lines" along the edges of the individual tiles. Use a seamless pattern as the Pattern image for the Flood Fill tool, for example, to fill an area with a texture. Or use a seamless pattern as the background tile for a Web page.

To create a seamless pattern, begin by making a selection in your textured image, leaving a border of unselected pixels around the entire selection. PSP will blend some of the pixels in the selection with some pixels outside the selection (not the best means of creating a seamless texture, but for soft-edged textures, it works well enough). Then, choose **S**elections, **C**onvert to Seamless Pattern. If your selection is too close to the edge of your image, PSP displays a warning and suggests that you make a selection farther from the edge of your image. Just follow that advice and try again.

Figure 3.17 shows both a large textured image with a selection and the resulting seamless tile. Figure 3.18 shows a large image canvas that was filled with the tile by using the Flood Fill tool set to the Pattern Fill Style.

Fig. 3.17
Creating a seamless tile
with Convert to
Seamless Pattern.

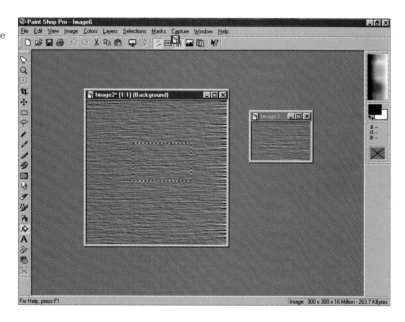

Fig. 3.18
The seamless tile used
to fill a large image.

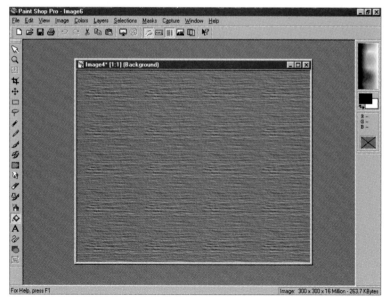

To create the large, patterned image in Figure 3.18, use the seamless tile
shown in Figure 3.17 as the Pattern for the Flood Fill tool. Then, click
the image with this tool, filling the image with repeating instances of
the tile. (See the discussion of the Flood Fill tool in Chapter 1, "Basic
Drawing and Painting Tools," for instructions on using this tool with the
Pattern setting.)

CHAPTER 3

Edit Operations

The Edit operations, which are all available from both the Edit menu and through keyboard shortcuts, include Cut, Copy, several Paste operations, and Clear. The basic Edit operations—Cut, Copy, and Paste as New Image—are also available as the standard Windows icons on the PSP toolbar.

Cut and Copy

Basically, two ways exist to copy pixels to the Windows Clipboard, thereby making those pixels available for insertion elsewhere. Pixels can be either *cut* from an image, which both deletes the pixels from the original image and places them on the Clipboard, or *copied* from the image to the Clipboard, leaving the pixels in the original image as they were.

To cut all the pixels from a flat image or from a layer, choose Edit, Cut or press Ctrl+X (the standard Windows shortcut for Cut). Alternatively, you can click the standard Windows Cut icon on the PSP toolbar. If you want to cut only some of the pixels from the image or layer, first select the area that you want to cut, and then use any of the methods just mentioned to remove the selection from the original and place those pixels on the Clipboard.

You can copy pixels to the Clipboard just as easily—and in just as many ways. To copy all the pixels from a flat image or a layer, choose Edit, Copy or press Ctrl+C (the standard Windows shortcut for Copy). You also can click the standard Windows Copy icon on the PSP toolbar. As with Cut, you can copy portions of the image or layer by first making a selection and then applying Copy in any of the ways just mentioned.

Cut and Copy will take only the pixels on a single layer. To copy the pixels from all visible layers in an image, choose Edit, Copy Merged or press Shift+Ctrl+C. No equivalent way exists to perform a one-step Cut on all visible layers. Probably the best approach for cutting a multilayered selection is to do a Copy Merged and then delete the selection on each individual layer by first making one layer active and pressing the Delete key, and then making the next layer active and pressing the Delete key, and so on.

When you cut or copy from a selection, keep in mind that antialiasing or feathering of a selection will affect the copy made. With antialiasing or feathering, the edges of the copied area will be softened, picking up or blending into the original image's background color or transparency. You can use this to your advantage when you later paste this material. But if you want a sharp edge on your copied material, be sure to uncheck

Antialias and set Feather to 0 on the Tool Options palette *before* you make your selection.

Paste

Five different Edit operations are available for pasting material from the Clipboard:

▶ **Edit, Paste, As New Image (Ctrl+V)**—Creates a new image from whatever material is currently on the Clipboard. The dimensions of the new image will be the minimal rectangle that can surround the pasted-in material, and the color depth will match that of the source of the pasted-in material. Any background areas not covered by the pasted-in material will be transparent if the color depth was 24-bit color or greyscale when PSP was loaded; otherwise, the background areas will be filled with the current background color set in the Color Palette.

TIP

Here's a convenient way to Paste, As New Image: Right-click on an empty area of the PSP workspace or on an image's title bar. Then, in the resulting menu, choose Paste As New Image.

The menu presented when you right-click on the title bar is more extensive than the one presented when you right-click on the workspace. On the title bar menu you can select any of the Cut, Copy, or Paste operations.

▶ **Edit, Paste, As New Layer (Ctrl+L)**—Places the pasted-in material on a new layer in the currently active image canvas. (This option is inactive for images with color depths other than 24-bit color or greyscale.) Any areas on the new layer that are not filled with the pasted-in material will be transparent. If the material is larger than the image canvas, the outer edges of the material "fall off the edges"—the material is still there, but it's outside the canvas area and thus can't be seen. Regardless of whether the material fits completely in the image canvas, it can be repositioned on its layer with the Mover tool.

▶ **Edit, Paste, As New Selection (Ctrl+E)**—Pastes the material on the Clipboard into the currently active image as a floating selection above the image's currently active layer. You can position the selection by dragging until you anchor it in place by clicking. The pasted-in selection can then be manipulated like any other floating selection. It can be defloated, repositioned by dragging with a selection tool or the Mover tool, modified by choosing **S**elections, **M**odify, and so on.

If the pasted-in selection is too large to fit inside the image canvas, it "falls off the edges," just like a pasted-in layer. As long as the selection is kept floating, the material outside the image canvas is not destroyed, and repositioning the selection can reveal hidden areas of the selection. However, once the selection is defloated (by choosing **S**elections, **D**efloat or pressing Shift+Ctrl+F), the areas outside the image canvas are deleted, and the shape of the selection changes to include only the areas visible in the image canvas.

▶ **Edit, Paste, As Transparent Selection (Shift+Ctrl+E)**—Similar to choosing Paste, As New Selection, except that any pixels in the material on the Clipboard that match the current background color (as set in the Color Palette) are eliminated from the pasted-in selection. Figure 3.19 shows an example of a pasted-in selection made by choosing Paste, As New Selection; Figure 3.20 shows the same material pasted in by choosing Paste, As Transparent Selection with white as the current background color.

Fig. 3.19
Results of choosing
Paste, As New
Selection.

Fig. 3.20
Results of choosing
Paste, As Transparent
Selection.

▶ **Edit, Paste, Into Selection (Shift+Ctrl+L)**—Great for filling a text selection or other irregularly shaped selection with an image. The pasted-in material is adjusted to fit inside the selection—if the selection is too big, the material is stretched; if the selection is too small, the material is compressed. Figure 3.21 shows both an image that was copied to the Clipboard and a text selection filled with that material by choosing Paste, Into Selection.

Fig. 3.21
Text selection filled
with material by
choosing Paste, Into
Selection.

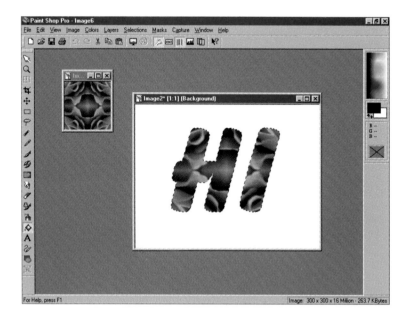

NOTE

When you fill a selection with a texture, remember that an important difference exists between using Paste, Into Selection and filling with a seamless pattern. When you use Paste, Into Selection, the copied pattern stretches to fit the dimensions of the selected area. When you add a seamless pattern with the Flood Fill tool, however, the pattern tile maintains its original dimensions and repeats to fill the selection. Compare Figure 3.22 with Figure 3.21.

The method you should choose in any given instance depends on the effect you want to produce.

CHAPTER 3

Fig. 3.22
The text selection filled with the seamless tile by using Flood Fill.

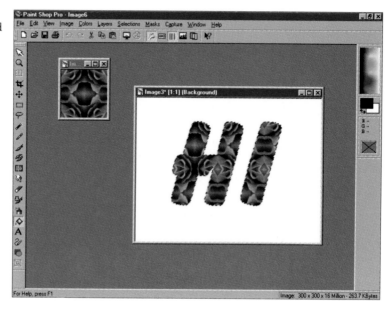

Clear

Choosing **E**dit, **C**lear (the keyboard shortcut for which is the Delete key) is an operation that you might find quite useful.

On a flat image or Background layer, Clear replaces pixels with the current background color set in the Color Palette. On a layer, Clear replaces pixels with transparency. If you want to replace all the pixels in a flat image or layer, make sure that either no selection is active or Select All is in effect, and then invoke Clear. Figure 3.23 shows an example of a text selection on a solid-white layer with all of the selection's pixels deleted with the Delete key, revealing the patterned layer underneath.

Fig. 3.23
Using Clear to eliminate pixels in a selection on a layer.

This completes your preliminary look at selections. You will return to the subject of selections in Chapter 10, "Selections, Masks, and Channels."

4

Mastering Layers and Blend Modes

One of the most popular features of Paint Shop Pro version 5 and 6 is *layers*, and for good reason. You'll probably find that you use layers in the majority of your PSP projects. And, if you're a graphic artist whose work involves a lot of compositing, nearly all of your image editing will involve layering.

Layers let you manipulate different components of your image independently. This can enable you to, for example, apply an effect or filter to only part of your image, reposition or rotate a figure in the image without affecting the background, or blend one part of your image into another.

Here's what you'll be exploring in this chapter:

▶ Examining the basics of layers

▶ Manipulating layers

▶ Using blend modes and opacity

PSP has three types of layers. In this chapter, you'll look at *raster layers*. You "paint" with pixels on a raster layer. PSP also has two other types of layers: vector layers and adjustment layers.

A *vector layer* is a special layer for holding vector objects. Vector objects aren't defined as pixels painted on the screen. Instead, a vector object is defined by a set of instructions to the computer that specify the object's characteristics. We'll look at vector layers and objects in the later sections of this chapter.

Adjustment layers provide a nonpermanent, editable way of adjusting the color, brightness, and/or contrast of one or more layers without actually changing those layers. You'll explore adjustment layers in Chapter 9, "Making Adjustments."

Layers

Think of a layer as a clear sheet of acetate on which you can paint. A multilayered image is like a stack of these acetate sheets, each with its own image elements. Areas of a sheet that are unpainted are transparent, allowing the image elements of lower sheets to show through. Areas of a sheet that are opaque block out image elements on lower sheets. Finally, areas of a sheet that are semitransparent partially reveal image elements on lower sheets.

Extending this analogy further, the order of the sheets in the stack can be changed. One or more sheets can be removed from the stack, either temporarily or permanently, and other sheets can be added to the stack.

Take a look at a simple example of a multilayered image to get a better idea of what layers are. Figure 4.1 shows an image with three layers, one named Background, one named Cat, and one named Yellow Planet.

Fig. 4.1
Simple multilayered image.

Figures 4.2a-c show each of the three layers separately. The layer named Background, which is totally opaque, is filled with a dark, starry sky. The Cat layer contains the head of a cat, with the rest of the layer transparent (the checkerboard pattern that you see "behind" the cat is what PSP shows by default to indicate transparent areas). The Yellow Planet layer contains a solid-yellow circle, with the rest of the layer transparent.

Fig. 4.2a
The Background layer.

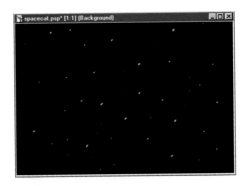

Fig. 4.2b
The Cat layer.

Fig. 4.2c
The Yellow Planet layer.

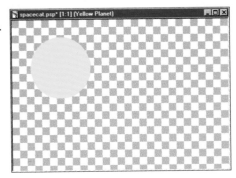

The Layer Palette

Did you notice the palette in the lower-right corner of Figure 4.1? This is the *Layer Palette*, which you can toggle on and off either by clicking the Layers button on the PSP menubar or by pressing the *L* key on the keyboard. Although quite a few ways exist to manipulate layers, using the Layer Palette is generally the easiest way to control layers. Examine the Layer Palette, shown in Figure 4.3.

Fig. 4.3
The Layer Palette.

> **NOTE**
> Figure 4.3 shows the Layer Palette with the palette window expanded so that all the tabs are showing. You might need to drag the edge of the palette to expand it so that the right side of the palette is completely revealed.

Take a look at some of the most commonly used controls on the Layer Palette. The left pane includes a column of rectangular, labeled buttons. These buttons, the *Layer buttons*, correspond to each of the layers in your image. The Layer button at the bottom of the column corresponds to the "lowest" layer in the stack of layers, and each Layer button up the column corresponds to an increasingly higher layer in the stack.

In the right pane of the Layer Palette are several more controls for each layer, including a Layer Opacity control. In the upper-left corner of the Layer Palette are three buttons, including the Add Layer button on the left and the Delete Layer button to its right.

The following is a quick summary of what the Layer Palette controls are used for. You'll try out each of these controls, along with a few others, later in the chapter.

▶ **Layer Button**

—Click a Layer button to make its layer the active layer. In most cases, PSP tools and operations affect only the active layer.

—Double-click a Layer button to open the Layer Properties dialog box, which is one means of manipulating a layer, and is the only means of naming/renaming a layer.

—Right-click a Layer button to open a menu that contains most of the commands available on the Layers menu on the PSP menubar.

—Position the mouse cursor over a Layer button, without clicking, to see a thumbnail of the button's associated layer. The thumbnail disappears when you move the cursor away from the Layer button.

NOTE

Be sure to click the Layer button itself to make a layer active. The layer icons to the left of the Layer buttons are there to help identify each layer's type (raster, vector, or adjustment). Only the Layer buttons, not the icons, are clickable.

▶ **Opacity Control**

—Nontransparent areas on a layer can be entirely opaque or semitransparent. To adjust the opacity of a layer, move the Opacity control. Moving the slider to the left makes pixels on the layer less opaque, and moving the slider to the right increases the opacity of the pixels. (Keep in mind, though, that you can't use the Opacity control to make pixels any more opaque than they were when they were painted on the layer.)

NOTE

The Background layer does not have an active Opacity control. This special layer, created when you either open a new image with an opaque background or flatten a layered image, does not have a transparency channel. If you have a Background layer and want it to have a transparency channel, right-click the Background's Layer button and in the resulting menu choose Promote to Layer. The layer's name will change from Background to Layer$n$, where n is a number determined by the current number of layers in the image.

An alternative way of promoting the Background to a layer is to double-click the Background's Layer button, which brings up the Layer Properties dialog box. Click OK—the Background will automatically be promoted and its name changed to Layer$n$.

▶ **Add New Layer Button and Delete Layer Button**

—Click the Add New Layer button to create a new, empty layer "above" the currently active layer.

—To create a copy of an existing layer, drag the Layer button of that layer to the Add New Layer button.

—Click the Delete Layer button to delete the currently active layer. You also can delete a layer by dragging its Layer button to the Delete Layer button.

CHAPTER 4

Layer Basics

It's time to return to the simple three-layer example shown in Figure 4.1. To add a new layer to this image, you click the Layer button labeled Yellow Planet to make this the active layer. Then, click the Add New Layer button, which opens the Layer Properties dialog box, shown in Figure 4.4.

Fig. 4.4
The Layer Properties dialog box.

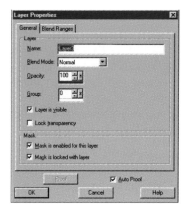

TIP

If you want to add a new layer without opening the Layer Properties dialog box, hold down the Shift key while you press the New Layer button.

Any layer that you create in this way will be given a default name of the form Layer1, Layer2, and so on. You can always give such a layer a more meaningful name later on by double-clicking the layer's Layer button and entering a new name in the Layer Properties dialog box.

Notice that, in addition to the Name text box, the Layer Properties dialog box presents quite a few other controls. Don't worry about these controls just yet. For now, all we are going to do with this dialog box is give a name to the new layer. Enter "Red Planet" in the text box labeled Name and then click OK.

An empty layer is now above the Yellow Planet layer. Since this layer is empty, the appearance of the image hasn't changed. If you look at the Layer Palette, though, you'll see a new Layer button labeled Red Planet above the Layer button labeled Yellow Planet. The new layer will automatically become the active layer.

NOTE
The Layer button of the currently active layer is highlighted.

To draw on the new layer, set the foreground color in the Color Palette to a shade of red. Then, select the Preset Shapes tool. If the Tool Options Palette isn't visible, press the letter O on the keyboard to display it. On the Tool Controls tab, select Circle and Filled, and be sure that *Create as vector* is not selected. Then, draw a small circle in the middle of the Red Planet layer. If your workspace now seems cluttered to you, you can press the O key again to hide the Tool Options palette.

CAUTION

Before you use a tool or perform an operation on a layered image, be sure the layer that you want to be affected is the active layer.

The image and the Layer Palette should now look something like Figure 4.5.

Fig. 4.5
Red planet drawn on the Red Planet layer.

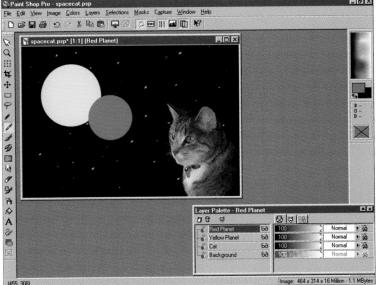

Next, try moving the figure that you just drew. Choose the Mover tool and click with it on the red planet figure. Drag the red planet to a new position. To return the figure to its original position, either click the Undo button on the PSP toolbar or press Ctrl+Z.

CAUTION

If you click the Mover tool on a figure that is on a layer other than the currently active layer, the Mover tool will affect that figure, and the figure's layer will become the active layer.

This can be quite handy when you do it intentionally, but be careful. It's very easy to click in the wrong place and unintentionally move an image element on the wrong layer. If you do make a mistake, don't forget that you can easily recover by clicking the Undo button or by pressing Ctrl+Z.

To ensure that the Mover tool affects only the current layer, hold down the Shift key while dragging with the Mover.

Now move the Yellow Planet layer above the Red Planet layer. You can move a layer up and down in the layer stack by dragging the layer's Layer button. Click the Layer button of the Yellow Planet and drag it to the top of the Layer button of the Red Planet, as shown in Figure 4.6. Keep an eye on the black line that shows up at the top or bottom of the moving layer's Layer button; this line indicates the position of the moving layer.

Fig. 4.6
Moving the Yellow Planet layer "above" the Red Planet layer.

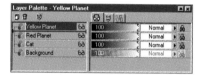

After you move the Yellow Planet layer, notice that the yellow planet figure appears to be "above" or "in front of" the red planet figure, as shown in Figure 4.7.

Fig. 4.7
The example image after restacking the layers.

NOTE
You also can move layers by using the Layers menu on the PSP menubar. Click the Layer button of the layer you want to move. Then, choose **Layers, Arrange** from the menubar and select any of the following: Bring to Top, Move Up, Move Down, or Send to Bottom.

The next step is to copy a layer. Click the Red Planet Layer button and drag it to the Add New Layer button. A new layer will be created just above the Red Planet layer, and this new layer will have a Layer button labeled "Copy of Red Planet." Nothing in the image appears different yet, however, because the copied layer is simply overlaying the original Red Planet layer. To see a difference, choose the Mover tool and drag the topmost red circle away from the red circle on the original Red Planet layer. Then, you'll see something like the image in Figure 4.8.

Fig. 4.8
Copy of Red Planet layer with its red circle moved up and to the right.

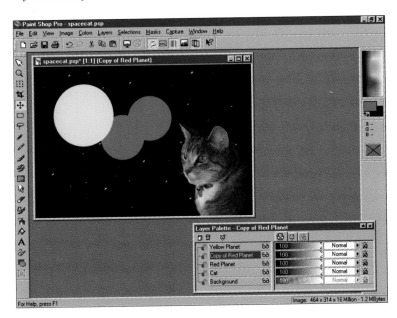

NOTE
You also can duplicate a layer by using the Layers menu on the PSP menubar. Click the Layer button of the layer that you want to duplicate and then choose **Layers, Duplicate**.

We now are going to edit the circle on the Copy of Red Planet layer, changing the red circle to green with PSP's Colorize operation. First, be sure that Copy of Red Planet is the current layer, clicking its Layer button if you need to. Then, choose **Colors, Colorize** from the menubar, and set Hue to 90 and Saturation to 150. After you click OK, you'll see something like the image in Figure 4.9.

Fig. 4.9
Colorize applied to the Copy of Red Planet layer.

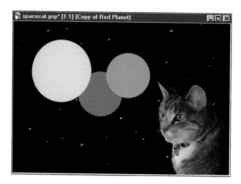

As you see, Colorize affected only the current layer.

This covers the basic Layer operations. The next two sections explore a few somewhat more advanced Layer features and operations.

Layer Visibility and Protect Transparency

Two controls on the Layer Palette that you haven't looked at closely yet are the Layer Visibility and Protect Transparency toggles.

Each layer has an associated *Layer Visibility toggle*, which you use to hide a layer temporarily. One reason to hide a layer is simply to get extraneous material out of your way while you're working on one or more layers of your image. Return to the example image as it was left in Figure 4.9. Suppose that you want to edit the Yellow Planet layer without looking at any of the other elements of your image. You can do so by hiding all the other layers, as in Figure 4.10.

Fig. 4.10
Layer Palette with all but the Yellow Planet layer hidden.

You may want to add some shading to the planet, perhaps by using the Airbrush tool to spray a darker-yellow color lightly along the bottom-right edge of the planet. You probably want to add color to the planet, but you don't want to add any paint to the transparent area surrounding the planet. You can accomplish this by using the Magic Wand to either select the planet, or select the transparent area and then invert the selection.

But there's an easier way to restrict your painting to the nontransparent areas: simply turn on the *Protect Transparency toggle.*

With Protect Transparency toggled on, only pixels that are already nontransparent will accept paint. With Protect Transparency toggled off, any area of the layer will accept paint. Figures 4.11 and 4.12 illustrate the difference.

Fig. 4.11
Painting with Protect Transparency toggled off.

Fig. 4.12
Painting with Protect Transparency toggled on.

In the example image, the version made with Protect Transparency on was used. If you're working on this example, you should use this version, too. You should then make all the layers visible again by clicking their Layer Visibility toggles on.

> **NOTE**
> You can easily hide all layers except the current one by using the Layers menu on the PSP menubar. Choose **Layers**, **View**, **Current Only**.
>
> To make all the layers visible again, choose **Layers**, **View**, **All**.

Layer Groups

Layer groups are used to keep elements on separate layers together so that when you move an element on one of the layers, all the elements on the other layers in the group move along, too. In the example image, you might want to keep the three planets together in the same relative alignment. To do this, you must add each of the planet layers to a single layer group.

Assigning a layer to a layer group is easy—just select the Group tab on the Layer Palette and click the layer's Layer Group toggle. The Layer Group toggle of a layer that is not a member of any layer group has "None" as its label. If no layer groups exist yet, clicking a layer's Layer Group toggle changes its label to **1,** and the layer is assigned to layer group 1. Click that same toggle after that to increment the layer group number and remove the layer from layer group 1. Each click further increments the number until the label returns to "**None.**" The number of times the layer group number is incremented until returning to "None" depends on how many layers are present in the image.

To assign each of the planet layers to layer group 1, click once on each planet layer's Layer Group toggle so that a **1** shows on each toggle, as in Figure 4.13.

Fig. 4.13
Planet layers assigned
to layer group 1.

Now, select the Mover tool and drag one of the planets around the image canvas. All three of the planets move together, maintaining their original positions relative to one another (see Figure 4.14).

Fig. 4.14
Members of a layer
group move together.

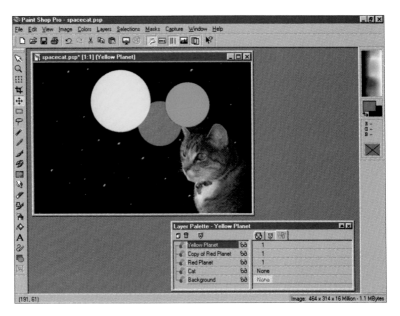

You can have more than one layer group. To add a new layer group,
select the first member of that group and click its Layer Group toggle
until the label is a number different from any other layer group. (If you
click too many times, the label returns to "**None,**" and the layer is
removed from any layer group.) Then, for the next member of the new
group, click its Layer Group toggle until the number matches that of the
first member of its layer group.

In our example, suppose that we decide that the red and green planets
should be in one layer group and the yellow planet should be in a
layer group with the Cat layer. To accomplish this, click the Layer
Group toggles for the red and green planets so that both are labeled **1**.
Then, click the Layer Group toggle of the Cat layer until it is labeled **2**.
Finally, click the toggle for the Yellow Planet layer until its toggle is also
labeled **2**.

Figure 4.15 shows these two layer groups and the effect of dragging the
red planet figure after these two groups are set.

Fig. 4.15
You can have multiple layer groups.

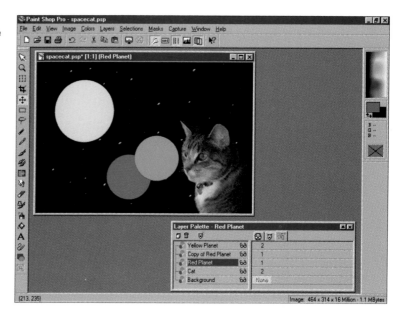

Layer groups are most useful when you have a complex figure—such as a car or a bird in a cage—with various components on separate layers. By keeping the layers of such a figure in a layer group, you can ensure that the components will not become misaligned if you move the figure.

Opacity and Blend Modes

You can dynamically adjust the opacity of a layer or the way a layer's pixels are blended with pixels on lower layers by using the layer's Opacity control and Blend Mode selector. If you save your layered image in a format that preserves layering, such as PSP or PSD, such settings are retrieved when you open the image and then are available for further adjustment.

Blend Mode and Opacity Basics

Opacity determines how much the pixels on one layer cover pixels on lower layers. The opacity for a layer can be set on the layer's Opacity control, anywhere from 0 (fully transparent) to 100 (fully opaque). Any layer with an opacity setting of less than 100 allows pixels from lower layers to show through to some extent. Figures 4.16 and 4.17 show a layer with some gold text above a layer that is entirely white. In Figure 4.16, the Opacity of the text layer is set to 100, and in Figure 4.17, the Opacity is set to 60.

Fig. 4.16
Text layer with Opacity set at 100.

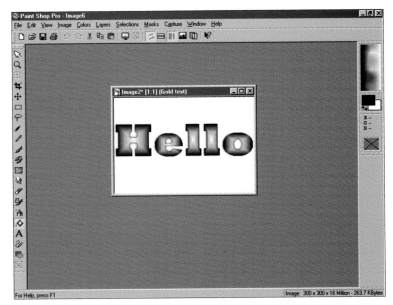

Fig. 4.17
Text layer with Opacity set at 60.

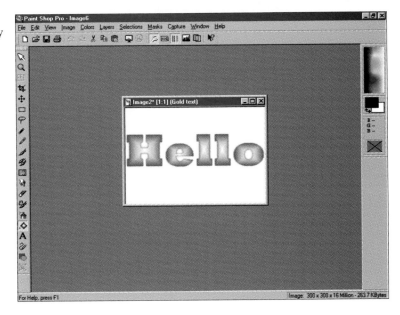

Blend Mode determines how the pixels of a layer are blended with those on lower layers. With Normal Blend Mode, pixels on the layer simply cover the pixels on lower layers. With the other blend modes, the pixels of the layer are combined with the lower pixels in various ways. For example, with Blend Mode set to Lighten, only the pixels that are lighter than the pixels on lower layers show up, whereas with Blend Mode set to Darken, only the pixels that are darker than the pixels on lower layers show up.

TIP

You also can use blend modes with the Flood Fill tool: Go to the Tool Controls tab of the Flood Fill tool's Tool Options palette and click the Options button. In the Fill Options dialog box, you can then set Blend Mode to any of the blend modes that are available with layers. This option is particularly useful with the Flood Fill tool's Match Mode set to None. Refer to Chapter 2, "More Painting Tools," for more information about the Flood Fill tool.

Figure 4.18 shows some of the results that you can create with blend modes, and Table 4.1 summarizes the effects produced by using the different blend modes.

Fig. 4.18
Blend Mode examples.

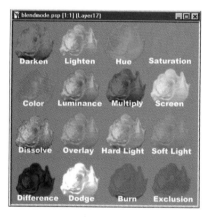

Table 4.1.
The Effects of
Using Different
Blend Modes

Blend Mode	Effect
Normal	Pixels cover pixels on lower layers; affected only by the Opacity setting.
Lighten	Only a pixel that is lighter than those on lower layers shows up.
Darken	Only a pixel that is darker than those on lower layers shows up.
Hue	Only a pixel's hue is applied to the layer.
Saturation	Only a pixel's saturation level is applied to the layer.
Color	Only a pixel's color (hue and saturation, without luminance) is applied to the layer.
Luminance	Only a pixel's luminance level is applied to the layer.
Multiply	The value of a pixel and the value of lower pixels are multiplied and adjusted so that no value exceeds 255. The overall result is darker than the separate layers.
Screen	The inverse of Multiply. The overall result is lighter than the separate layers.
Dissolve	At random intervals, pixels from lower layers are displayed. The degree of the dissolve effect increases as the layer's opacity decreases.
Overlay	Acts like Multiply for pixels with values greater than 128, and acts like Screen for all other pixels. Good for "painting" a pattern over a textured layer.
Hard Light	Similar to Overlay. Good for adding highlights and/or shadows.
Soft Light	Acts like Burn for pixels with values less than 128, and acts like Dodge for all other pixels.
Difference	Subtracts the values of the layer's pixels from the values of lower pixels, or vice versa, depending on which pixel value is lower. This modifies the hues of the image.
Dodge	Lightness values lighten underlying pixels. The lighter the areas, the more the resulting lightening.
Burn	Lightness values darken underlying pixels. The lighter the areas, the more the resulting darkening.
Exclusion	A "softer" version of Difference.

Blend Ranges

If you're new to layers, you probably should skip this section. If you're experienced with blend modes and really want to control how pixels on a layer are blended with pixels on lower layers, experiment with the Blend Ranges controls available on the Blend Mode tab of the Layer Properties dialog box. To access the Layer Properties dialog box for a layer, double-click the layer's Layer button.

There are three Blend Ranges controls (see Figure 4.19). First, in the drop-down list in the section marked *Blend if the _____ on this layer is:*, you can select whether to restrict the blend range to the Grey Channel (luminance) or to any of the three color channels (Red, Green, or Blue).

Fig. 4.19
Blend Ranges controls.

The other two controls each have two pairs of arrows, one at the top of the box and one at the bottom of the box. These arrows are used to define opacity ranges for the current layer and the underlying layers. The box under the words *this layer is:* can be used to make pixels on the current layer transparent if they have high and/or low values for the relevant channel, leaving just the intermediate pixels available for blending. The box under the words *and the underlying layer is:* can be used to make pixels on underlying layers transparent for blending if they have high and/or low values for the relevant channel, leaving just the intermediate pixels available for blending.

In both controls, the top arrows are used to set the range for pixels that are to be treated as 100% opaque. The bottom arrows are used to set the points at which Opacity is set to 0%. Opacity gradually rises between 0% and 100% at the lower value range and gradually falls off between 100% and 0% at the upper-value range.

Figure 4.20 shows a two-layered image with full Blend Ranges (from 0–255 for both the top layer and the bottom layer) and with Blend Mode set to Hard Light. Figure 4.21 shows the same image with the same Blend Mode, but with Blend Ranges set as indicated in Figure 4.22.

Fig. 4.20
Image with full Blend Ranges for Sphere layer.

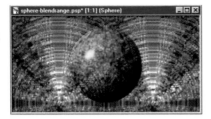

Fig. 4.21
Image with Blend Ranges of Sphere layer restricted.

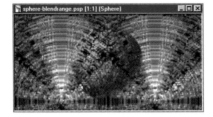

Fig. 4.22
Blend Ranges for Sphere layer.

NOTE

When a layer's Blend Ranges are restricted, a special symbol appears on the right side of the layer's Layer button on the Layer Palette.

Merging Layers

The two basic layer-merge operations are Merge All (flatten) and Merge Visible. You can access these operations either by choosing **Layers**, **Merge** or by right-clicking a layer's Layer button in the Layer Palette and choosing **Merge**.

Merge All (flatten) merges all the layers in an image and makes the image nonlayered. Any areas in the image that had been transparent are filled with white. Merge Visible merges only those layers that are visible, so it can be used to merge one or more layers while leaving other layers untouched. Merge Visible can be used when all layers or only some layers are visible.

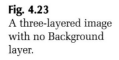

CAUTION

For most file formats, saving automatically flattens layers. When you open such a file again, you'll find that the layers are gone and cannot be retrieved.

If you want to save your file with the layers intact, use a file format that preserves layering, such as PSP (Paint Shop Pro native format) or PSD (Photoshop format).

Figure 4.23 shows an image with three layers. Compare Figure 4.24, in which Merge Visible has been applied with all the layers visible, with Figure 4.25, in which Merge All (flatten) has been applied.

Fig. 4.23
A three-layered image with no Background layer.

Fig. 4.24
Merge Visible applied
to all layers.

Fig. 4.25
Merge All (flatten)
applied.

Some of PSP's operations can behave as if layers were merged even when
they're not. For example, choosing **E**dit, **C**opy Merged will copy all
visible layers as if they were a single, nonlayered image. And the Magic
Wand, Clone Brush, Retouch tool, and Flood Fill tool can each be used
on a layered image as if the image were nonlayered—just check Sample
Merged in the tool's Tool Options palette before using the tool.

Suppose that you choose the Magic Wand to make a selection in an image that contains the two layers shown in Figures 4.26a and 4.26b.

Fig. 4.26a
Circle layer visible.

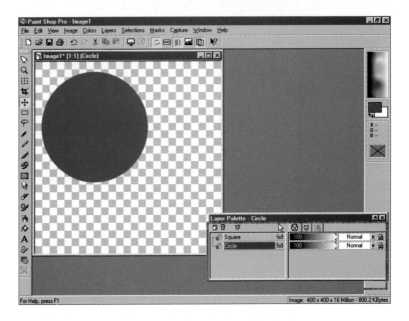

Fig. 4.26b
Square layer visible.

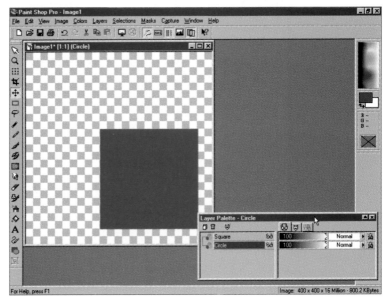

If the Square layer is active and Sample Merged is checked in the Magic Wand's Tool Options palette, clicking the square results in the selection shown in Figure 4.27. Clicking the square when Sample Merged is unchecked, however, results in the selection shown in Figure 4.28.

Fig. 4.27
Selection with Magic
Wand set to Sample
Merged.

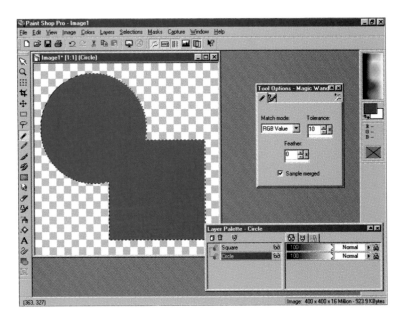

Fig. 4.28
Selection when Sample
Merged is not checked.

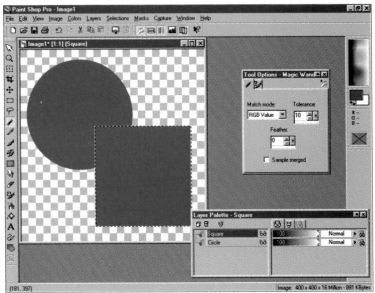

You've now covered nearly all of the layer operations and controls. In Chapter 10, "Selections, Masks, and Channels," you'll also examine the layer mask controls: the Layer Mask toggle and the Link Mask toggle, both of which appear on the Mask tab of the Layer Palette.

Layers are powerful tools for creating complex images with minimal effort. To get an even better idea of the power of layers, take a look at BOTTLE.PSP, one of the sample images on the PSP6 installation CD.

Toggle the individual layers of this image on and off in order to see how the image is constructed. And be sure to experiment with layers in your own graphics projects!

Table 4.2.
Layer Palette Summary

Layer Palette Element	Use
Add Layer button	Clicking this button when you're editing a greyscale or 24-bit image opens the Layer Properties dialog box with default settings for a raster layer. Click OK to create a new raster layer.
	Click this button when you're editing an image of any other color depth, and PSP warns you that only a vector layer can be created. (See chapter 5, "Working with Vectors.")
	Shift-click this button to create a new raster layer without first opening the Layer Properties dialog box.
	Right-click this button to open a menu where you can choose to create a New Raster Layer, a New Vector Layer, or a New Adjustment Layer.
Delete Layer button	Click this button to delete the current layer.
Create Mask button	Click this button to create a mask on the layer. (See Chapter 10, "Selections, Masks, and Channels.")
	Right-click this button to open a menu where you can choose among several options for creating a new mask on the layer.
Layer buttons	Click a Layer button to make its layer the current layer.
	Double-click a Layer button to open the Layer Properties dialog box for the layer.
	Right-click a Layer button to open a menu where you can choose various layer operations to apply to the layer.
Visibility toggle	Click a layer's Visibility toggle to hide the layer. Click a hidden layer's Visibility toggle to show the layer again.
Appearance tab	On this tab are the Opacity slider, Blend Mode list, and Protect Transparency toggle for each layer.
Mask tab	On this tab are the Enable Mask toggle and Link Mask toggle for each layer. (See Chapter 10, "Selections, Masks, and Channels.")
Group tab	On this tab is a Layer Group button for each layer.

5

Working with Vectors

Probably the biggest new feature of PSP6 is vector objects and vector layers. Vector objects aren't defined as collections of pixels, but instead are defined by instructions to the computer on how to draw the lines and/or shapes that make up an object. To create a vector line, shape, or string of text, select *Create as vector* in the Tool Options palette of the Draw or Preset Shapes tool, or select *As vector* in the Text Entry dialog box.

Vector objects reside on vector layers. Raster layers ("normal" layers) cannot hold vector objects, and if you try to add a vector object to a raster layer, PSP will immediately create a new vector layer above the raster layer, adding the vector object to the vector layer. In the Layer Palette shown in Figure 5.1, notice that the icon that identifies vector layers differs from the icon for raster layers:

CHAPTER 5

Fig. 5.1
Display for a raster and a vector layer in the Layer Palette.

NOTE
You can convert a vector layer to a raster layer, but raster layers can't be converted to vector layers. To convert a vector layer to a raster layer, right-click on the vector layer's Layer button and then choose Convert to Raster from the resulting menu.

TIP
Unlike raster layers, vector layers can be used with 8-bit, 256-color images. One difference, however, is that antialiasing doesn't work in 256-color images.

Vector Objects

To practice handling vector objects, create a vector shape:

1. Open a new image with a solid white background. This initial background layer is a raster layer.

2. If the Tool Options palette isn't visible, press the letter O on the keyboard to make this palette visible. Then select the Preset Shapes tool, and on the Tool Options palette, select Ellipse as the *Shape type* and Stroked as the *Style*. Also be sure to select *Create as vector* (see Figure 5.2.).

Fig. 5.2
Tool Options palette for Preset Shapes.

3. Draw an ellipse in the middle of your new image by dragging from the center of the image. When you release the mouse button, you'll see something like Figure 5.3.

Fig. 5.3
A vector ellipse.

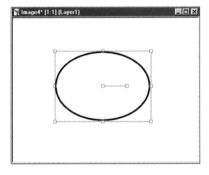

Notice the rectangular border around the ellipse, which indicates that the object is selected. Also notice the control handles on the top, bottom, corners, and sides of this border, and the bar radiating from the center of the circle, along with its control handles. The border and control handles can be used to move the object or deform it.

4. If the Layer Palette isn't visible, press the letter L on the keyboard to make that palette visible. Notice that there is a plus sign to the left of the vector layer icon, indicating that this layer contains at least one object. Click on the plus sign and the vector layer information will be expanded, showing a button for the new Ellipse object (see Figure 5.4).

Fig. 5.4
Layer Palette display
for a vector object.

5. When an object is selected, its name appears in boldface on its Object button in the Layer Palette. To deselect an object, right-click the Object button for the selected object and choose Select None: The label on the button becomes unbolded, and the object becomes deselected. Click the Object button of the object again and that object becomes selected again.

Deforming a Shape

Now try moving, resizing, rotating, and deforming the vector object. Before beginning, be sure that the Ellipse object is selected and that you're using one of the drawing tools or the Vector Selection tool.

1. If you're using one of the drawing tools, reposition the object by placing the mouse cursor on the center handle. If you're using the Vector Selection tool, you also can place the cursor anywhere along the edge of the object (except on a node). When the cursor is in the correct position, the shape of the cursor will change to the double-headed crossed arrows of the Mover tool. Then drag to move the object (see Figure 5.5). Until you release the mouse button, you'll see both the original object in its original position and a thin moving outline of the object.

Fig. 5.5
Moving a vector object.

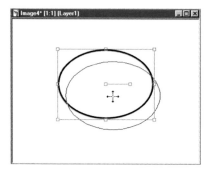

CHAPTER 5

2. To resize the object, place the mouse cursor on one of the control handles on the selection border and drag. Dragging the top or bottom handle alters the height of the object, whereas dragging the side handles alters the width. To change both the height and width at the same time, drag a corner handle (see Figure 5.6).

Fig. 5.6
Resizing a vector object.

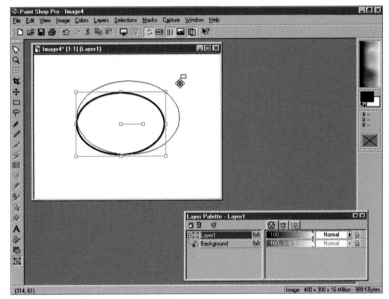

TIP
To maintain the aspect ratio while resizing your object, right-drag on one of the corner handles.

3. To rotate the object, position the mouse cursor on the handle at the outer end of the bar radiating from the center of the object. When the cursor is in the correct position, the shape of the cursor changes to two arrows forming a circle (see Figure 5.7).

Fig. 5.7
Rotating a vector object.

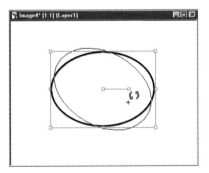

4. There are several ways you can deform an object, just as you would with the Deformation tool on a raster layer (discussed in Chapter 7, "PSP Deformations"): Drag on a handle with either the Shift key, the Ctrl key, or both keys depressed, as shown in Figures 5.8a-c. The shape of the cursor when the mouse is positioned over a handle will give you a clue about what will happen when you drag with that particular handle. When you release the mouse, the object will take on its new shape.

Fig. 5.8a
Deform with Shift+drag.

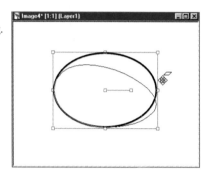

Fig. 5.8b
Deform with Ctrl+drag.

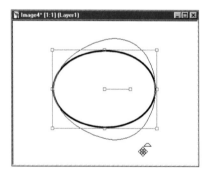

Fig. 5.8c
Deform with
Shift+Ctrl+drag.

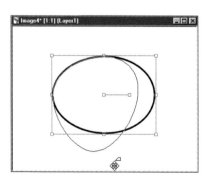

Modifying an Object's Properties

There are three ways to access an object's properties:

▶ Double-click on the object's Object button on the Layer Palette.

▶ Right-click on the object's Object button on the Layer Palette, and then select Properties from the resulting menu.

▶ Choose the Vector Object Selection tool, select the object that you're interested in (either by clicking its Object button or by dragging the tool across the object), and then right-click anywhere within the object's selection border and select Properties.

The Properties box of the Ellipse object looks something like Figure 5.9.

Fig. 5.9
The Vector Properties
dialog box.

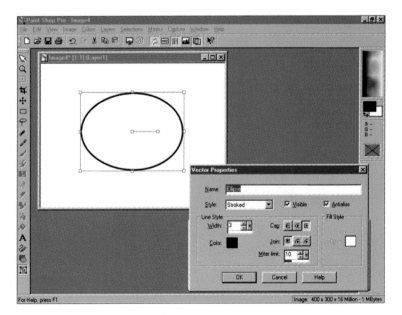

You can modify any of the vector object's properties. For example, change the black Stroked ellipse to blue Filled (see Figure 5.10).

Fig. 5.10
Modifying a vector
object's properties.

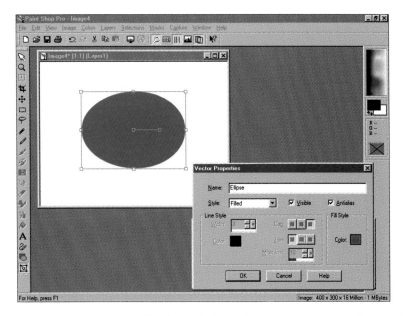

To change the line or fill colors, click on the appropriate color box in the
Vector Properties dialog box and then select the color you want with the
Color dialog box.

Now, try changing the ellipse object to Stroked & Filled, filled with blue
and outlined with black. Also increase the width of the outline to 10 (see
Figure 5.11).

Fig. 5.11
Additional
modifications to the
vector object's
properties.

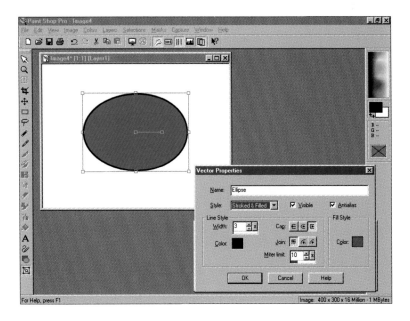

CHAPTER 5

NOTE

The Cap and Join properties aren't really relevant for ellipses and circles. You should experiment with these two properties on vector lines, however.

Making Text Follow a Path

To make text conform to a path, you need to define a path by drawing a vector line or preset vector shape and then "attach" the vector text to the path:

1.   Begin by creating a path. For this example, draw a bowl-shaped Bézier curve for the path. Choose the Draw Tool and in the Tool Options palette, select Bézier Curve as the *Line type* and Stroked as the *Style*; be sure that *Create as vector* is selected.

2.   To begin the path, click about halfway down on your image canvas a few pixels to the right of the left edge. Drag horizontally until you are within a few pixels from the right edge. Define the curve's first control point by clicking below and to the right of the line's starting point. Then define the second control point by clicking below and to the left of the line's endpoint (see Figure 5.12).

Fig. 5.12
Defining the path.

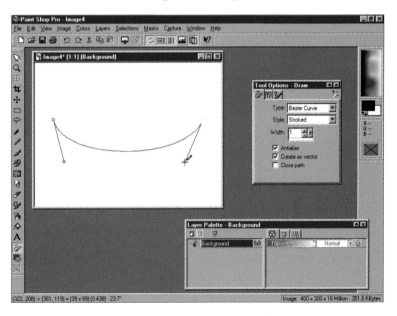

3.   Choose the Text tool, and position it anywhere on your vector curve. When the tool is positioned correctly, the **A** of the cursor icon will tilt to the left with a curve below it (see Figure 5.13).

Fig. 5.13
Positioning the text on
the vector curve.

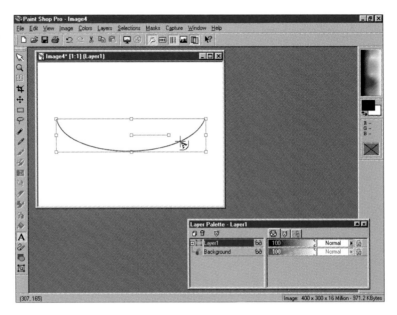

4. Click on the vector curve when the cursor is positioned correctly.
    The Text Entry dialog box appears, as shown in Figure 5.14.

Fig. 5.14
Text Entry dialog box.

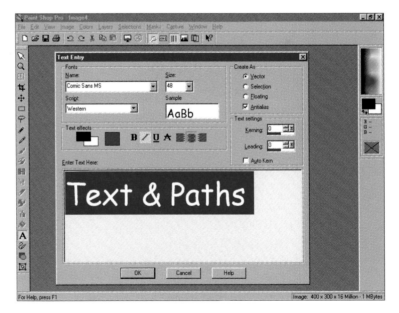

In the Text Entry dialog box, choose the font and font size you want.
In the Create As pane, you can choose Selection, Floating, or Vector;
you also can select Antialias here, if you like.

CHAPTER 5

NOTE

If you select Floating for *Create as* and you then defloat the selection, the text will be placed on the first raster layer below the current vector layer. If there is no raster layer below the vector layer, defloat will not be an option and you'll need to promote the floating selection to a layer instead.

6.   In the *Text effects* pane, click on the *Color* box to bring up the Color dialog box. Select the color you want for your text. For fonts supporting them, you also can choose among several attributes for your text: Bold (**B**), Italics (*I*), Underline (U), or Strikethrough (A).

7.   Choose the alignment for your text. Align Left positions your text so that it begins at the curve's left end; Center centers the text on the line; and Right Align positions the text so that it ends at the curve's right end.

8.   Enter the text you want in the text box and click OK. You'll then see something like the image shown in Figure 5.15.

Fig. 5.15
Text conforming to a path.

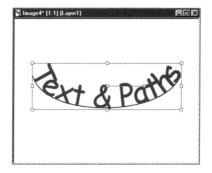

Notice that both the curve and the text are selected. You can move, resize, or deform them just as you can any other vector object. You also can modify the curve with Node Edit, which you will explore in the next section of this chapter.

TIP

Notice how the text along the curve is squashed together in places. You can adjust the spacing of the whole string of text, or character by character, with *kerning*.

In the Text Entry dialog box, select the string of text or position the cursor between the characters that you want to add space between. Then, in the Text Settings pane, set Kerning. The units here are 1000th of an *em* (the space that a lowercase "m" takes up in the font and size you're using), so you'll need to set the kerning fairly high in order to see much of a difference in the spacing.

9. You probably don't want the curve itself to be visible. There are a couple ways to make the path invisible. If you expand the vector layer information on the Layer Palette, you can just click the Visibility toggle on the curve's Object button (see Figure 5.16).

Fig. 5.16
Hiding the path with
the Visibility toggle.

Another alternative is to access the curve's Properties dialog box and deselect Visible. Figure 5.17 shows the example with the path invisible and the text object deselected.

Fig. 5.17
Text on a path.

Node Editing

To really exploit the power of vectors, try Node Edit. Any vector object is made up of at least two nodes, with pairs of nodes connected by segments. Entering Node Edit mode gives you access to an object's nodes, enabling you to reshape and refine the object.

The best way to learn about node editing is to jump right in, so try working through a few examples.

Modifying a Simple Shape

With Node Edit, you can make complex shapes from relatively simple shapes. For example, starting with a five-pointed star, you can make a gingerbread man like the one in Figure 5.18.

CHAPTER 5

Fig. 5.18
A vector gingerbread
man.

Here's how you can tackle this project:

1. With the Preset Shapes tool set to *Create as vector*, draw a filled five-
    pointed star (see Figure 5.19).

Fig. 5.19
A five-pointed vector
star.

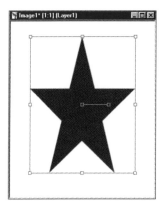

2. Choose the Vector Object Selection tool. Right-click in the image
    canvas and select Node Edit to see the nodes and segments of the
    star, as shown in Figure 5.20.

Fig. 5.20
The star in Node Edit
mode.

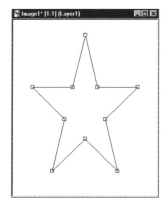

3. Now, add a few more nodes to the star. To add a node, depress the Ctrl key and click on the path of the star wherever you want a new node (see Figure 5.21a).

4. Add nodes for the head and neck, as shown in Figure 5.21b.

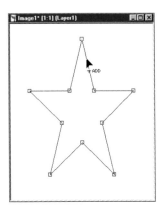

Fig. 5.21a
Adding a new node.

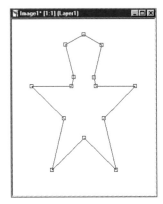

Fig. 5.21b
Adding nodes for the head and neck.

5. Add two more nodes for the points where the torso meets the legs (see Figure 5.22).

Fig. 5.22
Adding nodes for the torso and legs.

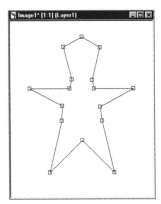

CHAPTER 5

6. At this point, all of the nodes are *cusps,* connecting lines that meet at sharp angles, but what you want instead are the nodes for the head and the ends of the arms and legs to connect as smooth curves.

To convert a node, select the node and right-click to bring up the Node Edit menu. Highlight Node Type and select Symmetric. This changes the node to a Symmetric, Smooth/Tangent, connecting two curves. Repeat for each of the other nodes that you want to convert. Notice how the shape of the path near these nodes has become rounded, as in Figure 5.23.

Fig. 5.23
Changing some of the lines to curves.

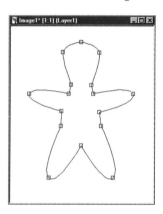

7. Now, fine-tune the curves of the head, arms, and legs. Click a node to select it. A selected node that connects two curves will display an arrow-shaped control. Pull on the head or tail of the arrow to adjust the length of the segments connected to the node. Rotate the head or tail of the arrow to adjust the curvature of the path near the node. When you finish adjusting each of the nodes of the head, arms, and legs, the shape will look like a gingerbread man (see Figure 5.24).

Fig. 5.24
The completed gingerbread man shape.

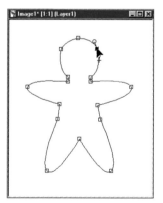

8. Exit Node Edit mode by pressing Ctrl+Q, or by pressing the Node Edit button on the Tool Options palette, or by right-clicking in the image canvas and selecting Quit Node Editing or clicking anywhere outside the image canvas.

9. Use the Preset Shapes tool to add Stroked vector circles for the gingerbread man's eyes and buttons. You can draw each eye and button separately, but it might be easier to draw one eye and one button, and then copy and paste as needed (see Figures 5.25a-b).

Fig. 5.25a
Add one eye and one button.

Fig. 5.25b
Copy and paste to add the remaining eye and buttons.

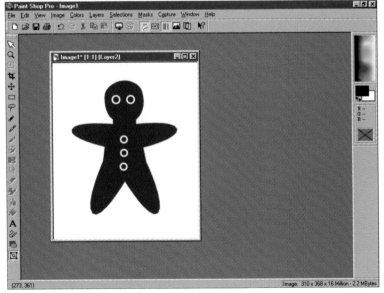

10. To copy a path and add it to an existing vector object, select the object with the Vector Object Selection tool. Right-click and select Node Edit. To select the object, drag across the object with the Vector Object Selection tool, or simply press Ctrl+A. To copy the selected nodes, press Ctrl+C and then press Ctrl+V to paste in a new copy. Repeat as needed.

11. Add a nose and mouth. The nose can be added with the Preset Shapes tool set to Triangle, and the mouth can be added with the Line tool set to Bézier Curve, with *Close path* selected. The basic gingerbread man is complete (see Figure 5.26).

Fig. 5.26
Gingerbread man with its nose and mouth added.

12. It's just about time for the finishing touches. Gingerbread men are usually iced around their edges, too, so you'll want some icing along the edges. White icing won't show up on the white background, but the color of the background can easily be changed: Click the Background's Layer button to make the Background the active layer. Select a color on the Color Palette and then fill the Background layer with the Flood Fill tool.

13. To make the icing along the gingerbread man's edges, change the modified star to Stroked & Filled rather than just Filled. Double-click the Star Object button on the Layer Palette to bring up the object's Vector Properties dialog box. Change the Style from Filled to Stroked & Filled. Be sure that the Line Style color is white and the Fill Style color is brown (see Figure 5.27).

Fig. 5.27
Modifying the object's properties.

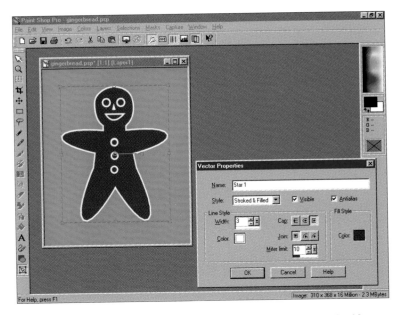

14. Finally, rasterize your vector layer so that you can apply filters and/or effects to the layer. Right-click the Layer button of the vector layer and choose Convert to Raster. (Or if you'd rather keep your vector layer for possible editing later, copy the layer by right-clicking its Layer button and choosing Duplicate. You can then convert the duplicate layer to a raster layer.)

15. Apply whatever filters or effects you like. The example at the beginning of this section, Figure 5.18, shows the gingerbread man enhanced with the Texture, Inner Bevel, and Drop Shadow effects.

Combining Objects

In the next example, you'll combine objects to create the pear image in Figure 5.28.

Fig. 5.28
A vector pear.

1. Begin with a new image with a white background. Use the Preset Shapes tool to create two green vector circles, as shown in Figure 5.29.

Fig. 5.29
Creating the basic shapes for the pear.

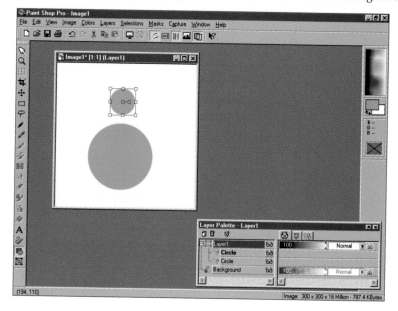

2. With the smaller of the two circles selected and the Vector Object Selection tool active, enter Node Edit mode. Drag around the small circle to select all its nodes. Then, right-click to open the Node Edit menu, and select **E**dit, **C**opy, as in Figure 5.30. (Alternatively, just press Ctrl+C to copy the selected nodes.)

Fig. 5.30
Copying the nodes of the small circle.

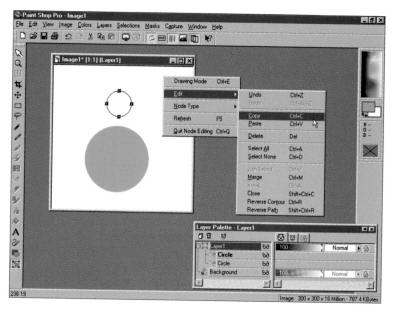

3. Delete the small circle object by right-clicking its Object button on the Layer Palette and then selecting Delete from the pop-up menu.

4. Select the large circle with the Vector Object Selection tool and enter Node Edit mode. Right-click to open the pop-up menu, and select **E**dit, **P**aste (or just press Ctrl+V) to paste the copied nodes into the current object. The pasted-in nodes will all be selected, and you can move the small circle by dragging it into place, as shown in Figure 5.31.

Fig. 5.31
Positioning the pasted-in circle.

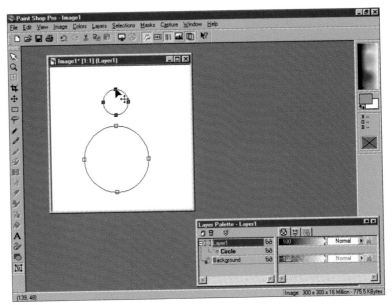

5. Delete the bottom node of the small circle and the top node of the large circle by selecting one of these nodes and then selecting **E**dit, **D**elete from the pop-up menu (or just press the Del key). Select the other node and delete it as well. Figure 5.32 shows the small circle with its bottom node deleted and the large circle with its top node selected and ready for deletion.

Fig. 5.32
Deleting nodes.

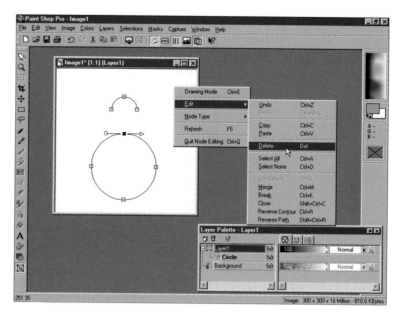

6. To produce the basic pear shape, all you need to do now is join the unattached nodes of the large and small circles. Begin by selecting the lower-left node on the small circle, and then Shift+click on the upper-left node of the large circle to select that node, too. Next, on the Node Edit menu, select **E**dit, **J**oin Select, as shown in Figure 5.33, or just press Ctrl+J. Perform the same action on the unattached nodes on the right.

Fig. 5.33
Joining nodes.

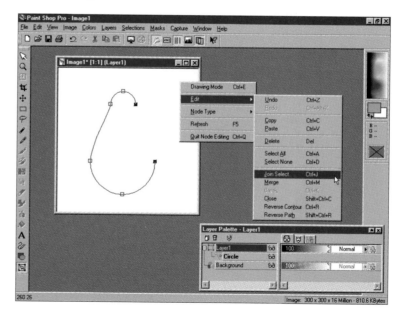

7. Add the dimple at the end of the pear. Select the bottom node. This node, like any node of a Preset Shape, is a cusp. A cusp is a node that connects segments at an angle rather than on a smooth curve. You can use each end of the arrow-shaped control to adjust the angle of the joined segments, as in Figure 5.34.

Fig. 5.34
Adjusting the angle of the joined segments at a cusp.

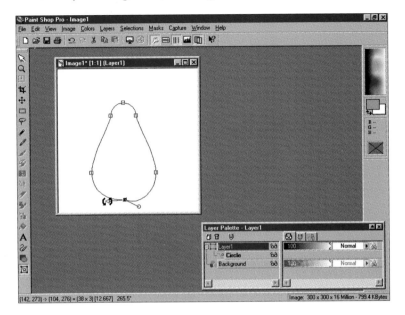

8. Adjust each end of the control and reposition the node as needed.

9. Add a new vector layer for the leaf and stem. An easy way to add a new vector layer is to right-click the New Layer button on the Layer Palette and then select New Vector Layer. For the leaf, use the Preset Shapes tool to create a vector hexagon on the new vector layer, as shown in Figure 5.35.

Fig. 5.35
The leaf begins as a hexagon.

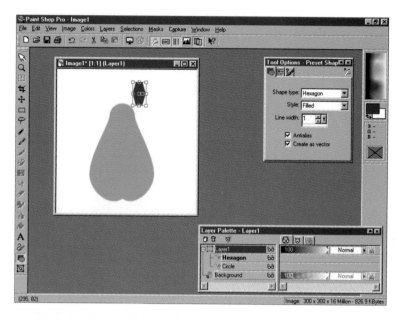

10. With the Vector Object Selection tool, enter Node Edit mode. All of the nodes start out as cusps. Use Node Type to change some of the nodes to Smooth/Tangents. You can achieve this either by changing the Node Type to Symmetric, or by changing the Node Type to Curve Before, Curve After, and Smooth/Tangent. Figure 5.36 shows Curve Before being applied to a selected node. Change the Node Type of each of the nodes that should define the curved parts of the leaf.

Fig. 5.36
Editing nodes to create curves.

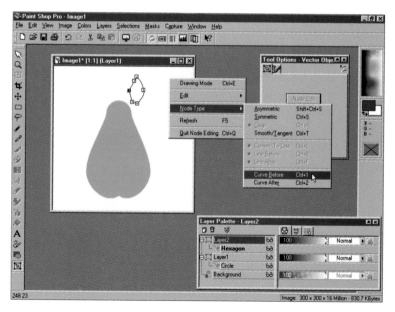

11. Adjust the position of the nodes and the curvature of the segments as needed.

12. Exit Node Edit mode. The easiest way to do that is to click anywhere outside the image canvas. (In fact, you might find that it's all too easy to exit Node Edit mode. Don't be too concerned if you exit the mode inadvertently, however. When you accidentally exit, just enter Node Edit mode again and continue with your work.)

13. Use the Vector Object Selection tool to rotate and position the leaf, as shown in Figure 5.37.

Fig. 5.37
Rotating and positioning the leaf object.

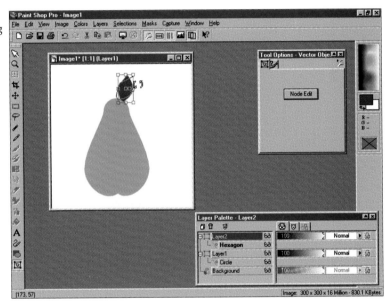

14. Create the stem as a vector triangle with the Preset Shapes tool, as shown in Figure 5.38. The triangle will be pointed up rather than down, but you'll take care of that with Node Edit.

Fig. 5.38
The stem begins as a triangle.

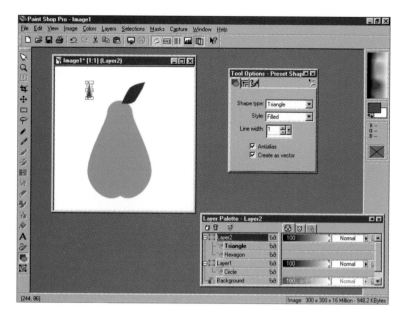

15. Select the Vector Object Selection tool, and enter Node Edit mode. Select the top node of the triangle and drag it down past the triangle's base, as shown in Figure 5.39. You can then change the type of any of the cusp nodes and adjust the curvature of the triangle's segments as appropriate.

Fig. 5.39
Modifying the triangle.

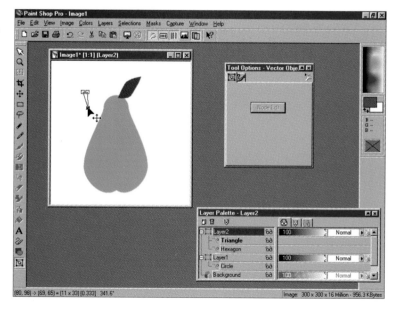

16. Exit Node Edit mode and then drag the stem into position. Rotate the stem if you need to. Your image will look something like Figure 5.40.

Fig. 5.40
The pear with its leaf and stem.

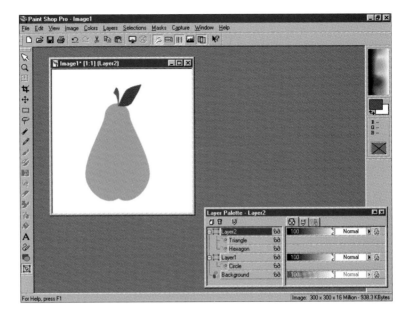

As a last touch, add a shadow to the pear with the Airbrush. The Airbrush isn't available for use on a vector layer, but there are a couple ways to create a shadow on the pear anyway. For example, you can rasterize the pear layer by right-clicking on that vector layer and choosing Convert to Raster. You can then use the Airbrush on the rasterized layer.

The disadvantage with this approach is that you then would lose the raster information for that layer, with no way of getting it back. If you want to retain the pear's layer as a vector layer, there's another way to approach things:

CHAPTER 5

1. Click the pear layer's Layer button to make it the active layer.

2. Use the Magic Wand to select the pear.

3. With the selection still active, click the New Layer button to create a new raster layer above the pear's layer.

4. Use the Airbrush to spray the shadow on the raster layer, as shown in Figure 5.41.

Fig. 5.41
Adding a shadow to a raster layer above the vector layer.

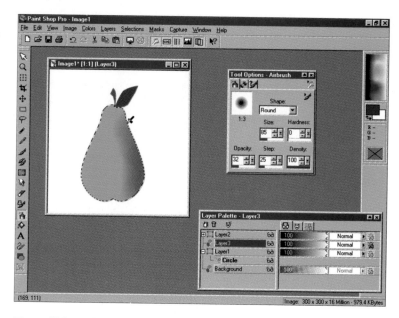

Turn off the selection, and there you are! A lovely vector pear, good enough to eat.

Converting Text to Curves

Text that is created as a vector can be converted to curves. The text can be converted as one multi-path object or as individual objects for each character in the text string. To convert vector text to a curve, select the text and right-click on the image canvas with the Vector Object Selection tool. On the pop-up menu, select either **C**onvert Text to Curves, As **S**ingle Shape or **C**onvert Text to Curves, As C**h**aracter Shapes.

Figure 5.42 shows the text-on-a-path example converted to character shapes. Here, the "T" of the word "Text" is selected and is ready to be edited in Node Edit mode.

Fig. 5.42
A character shape ready to be edited in Node Edit mode.

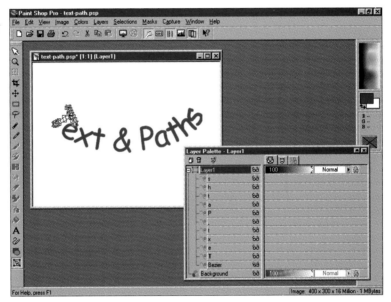

NOTE

Immediately after you convert text to a curve as individual character shapes, the entire vector layer containing the character shapes is selected. To enter Node Edit mode, you need to select a single character: Click the character's Object button on the Layer Palette or select the character with the Vector Object Selection tool.

You can convert characters from dingbats fonts as well as regular text to curves. This can be very useful for creating complex shapes for digital drawings or making fancy buttons for a Web site.

Figure 5.43 shows the Text Entry dialog box with a dingbat character from Astigmatic One Eye's ButtonButton font (the character you get by typing "c"). You'll use this character to create a more complex shape.

Fig. 5.43
Entering a dingbat character as a vector.

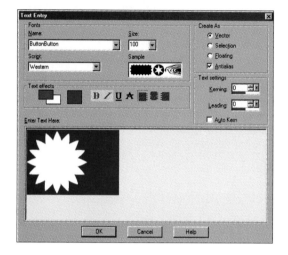

Figure 5.44 shows one of the advantages of vector text: You can scale the text without affecting the quality of the text. If the character isn't the size you want, just use the Vector Object Selection tool to drag it to the proper size.

Fig. 5.44
Resizing vector text.

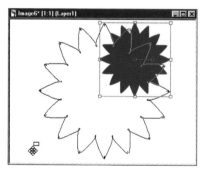

The next step is to convert the text to a curve, as shown in Figure 5.45.

Fig. 5.45
Converting the dingbat
to a curve.

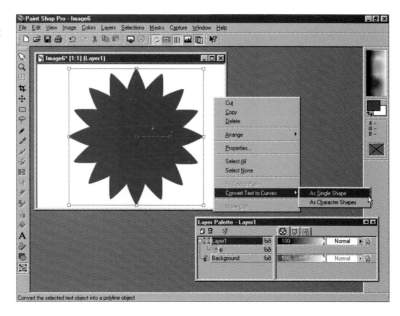

Now you're ready to edit away! Enter Node Edit mode and edit the
dingbat object just as you would any other vector object. Figure 5.46
shows an example of what you might do with this dingbat character.
Figure 5.47 shows the final result of what you might produce with this
example.

Fig. 5.46
Editing the dingbat in
Node Edit mode.

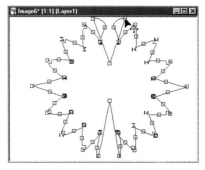

Fig. 5.47
The edited dingbat
character.

CHAPTER 5

Making Cutouts with Vectors

Another nice effect you can create with vectors is cutouts, as shown in Figure 5.48.

Fig. 5.48
A cutout effect created with vectors.

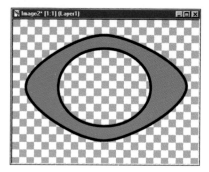

To create this effect, you take advantage of the direction of independent elements (or "contours") of a vector object. By default, the path of an object made with the Preset Shapes tool goes clockwise from its Start point to its Close point. The direction of the path of a shape that you draw by hand depends on how you draw the shape: Proceed clockwise, and the path goes clockwise; proceed counterclockwise, and the path goes counterclockwise. The direction of a path is indicated by the arrow controls on a node—the arrow points in the direction of the path, as shown in Figure 5.49.

Fig. 5.49
A vector path has a direction.

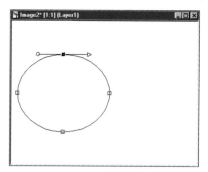

Now consider what happens when you have two independent contours in an object—elements of the object whose nodes aren't connected to any nodes of the other element. Figure 5.50 shows an object made of the original shape shown in Figure 5.49 and a copy of that shape. (The copy was made by selecting all the nodes of the first shape in Node Edit, then using Ctrl+C and Ctrl+V to copy and paste those nodes.)

Fig. 5.50
An object with two
contours.

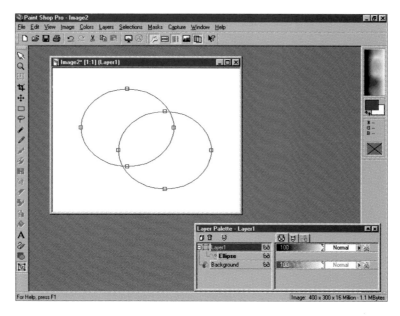

Now for the nifty part. In Node Edit mode, select one node on one of the
contours. Right-click to bring up the menu, and select **E**dit, Reverse
Contour (or instead of using the menu, just press Ctrl+R). You'll see that
the arrow control has switched to indicate counterclockwise direction for
the contour the node is on (see Figure 5.51).

Fig. 5.51
Reversing the contour.

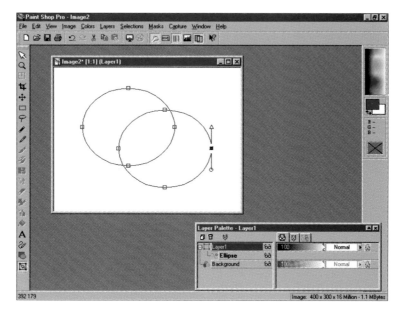

Exit Node Edit mode and deselect the object. You'll see something like Figure 5.52.

Fig. 5.52
The cutout effect.

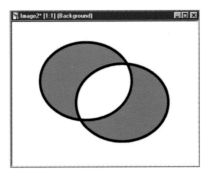

At the point where the two contours overlap, the intersection will be treated as being "outside" the object. In this example, the contours partially overlap, so each contour produces solid areas (where they don't overlap) and a hole (where they do overlap). In the example in Figure 5.48, at the beginning of this subsection, one contour is entirely contained in the other. Since the inner contour's path goes in the opposite direction as the path of the outer contour, what you get is a continuous object that looks like it has a hole in the middle.

NOTE

If you're trying to make a cutout with vectors but no cutout appears, it may be that you accidentally chose Reverse Path instead of Reverse Contour. Reverse Path reverses the path direction for all contours of an object. Reverse Contour reverses the path direction of only the contour that contains the currently selected node.

To get the cutout, try Reverse Contour again on one of the nodes of one of the contours: In Node Edit mode, select a single node on the contour. Right-click to bring up the Node Edit menu, and choose **E**dit, Reverse Contour.

You're now ready to create all sorts of simple and complex vector drawings. Try using vector lines and preset shapes to make your own scalable buttons for a Web site or scalable versions of your company logo, saving raster copies when you have just the size you want. Combine multiple vector layers to create high-quality illustrations, such as VECTOR FISH.PSP, one of the sample images available on the PSP6 installation CD. You'll be amazed at what you can achieve with vectors.

6

PSP Effects

PSP Effects are built-in operations that you can use to transform your images. The Effects give your images a 3D look, perfect for adding depth and interest to text and objects. Use the Effects to create buttons and banners for a Web site, to simulate naturalistic effects, or to produce wild and unnatural effects.

Here's what you'll be exploring in this chapter:

▶ Producing simple 3D effects

▶ Creating complex effects

Version 6 of PSP has a whole new set of Effects, along with the old standbys from previous versions. All of the Effects add depth to your images, some simply by adding shadows and others by applying a pattern or texture to your image.

You access the Effects by choosing Image, Effects from the PSP menubar. A list then appears from which you can select one of the many Effects discussed in this chapter.

NOTE

You can use PSP Effects only on raster layers and only with greyscale and 24-bit color images. Some Effects—Cutout, Drop Shadow, and Inner Bevel—are available only if your image has a selection or the active layer contains some transparent areas. Outer Bevel is even more picky: It's available only if there's a nonfloating selection.

If you have trouble applying an Effect, check the color depth of your image and make sure that there is a selection, if one is needed. In layered images, also be sure that the current layer is a raster layer.

Simple 3D Effects

One of the quickest and easiest ways to add nice-looking text and other accents to your images is to use one of the simple 3D-type Effects: Buttonize, Drop Shadow, Chisel, Cutout, Inner Bevel, and Outer Bevel. If you've used earlier versions of PSP, you're probably at least somewhat familiar with the first four of these Effects.

Buttonize

Web graphic designers and print artists will find the Buttonize Effect useful. For example, using the Buttonize Effect is the easiest way to create attractive rectangular buttons and other beveled rectangular elements in PSP.

You can create your button either by using an entire image or by making a rectangular selection in an image. Choose **I**mage, **E**ffects, **B**uttonize to access the Buttonize dialog box, as shown in Figure 6.1.

Fig. 6.1
The Buttonize dialog box.

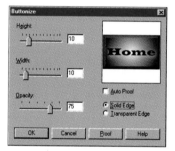

The Buttonize dialog box contains several controls that you can set to change the look of your button. Choose either Solid Edge, for a sharply defined bevel edge, or Transparent Edge, for a softer beveling effect. You define the height and width of the bevel by dragging the Height slider (for the top and bottom beveling) and the Width slider (for the side beveling). Opacity can also be set, to vary the darkness of the bevel's shadow.

Try adjusting the controls in the Buttonize dialog box to see how they affect your button.

NOTE
The bevel is set to the background color that was selected in the Color Palette before you chose Buttonize.

There are several ways to proof your button before you actually apply the Buttonize Effect. You can get an idea of how your button will look by examining the Preview window in the Buttonize dialog box. You also can preview your entire image by clicking the Proof button in the dialog box. If you want to proof your work dynamically, to see the results of changes as you make them, check the Auto Proof box in the Buttonize dialog box. Keep in mind, though, that Auto Proof requires considerable resources and can slow down PSP's responsiveness.

After you preview your button and establish the look that you want, click OK to apply the Effect. Figures 6.2 and 6.3 show the same rectangular image before and after Buttonize is applied (with Transparent Edge selected, Height and Width both set to 20, and Opacity set to 100).

Fig. 6.2
Rectangular image before Buttonize is applied.

Fig. 6.3
Buttonized image.

Figure 6.4 illustrates another use for Buttonize. Here, a rectangular selection was feathered 10 pixels by choosing Selections, Modify, Feather and then applying Buttonize to the image. The result is a raised rectangular area that seems to gradually rise from the background.

Fig. 6.4
A Buttonized, feathered selection.

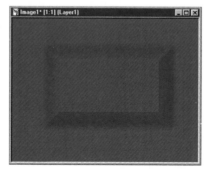

You also can use Image, Add Borders in combination with Buttonize to produce frame-like effects. Figure 6.5 shows an example in which a 10-pixel red border was added to the rose image, and then Buttonize was applied with Transparent Edge selected and Height and Width set to 10.

CHAPTER 6

Fig. 6.5
A Buttonized border
added to an image.

Use multiple Buttonized borders to make even fancier frames. In the
examples in Figures 6.6a and 6.6b, a red border was added and Buttonized,
and then another red border was added and Buttonized. In Figure 6.6c,
a third border was added and Buttonized.

Fig. 6.6a
A fancier Buttonized
border frame.

Fig. 6.6b
A variation on the
Buttonized border
frame.

Fig. 6.6c
A frame made with
three applications of
Add Borders and
Buttonize.

NOTE
You can apply Image, Add Borders only to flat images. When you try to add a
border to a layered image, PSP warns you that the image will be flattened if
you proceed.

Drop Shadow

Another easy-to-use Effect is Drop Shadow, which creates an illusion of
depth in your images. By using this Effect with text or objects, you can
make them appear to "float" above the background and cast a shadow.

To use Drop Shadow, you need to have either a selection or a transparent
background.

To apply Drop Shadow, choose **I**mage, Effects, **D**rop Shadow. The Drop Shadow dialog box appears, as shown in Figure 6.7.

Fig. 6.7
The Drop Shadow dialog box.

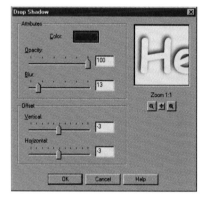

Set the shadow color by clicking the color swatch at the top of the dialog box; this brings up the Color dialog box. Alternatively, right-click to bring up the Recent Colors dialog box.

Set the opacity of the shadow from 1 to 100 percent with the Opacity slider. Use Blur to set the softness/blurriness of the shadow, and use the Vertical and Horizontal Offsets, which range from −100 to 100 pixels, to position the shadow. Negative Offset values push the shadow up or to the left, whereas positive values push the shadow down or to the right. When you're satisfied with the effect, click the OK button to apply the Drop Shadow.

CHAPTER 6

Figure 6.8 shows a few examples of Drop Shadow applied to images.

Fig. 6.8
Examples of Drop
Shadow.

The top example in Figure 6.8 shows a black shadow with positive Horizontal and Vertical Offsets. In the middle example, the shadow is red; the Horizontal and Vertical offsets are set to 0; and Blur is set to a high setting. For the bottom example, the blue shadow's Horizontal Offset is set to a large negative value and its Vertical Offset is set to a large positive value.

You also can produce some interesting 3D effects by inverting a text selection to apply a Drop Shadow *inside* your text. This can give the edges of your text a rounded effect, creating a bas relief look. Figure 6.9 shows one example of this technique.

Fig. 6.9
Bas relief effect created
with Drop Shadow on
an inverted text
selection.

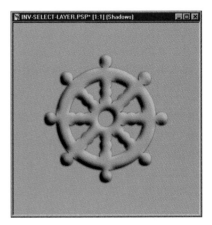

Here's how the effect was produced in this example:

1. Add a dingbat character with the Text tool. Be sure that Selection is checked. (The Wingding] character was used here, set to a size of 250 points.)

2. Invert the selection by choosing **S**elections, **I**nvert or by pressing Shift+Ctrl+I. The marquee will then look something like the one in Figure 6.10.

Fig. 6.10
An inverted text
selection.

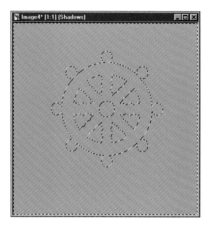

3. Choose **I**mage, **E**ffec**t**s, **D**rop Shadow. Set the Color to Black, Opacity to 80, Blur to 14, Vertical Offset to −6, and Horizontal Offset to 6.

4. Again, choose **I**mage, **E**ffec**t**s, **D**rop Shadow. Set the Color to White, Opacity to 50, Blur to 8, Vertical Offset to 6, and Horizontal Offset to −6.

5. Invert the selection again. Choose **I**mage, **E**ffec**t**s, **D**rop Shadow. Set Color to Black, Opacity to 80, Blur to 5, Vertical Offset to 1, and Horizontal Offset to −1 to create the effect shown in Figure 6.9.

TIP
You can use this same technique on an empty layer and then insert any textured layer under the Drop Shadow layer to produce the bas relief effect on the texture, as in Figure 6.11.

Fig. 6.11
Bas relief Drop Shadow
layer above a textured
layer.

CHAPTER 6

Chisel

The Chisel Effect usually is used to give text or some other selected object a raised-border effect. To try out Chisel, add text with the Text tool and then choose Image, Effects, Chisel. You'll then see the Chisel dialog box, as shown in Figure 6.12.

Fig. 6.12
The Chisel dialog box.

You can adjust two settings in the Chisel dialog box: By dragging the Size control slider, you can change the size of the chiseling; by selecting either Transparent or Background Color, you can control whether the chiseled area is transparent (letting the color of the image show through) or painted on in the current background color.

Figure 6.13 shows some chiseled text with the Transparent option selected, and Figure 6.14 shows the same text with Background Color selected instead. In each case, Size is set to 10.

Fig. 6.13
Chisel with Transparent setting.

Fig. 6.14
Chisel with Background Color setting.

A slight variation on the Chisel Effect works particularly well with nonlayered images. Instead of applying Chisel to a text selection itself, try inverting the selection and then applying Chisel. The result of this technique is shown in Figure 6.15.

Fig. 6.15
Inverted Chisel
technique.

Although the inverted Chisel technique does not work in this way on layers, it often produces very nice results on flat images. And don't limit your use of the inverted Chisel technique to text selections; you also can try this technique with rectangular or square selections to create buttons or frames, as shown in Figure 6.16.

Fig. 6.16
Inverted chiseled
button.

You might also want to create a glow around text by using Chisel on a layered image, as shown in Figure 6.17.

Fig. 6.17
A glow effect created
with Chisel.

CHAPTER 6

NOTE

If you are unfamiliar with layers, work through the examples in Chapter 4, "Mastering Layers and Blend Modes," before beginning the following example.

Here's how to produce the glow effect:

1. Begin with a solid-colored, 24-bit image. Change the foreground color in the Color Palette to the background color of your image by clicking the Dropper tool in the image canvas.

2. Select a new background color by clicking the background tile on the Color Palette and then selecting a color on the Color Wheel. This will be the color of your glow.

3. Add a new layer above the solid-colored Background. (Either click the New Layer icon on the Layer Palette or choose **L**ayers, New Raster **L**ayer.) When the Layer Properties dialog box appears, click OK.

4. With the Text tool, add text to the new layer. Make sure that Selection in the Add Text dialog box is checked.

5. Apply the Chisel Effect by choosing **I**mage, Effe**c**ts, **C**hisel. In the Chisel dialog box, set a fairly large value for Size (33 was used to create the effect in Figure 6.17) and select the Transparent option.

6. Keep the text selection active. Add another layer, this one above the layer used for the Chisel Effect. Use the Flood Fill tool to fill each letter of the selection with the same fill that you used for the solid-colored background. When the text selection is completely filled, deselect the text by right-clicking with a selection tool, by pressing Ctrl+D, or by choosing **S**elections, Select **N**one.

TIP

To fill all areas of a discontinuous selection at once, set the Match Mode for the Flood Fill tool to None.

7. Make the layer with the Chisel Effect the active layer by clicking its Layer button in the Layer Palette. Then, apply a blur by choosing either **I**mage, **B**lur, **B**lur or **I**mage, **B**lur, **B**lur More. Your glowing text is complete!

Try out Chisel on your photorealistic images, too, to add a decorative edge. For example, define an elliptical, feathered selection around the main figure of a photo, and then apply Chisel to produce something like the effect shown in Figure 6.18, where Chisel was applied to a layer above the photo's layer.

Fig. 6.18
Add a decorative edge
to a photo with Chisel.

These are just some of the results you can create with Chisel. Be sure to
experiment with this Effect to discover others for yourself.

Cutout

For many PSP users, Cutout is mysterious and troublesome, but after you
master this Effect, it will be one of your most frequently used tools. You
can use Cutout not only to create various shadowed cutout effects but
also to produce raised 3D effects, such as those created when you apply
Drop Shadow to an inverted text selection.

As a first example, consider an image with a solid-blue background and a
rectangular selection. Choose Image, Effects, Cutout to access the Cutout
dialog box, as shown in Figure 6.19.

Fig. 6.19
The Cutout dialog box.

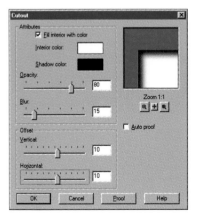

In this example, check the Fill interior with color checkbox so that the selection will be filled with a new color. Click the Interior color swatch and choose white in the Color dialog box. For Shadow color, click the Shadow color swatch and choose black in the Color dialog box.

Set Opacity, which determines how opaque the shadow appears (from 1–100 percent opaque), to 80, and set Blur, which determines how blurry the shadow appears, to 15.

The Horizontal and the Vertical Offsets are used to position the interior of the Cutout, affecting where the shadow appears. (This can be confusing, because the Offsets don't directly position the shadow, but they do affect the position of the shadow.) Both the Horizontal and the Vertical Offset controls can be set anywhere between −100 and 100 pixels. For this example, use 10 for each Offset control.

You can preview the results in the dialog box's Preview window, clicking + or − below the Preview window to zoom in and out. You also can drag inside the Preview window to shift the position of the thumbnail, or you can click the Proof button to proof the effect on your actual image. And, as with Buttonize, you can check Auto Proof to see the image change dynamically as you modify the settings.

Click OK to apply the Cutout, and the result appears in Figure 6.20.

Fig. 6.20
Cutout on a flat image, with Fill interior with color checked.

Now you are ready to learn how to use Cutout to simulate a carved-out effect on a flat image:

1. Begin with a nonlayered, textured image and add text with the Text tool, making sure that Selection is checked.

2. With the text area still selected, choose **C**olors, **A**djust, **B**rightness/ Contrast. Decrease the Brightness a bit, about −15% or so, with Contrast set at 0%. Darkening the text in this way adds to the recessed effect that you're trying to achieve.

3. With the text area still selected, choose **Image**, **Effects**, **Cutout**. This time, make sure that the Fill interior with color checkbox is *not* selected, and choose White as the Shadow color. Set Opacity to 75%, Blur to 0, and both Horizontal and Vertical to –1.

4. With the text area still selected, choose **Image**, **Effects**, **Cutout** again. Use 80% for the Opacity and set Blur to 15; use Black as the Shadow color and set Horizontal and Vertical to 4. (For this step and for Step 3, experiment to see what settings work best for your specific font and font size.)

5. After you apply this Cutout, deselect the text area by right-clicking anywhere in your image or by pressing Ctrl+D. Figure 6.21 shows the final result.

Fig. 6.21
Carved-out effect created with Cutout.

Experiment with this technique on text selections. Depending on the settings that you choose, especially for Blur and Opacity, you'll produce either a carved-out effect or a raised 3D effect.

So far, you've been using Cutout on nonlayered images or opaque backgrounds. Cutout behaves a bit differently, though, if you use it on a floating selection or on a real layer—one that allows transparency. To see the difference, compare Figures 6.22 and 6.23.

Fig. 6.22
Cutout applied on a flat image.

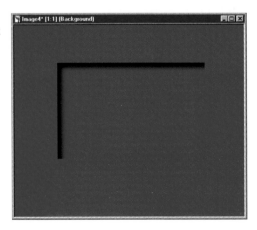

CHAPTER 6

Fig. 6.23
Cutout applied on a
layer.

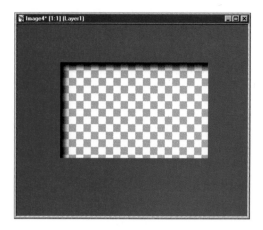

In both cases, the following options were set:

Fill interior with color = unchecked

Shadow color = Black

Opacity = 75

Blur = 20

Horizontal and Vertical Offsets = 10

One way to create the effect shown in Figure 6.22 on a layered image
is to make a selection and then float the selection (with Ctrl+F) before
applying Cutout. Another approach is to switch on the layer's Protect
Transparency toggle on the Layer Palette before applying Cutout to
the layer.

A somewhat more flexible alternative is to make sure that you apply the
Cutout to a new layer *above* the original layer. That new layer can be
either a duplicate of the original layer or a completely empty layer.

First, make the selection for the Cutout. Then, add the new layer. The
selection will be active no matter what the active layer is. With the new
layer active, apply Cutout. If Fill interior with color is left unchecked,
only the shadow of the Cutout will be present on the new layer, and the
rest of the layer will be transparent. If you want to add an additional
Cutout, add another layer and apply Cutout while the new layer is active.

Inner Bevel

All four of the Effects described in the preceding sections were also available in PSP5. Version 6 of PSP also includes Inner Bevel, which you can use to easily add beveled effects to selections of any shape.

Although the effects produced by Inner Bevel seem quite simple, the controls available are pretty complex. At first, the Inner Bevel dialog box (see Figure 6.24) might seem a little intimidating, but after you've used this effect a few times, it will be second-nature to you.

Fig. 6.24
The Inner Bevel dialog box.

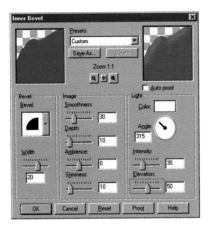

At the top of the dialog box is a pair of Preview windows, with the original image displayed in the left window and the version with the effect applied shown in the right window. Between these two windows, there's also a drop-down list of presets (saved settings that you can call up to use again).

On the lower left of the dialog box is a section labeled *Bevel* in which you choose the shape of the bevel and its width. To the right of the Bevel section is one labeled *Image*, which contains controls for Smoothness, Depth, Ambience, and Shininess, defined as follows:

▶ **Smoothness**—Determines to what degree the bevel is sharply edged or blends smoothly in with the flat part of the image. The higher the Smoothness, the rounder the edges of the bevel.

▶ **Depth**—Determines how pronounced the edges of the bevel are. The higher the Depth, the more pronounced the edges.

▶ **Ambience**—Determines the overall brightness of the image.

▶ **Shininess**—Determines how glossy the bevel appears. The higher the Shininess value, the more pronounced the highlights on the bevel are.

CHAPTER 6

The lower-right section of the dialog box, labeled *Light*, contains controls for setting the light shining on the image. At the top of this section is a color swatch. Click this swatch to call up the Color dialog box, where you can select the color for your light.

Below the color swatch are two controls that you can use to set the angle of the light: a dial and a textbox labeled Angle. To set the light's angle, you can either drag the hand of the dial or enter a number of degrees in the textbox.

Next are two sliders, one labeled *Intensity* and the other labeled *Elevation*. Intensity determines the brightness of the light shining on the object. Note that this will be added to the ambient brightness set with Ambience, so adjustments to Intensity might require you to also adjust Ambience in order to maintain a certain overall brightness.

Elevation determines the vertical position of the light source. A setting of 90 places the light source directly overhead. The lower the elevation, the closer the light source is to the "ground."

NOTE

Five of PSP's Effects use Smoothness, Depth, Ambience, Shininess, and the Light controls: Inner Bevel, Outer Bevel, Sculpture, Texture, and Tiles.

A few examples of Inner Bevel are shown in Figures 6.25a-c. Figure 6.25a shows an irregularly shaped beveled button; Figure 6.25b shows an edged oval; and Figure 6.25c shows a picture frame.

Fig. 6.25a
An irregularly shaped button made with Inner Bevel.

Fig. 6.25b
An edged oval made with Inner Bevel.

Fig. 6.25c
A picture frame made with Inner Bevel.

TIP

You can add to a beveled figure's feeling of depth by also applying Drop Shadow to the figure.

After you start experimenting with Inner Bevel, you're sure to find all sorts of uses for it, beyond frames and buttons. You can produce some very nice gold text, for example, by filling a text selection with the Yellow Metallic gradient supplied by Jasc and then applying Inner Bevel with settings like those in Figure 6.26.

Fig. 6.26
Making gold text with Inner Bevel.

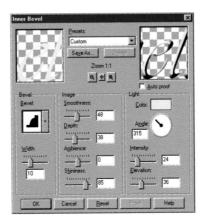

TIP

Several of the PSP Effects, including Inner Bevel, come with a variety of *presets*—saved settings that you can load and apply. If an Effect supports presets, be sure to experiment with the presets that accompany it.

To save your own preset, select your settings and then click the Save As button under the Presets drop-down list. Enter a name for your preset when prompted to do so, and then click OK. This creates a new preset file in PSP's Presets folder.

The filename of your new file is the name you gave your preset. The extension indicates which preset the file is for:

.PBV = Inner and Outer Bevel

.PSC = Sculpture

.PTL = Tiles

.PTX = Texture

To install a preset file that you've received from someone else, just copy the file to the Presets folder.

CHAPTER 6

Outer Bevel

Another new Effect added to PSP6 is Outer Bevel. In some ways this Effect is similar to Chisel, but you have a lot more options with Outer Bevel.

The controls for Outer Bevel are just like those for Inner Bevel. The difference is that with Inner Bevel the beveling is applied within the border of a selection, and with Outer Bevel the beveling is applied outside the selection border. Outer Bevel most resembles Chisel when the setting for Smoothness is set very low.

Figure 6.27 shows the dialog box for Outer Bevel, along with an example created by applying this Effect.

Fig. 6.27
An example of Outer Bevel.

NOTE
Outer Bevel is available only if you have a nonfloating selection.

Simple Artistic Effects

PSP6 also adds a number of simple artistic edge effects: Black Pencil, Charcoal, Chrome, Colored Chalk, Colored Pencil, Glowing Edges, and Neon Glow. Black Pencil, Charcoal, Colored Chalk, and Colored Pencil can add sketch-like textures to your images. Chrome, Glowing Edges, and Neon Glow add other interesting effects.

Black Pencil and Colored Pencil

These Effects can be used to make an image look as though it's been drawn either with a black pencil or with colored pencils. How successfully this effect is achieved depends on the particular image you use and the settings you choose. In general, photorealistic images that include figures that are distinct from the background are good candidates for these filters.

Both Effects use the same controls. Figure 6.28 shows an example with Black Pencil.

Fig. 6.28
An example of Black Pencil.

Increasing Detail adds more and heavier pencil lines. Decreasing Opacity lets more of the original image's color show through.

Charcoal and Colored Chalk

By using the Charcoal and Colored Chalk Effects, you can produce results very similar to those produced by using the Black Pencil and Colored Pencil, but with broader lines and less fine detail. The controls for these Effects are the same as those for Black Pencil and Colored Pencil. Figure 6.29 shows an example created with Colored Chalk.

Fig. 6.29
An example created with Colored Chalk.

Neon Glow

Neon Glow is another Effect that produces results similar to those produced with the pencil Effects. As its name implies, Neon Glow creates a bright, glowing effect.

To apply this Effect, choose **I**mages, Effects, **N**eon Glow. The Neon Glow dialog box, which includes the same controls as those used for the pencil Effects, appears. Figure 6.30 shows an example created with Neon Glow.

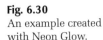
Fig. 6.30
An example created
with Neon Glow.

Chrome

Chrome, which is quite useful on color and greyscale photorealistic
images, is used to make shiny metallic effects. Because Chrome locates
areas of contrast in order to produce a shiny effect, using Chrome on a
solid-colored object produces very disappointing results. To see Chrome
at its best, try it on relatively complex images with areas of contrast.

NOTE

Folks who use Alien Skin's Eye Candy filters should note that Eye Candy's
Chrome filter works quite differently from PSP's Chrome Effect. The Eye
Candy filter makes use of selection edges or areas of transparency rather than
contrast. It gives pleasing results on solid-colored figures and text, but isn't
appropriate for use on the more complex images that work best with PSP's
Chrome Effect.

Call up the Chrome dialog box by choosing Image, Effects, Chrome.
There you'll find several controls that work together to produce different
metal-like effects: Flaws, Brightness, Use original color, and Color (see
Figure 6.31).

CHAPTER 6

Fig. 6.31
The Chrome dialog box.

Flaws determines the amount of banding, and Brightness is used to adjust brightness. You have the choice of having the filter retain the original color of the image or to change the image to monochrome. To make the image monochrome, click the Color box to call up the Color dialog box and then select the color you want.

Figures 6.32a-c show some examples of Chrome.

Fig. 6.32a
Chrome applied to a color photorealistic image.

Fig. 6.32b
Chrome applied to a greyscale photorealistic image.

Fig. 6.32c
Chrome applied to a
drawing.

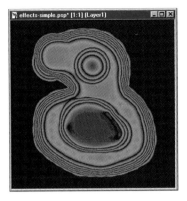

Glowing Edges

Glowing Edges lets you easily apply a whole range of edge detection
effects to your images. If you want an object or string of text to look like a
neon sign, Glowing Edges is the ticket.

There are two controls in the Glowing Edges dialog box, which you
access by choosing **I**mages, **E**ffects, **G**lowing Edges: *Intensity* determines
the amount of banding, and *Sharpness* determines how soft or sharp the
edges are.

Figures 6.33a-b show examples created with Glowing Edges.

Fig. 6.33a
Glowing Edges applied
to a photorealistic
image.

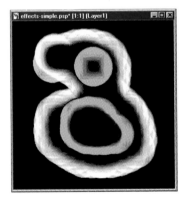

Fig. 6.33a
Glowing Edges applied to a photorealistic
image.

Fig. 6.33b
Glowing Edges applied to a
drawing.

Simple Texture Effects

Blinds, Feedback, Kaleidoscope, Mosaic – Antique, Mosaic – Glass, Pattern, and Weave all produce simple texture effects. Blinds, Kaleidoscope, the Mosaic Effects, and Weave produce effects similar to their real-world correlates. Pattern lets you create your own repeating patterns, like printed fabric. Feedback superimposes your image on itself, in smaller and smaller concentric copies.

Blinds

Care to do a little home decorating in your images? Blinds, which you apply by choosing Images, Effects, Blinds, can at least help with the window dressing, as Figure 6.34 shows.

Fig. 6.34
The Blinds dialog box, with an example behind.

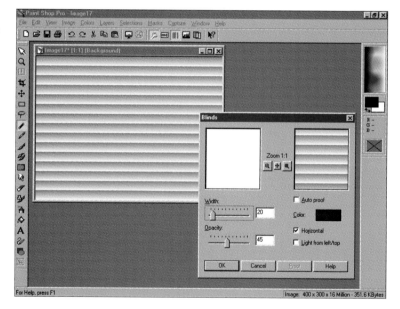

Don't care for horizontal blinds? Uncheck the *Horizontal* control in the Blinds dialog box and you'll get vertical blinds instead, as shown in Figure 6.35.

Fig. 6.35
An example of vertical blinds.

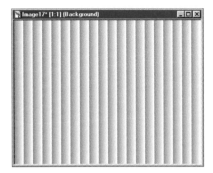

Don't think that window blinds are all you can make with this effect. Figure 6.36 shows a nice log cabin effect made by applying Blinds to a woodgrain texture.

Fig. 6.36
A log cabin effect made with Blinds.

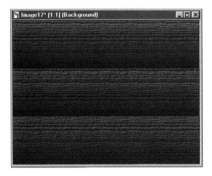

Begin with any wood texture. Creating the effect is then quite simple:

1. Choose Image, Effects, Blinds.
2. Set Width fairly high. How high will depend on the size of your image and on how thick you want your logs to be.
3. Set Color to a dark brown. Click the Color color swatch in the Blinds dialog box, and then choose the color you want in the Color dialog box. The Color setting determines the color both of the logs' outlines and of the shading.
4. Select Light from left/top and Horizontal.

The log cabin effect is then complete.

CHAPTER 6

Another effect to try is applying Blinds twice to the same image, varying the settings each time. Figure 6.37 shows a texture made by combining horizontal and vertical blinds.

Fig. 6.37
Combining horizontal and vertical blinds.

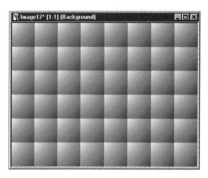

Feedback

Feedback can produce a number of strange, sometimes eerie, effects. Be sure to experiment with different Opacity and Intensity settings, and vary the Horizontal and Vertical center.

Figure 6.38 shows the Feedback dialog box, with an example of Feedback with Elliptical selected. Figure 6.39 shows another example, this time with Elliptical not selected.

Fig. 6.38
The Feedback dialog box and an example with Elliptical selected.

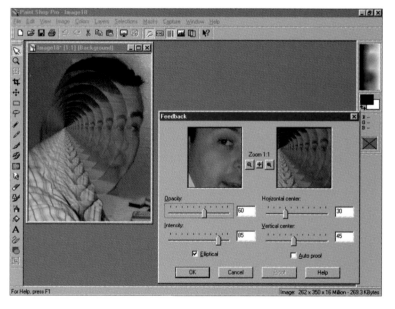

Fig. 6.39
An example of
Feedback, with
Elliptical unselected.

In each of these examples, Opacity is set rather low, allowing underlying copies of the image to show through the higher copies. Also, the Horizontal and Vertical offsets are set so that the vanishing point of the feedback copies is off-center. Experiment with different combinations of the Feedback settings to see what other sorts of effects you can achieve.

Kaleidoscope

To create nifty kaleidoscopic effects, use Kaleidoscope on just about any image that has two or more colors. Try greyscale images as well as color images. In fact, using Kaleidoscope on a greyscale image is a great way to produce interesting Paper Textures for use with PSP's painting tools. (See Chapter 11, "Adding to Your Toolkit" for instructions on creating your own textures.)

Kaleidoscope takes a wedge-shaped portion of your image and repeats and mirrors it to simulate a kaleidoscope. Figure 6.40 shows an example and the Kaleidoscope dialog box, which you access by choosing Images, Effects, Kaleidoscope.

CHAPTER 6

Fig. 6.40
The Kaleidoscope dialog
box, with example
behind.

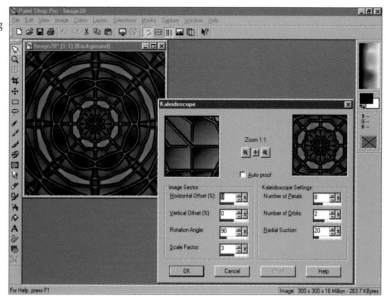

You can set the following controls in the Kaleidoscope dialog box:

▶ **Image Sector**—This setting determines what section of your image is used for the wedge that serves as the basis of the pattern.

▶ **Kaleidoscope**—This setting determines how many times the pattern is repeated, both around the circle and from the center out.

▶ **Radial Suction**—The most mysterious sounding of the controls, this setting determines how close or far away from the center of your image the sampling for the pattern begins. The larger the Radial Suction value, the farther from the center of the image the sampling begins. The sampled areas are pulled toward the center of your kaleidoscopic image.

The example in Figure 6.40 was made from an abstract image, but don't hesitate to use photos with Kaleidoscope. Figure 6.41 shows an example of Kaleidoscope applied to a photo of prairie daisies (Rotation Angle 90, Scale Factor –20, Number of Petals 8, Number of Orbits 0, Radial Suction 48).

Fig. 6.41
An example of Kaleidoscope applied to a photorealistic image.

Mosaic – Antique

Mosaic – Antique makes your image look like it's made from old mosaic tiles. Figure 6.42 shows an example, along with the Mosaic—Antique dialog box, which you access by choosing Image, Effects, Mosaic—Antique.

Fig. 6.42
The Mosaic – Antique dialog box, with example behind.

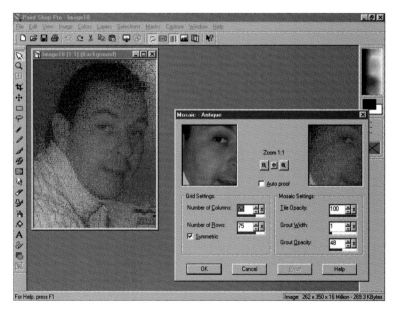

Vary the Tile Opacity, Grout Width, and Grout Opacity for different effects. For example, a high Tile Opacity combined with a Grout Width of 0 produces a pixelated or tiled effect similar to PSP's Mosaic filter (discussed in Chapter 8, "Filters"). In contrast, a lower Tile Opacity can produce an effect similar to frosted glass.

Figure 6.43 shows a glassier version of the previous example, this time with the Number of Columns and Number of Rows set to 50; Tile Opacity set to 65; Grout Width set to 2; and Grout Opacity set to 20.

Fig. 6.43
Another example of
Mosaic – Antique.

Mosaic – Glass

Mosaic – Glass can make your image look like its being viewed through small glass blocks. This effect is as nice with greyscale images as it is with color images, as Figure 6.44 shows.

Fig. 6.44
The Mosaic – Glass
dialog box, with
example behind.

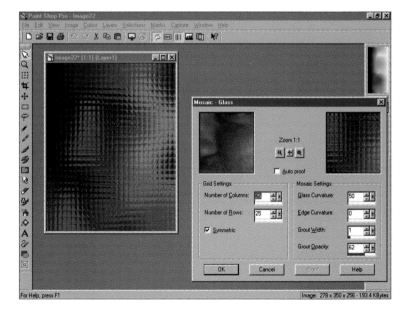

Notice how portions of the image are reflected in the glass blocks: The eye is made up of small reflections of the eye, the nose of small reflections of the nose, the mouth of small reflections of the mouth.

To achieve the etched glass look shown in Figure 6.45, open the Mosaic – Glass dialog box by choosing Image, Effects, **M**osaic – Glass and then set the *Number of Rows* and *Number of Columns* to a large value, and the *Grout Width* to 0.

Adjust the brightness and contrast of an image like this one to produce misty, romantic effects. Combine it with the Erode or Dilate filters (discussed in Chapter 8, "Filters") to make a digital painting from a photo.

Pattern

Use Pattern to make your own repeating patterns, using any image at all. Figure 6.46 shows an example and the Pattern dialog box.

CHAPTER 6

Fig. 6.46
The Pattern dialog box,
with example behind.

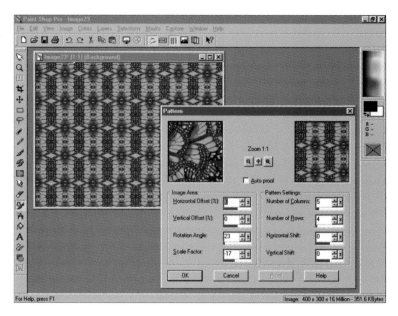

One technique that works well is to fill an empty image canvas by painting with a Picture Tube. Set the Step of the Picture Tube rather low and drag randomly around the canvas. When the canvas is filled, apply Pattern. That's the technique used to produce the image in Figure 6.46, using the Monarch Picture Tube supplied by Jasc.

Figure 6.47 shows a variation using the same tube-filled image with the following settings:

> Rotation Angle = 100
>
> Scale Factor = 0
>
> Number of Columns = 8
>
> Number of Rows = 6

Fig. 6.47
Another example
created with Pattern.

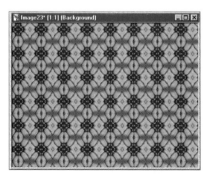

Weave

Weave makes your image look like it's made from woven strips. Figure 6.48 shows the Weave dialog box, along with an example of Weave applied to the Pattern shown in Figure 6.47.

Fig. 6.48
The Weave dialog box, with example behind.

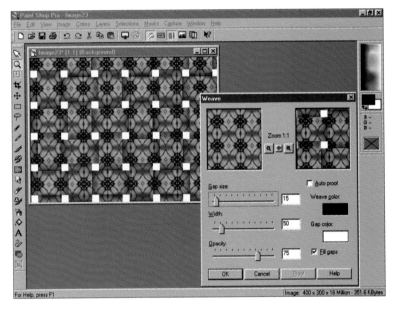

You can even apply Weave to a solid-colored image to produce a nice effect, as in Figure 6.49.

Fig. 6.49
Another example of Weave.

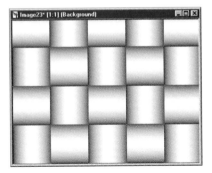

Here, Weave is applied to a pure white image, with Gap Size set to 1; Width to 80; and Opacity to 90.

CHAPTER 6

Complex Texture Effects

The remaining Effects are the most complex both in terms of their controls and in terms of the results they produce. All come with a set of presets, and you can save your own presets for future use, too. To get a feel for these Effects, be sure to try out the presets, noting the settings each uses and what results they yield.

Sculpture

The controls for Sculpture are very much like those for Inner Bevel, as Figure 6.50 shows.

Fig. 6.50
The Sculpture dialog box.

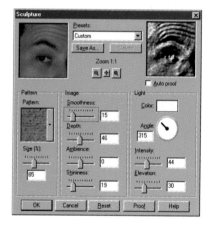

The only difference between the Sculpture and Inner Bevel dialog boxes is in the leftmost panel of controls. With Sculpture, contrasting edges in your image are "sculpted" into a pattern. You select the pattern and scale it with the Pattern controls.

The patterns available for Sculpture are stored in PSP's Patterns folder, as shown in Figure 6.51.

Fig. 6.51
The patterns available for Sculpture.

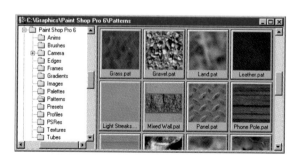

As discussed in Chapter 11, "Adding to Your Toolkit," you can add your own patterns, too.

Figure 6.52 shows a few examples of what you can do with Sculpture.

Fig. 6.52
Sculpture examples.

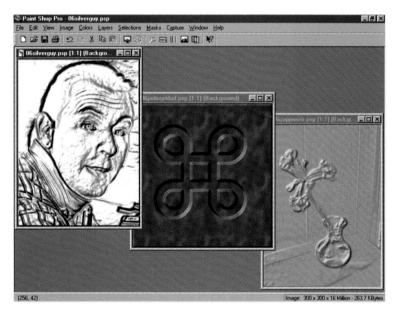

Here, the Silver preset was used for the image on the left; Jade was used for the middle image; and Copper was used for the image on the right.

Texture

Texture is another Effect with controls that are very similar to those of Inner Bevel, as Figure 6.53 shows.

Fig. 6.53
Texture dialog box.

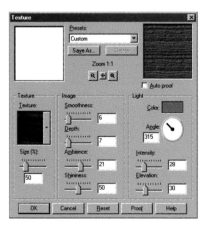

The unique controls here, in the leftmost panel, are *Texture* and *Size (%)*.

Use Texture to add a texture to your image. This is a lot quicker and easier than using the Clone Brush to paint your image onto a new canvas with a Paper Texture, as you did in Chapter 2, "More Painting Tools."

And it's no coincidence that the textures and the Paper Textures look so similar—the fact is, they're identical. Any of the textures available as Paper Textures with the painting tools are also available here, although some textures work best as paper textures while others work best with the Texture Effect.

Figure 6.54 shows an example of Texture applied to a photorealistic image.

Fig. 6.54
An example of Texture.

As you'll see in Chapter 11, "Adding to Your Toolkit," you can add your own textures for use as Paper Textures or as textures for the Texture Effect.

Tiles

Tiles is a very versatile Effect. You can create anything from simulated crewel work (see Figure 6.55a) to something like ceramic tile (see Figure 6.55b) to a leathery look (see Figure 6.55c).

Fig. 6.55a
Crewel work made with Tiles.

Fig. 6.55b
Ceramic tile made with
Tiles.

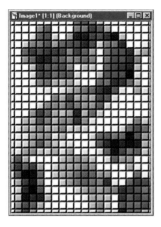

Fig. 6.55c
Leather made with
Tiles.

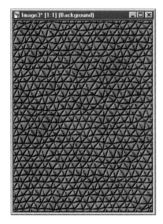

As Figure 6.56 shows, Tiles uses many of the controls familiar to you
from Inner Bevel and other Effects. The Tile controls, in the leftmost
panel of the Tiles dialog box, are the controls unique to Tiles.

Fig. 6.56
The Tiles dialog box.

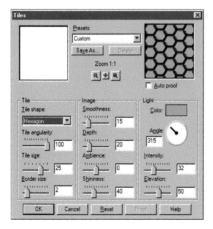

CHAPTER 6

▶ **Tile Shape**—As its name implies, this control sets the shape of the tiles. For example, you can set the tiles to Hexagon (as in Figure 6.55a), Square (as in Figure 6.55b), or Triangle (as in Figure 6.55c).

▶ **Tile Angularity**—This control determines whether the tiles are made in a regular, rigid matrix or are made to conform somewhat to the shape of your image; the higher the value, the more the tiles conform to the shape of your image. In Figures 6.55a-c, the crewel work and leather have high values for Tile Angularity, while the ceramic tiles have a value of 0.

▶ **Tile Size**—This control sets the size of the individual tiles.

▶ **Border Size**—This control sets the size of the spacing between the tiles. This spacing is always filled in with black.

Here's how to produce the leather-like effect shown in Figure 6.55c:

1.   Start with a tan or brownish solid-colored image.

2.   Use the Airbrush with Opacity set to 50% or less to spray on a barely perceptible irregular pattern that is only slightly darker than the image's original color. You need to have something other than a solid color in your image in order for Tile Angularity to have an effect.

3.   Apply the Tile Effect:

   ▶ Choose Image, Effects, Tiles to open the Tiles dialog box.

   ▶ Set Shape to Triangle, and set Tile Angularity to a rather high value. Use the Preview window in the dialog box or press the Proof button in order to see what value works best for your particular image.

   ▶ Set the Tile Size and Border Size to whatever values give you the effect you want. In general, you'll get the best leathery effect with a small value for Border Size—just enough to suggest the characteristic cracks of leather.

In your own experiments, be sure to try out all the Tiles presets and have fun doing your own exploring. You might be quite surprised by the range of possibilities with Tiles!

7

PSP Deformations

Like PSP Effects, PSP Deformations are built-in operations that you can use to transform your images. The Deformations warp the shape of your images, which is particularly useful when you want to add perspective to an image, wrap a texture around an object, or modify a figure's shape.

Here's what you'll be exploring in this chapter:

▶ Generating useful effects with PSP Deformations

▶ Creating free Deformations

Transforming Your Images with Deformations

PSP has seventeen built-in Deformation filters, which you can access by choosing **I**mage, **D**eformations and then selecting the particular Deformation you want to use. The Deformation filters can be applied to an image, layer, or selection—singly or in combination—to achieve sometimes odd and sometimes quite useful effects.

NOTE

You can use PSP Deformations and the Deformation tool only with greyscale and 24-bit color images.

The Deformation tool is available only on a layer or floating selection. If the Deformation tool is greyed out, check the color depth of your image and make sure that you have a layer or floating selection active. If you have a standard selection that isn't on a real layer, you can use the Deformation tool on the selection if you first choose **S**elections, **F**loat to float the selection.

TIP

You can use the Deformation Browser (choose Image, Deformations, Deformation Browser) for a rough preview of how the Deformation filters will affect your image.

If you find a Deformation filter that produces an effect you like, click Apply. With the two Deformation filters that have no setting controls, Circle and Pentagon, the deformation is applied immediately to the image. With the other Deformation filters, which all have setting controls, the Deformation dialog box pops up so that you can change the settings before you apply the effect.

Simple Warping Deformations

Most of the Deformations produce simple warping of the shape of a target image, layer, or selection. Some of these simple Deformations compress the target into a shape that doesn't fill the entire image canvas. In that case, areas outside the deformed figure are filled with the current background color (on a flat image or Background) or with transparency (on a layer).

Here's a summary of the simple warping Deformations:

▶ **Circle**—Warps the source into a circle, seeming to wrap it around the front of a sphere (see Figure 7.1). This is useful for adding texture to a ball or globe. Applying Circle to a circular figure produces a diamond shape.

Fig. 7.1
Circle deformation (with original image behind).

▶ **Cylinder – Horizontal and Cylinder – Vertical**—Appears to wrap the source around the front of a horizontal or vertical cylinder, respectively (see Figure 7.2). This can be useful if you want to add a label to a can or add a pattern to a mug or cylindrical vase.

Fig. 7.2
Cylinder – Horizontal deformation (with original image behind).

▶ **Pentagon**—Warps the target into a pentagon (see Figure 7.3).

Fig. 7.3
Pentagon deformation (with original image behind).

▶ **Perspective – Horizontal and Perspective – Vertical**—Alters the horizontal or vertical perspective of the target, respectively (see Figure 7.4). This can be useful if you want to add exaggerated perspective to your image. When applied to a circular figure, these Deformation filters produce an egg or teardrop shape.

Fig. 7.4
Perspective – Horizontal deformation (with original image behind).

▶ **Skew**—Skews the target up to 45 degrees either horizontally or vertically (see Figure 7.5).

Fig. 7.5
Skew deformation (with original image behind).

▶ **Pinch**—Makes the target look like it's been pinched in the middle, shrinking the image in the middle and pulling the rest of the image in toward the center (see Figure 7.6).

CHAPTER 7

Fig. 7.6
Pinch deformation (with original image behind).

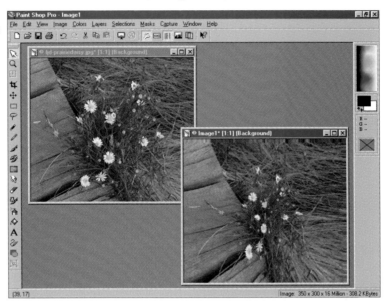

▶ **Punch**—Makes the target look like it's been punched from behind, making the middle of the image larger and bending the rest of the image toward the back (see Figure 7.7). This Deformation filter, applied to a circular or elliptical figure, can be used to create a slightly misshapen square or rectangle with rounded corners.

Fig. 7.7
Punch deformation (with original image behind).

▶ **Warp**—Warps the target so that part of it seems either to pop out like a bubble (see Figure 7.8a) or to sink down like a dent (see Figure 7.8b). Warp has controls for Size and Strength settings and for Horizontal and Vertical offsets. Size determines how much of the image is affected. A positive Strength value produces the bubble effect, while a negative value produces the dent effect.

Fig. 7.8a
Warp deformation, Strength set to 20 (with original image behind).

Fig. 7.8b
Warp deformation, Strength set to −20 (with original image behind).

As an example of a practical use for the simple warping Deformations, try using a Deformation to wrap a texture around an object.

1. Make a selection around the portion of an object that you want to wrap the texture around, as shown in Figure 7.9a.

Fig. 7.9a
Selecting an area to wrap a texture around.

2. Add a new layer by clicking the Add New Layer button on the Layer Palette. With the new layer as the empty layer, either paste the texture into the selection or paint the texture on with the Clone Brush or the Picture Tube tool. Figure 7.9b shows roses from a Picture Tube being painted on.

Fig. 7.9b
Applying the texture on its own layer with the Picture Tube tool.

3. Apply one of the Cylinder Deformations. Because the mug used here is a vertical cylinder, choose I**mage, D**eformations, Cylinder – **V**ertical to create the effect in Figure 7.9c.

Fig. 7.9c
Apply Cylinder –
Vertical to wrap the
texture around the mug.

4. In the Layer Palette, adjust the Opacity and Blend Mode on the upper layer to blend the texture into the object that you're texturizing. The result is shown in Figure 7.9d, with the texture layer's Opacity set to 44, and Blend Mode set to Multiply.

Fig. 7.9d
The completed
texturized image.

Special Effects Deformations

The rest of the Deformations alter the target image, layer, or selection to produce special effects. The following Deformations might be used to produce abstract textures or to simulate natural phenomena such as a ripple in water:

▶ **CurlyQs**—Turns the target into a collection of curls arranged in columns and rows. Besides being able to set the number of columns and rows, you can set the Size and Strength of the curls, and whether the curls turn Clockwise or Counterclockwise (see Figure 7.10).

Fig. 7.10
Examples of CurlyQs (with original image at left).

▶ **Ripple**—Makes the target appear to be reflected in a pool of water that has been disturbed by a small object falling into it (see Figure 7.11).

Fig. 7.11
Examples of Ripple
(with original image
at left).

▶ **Rotating Mirror**—Reflects part of the target along an axis (the line of reflection). By setting the Rotation Angle, you determine the slope of the line of reflection. A value of 0, 180, or 360 degrees creates a vertical line of reflection, while a value of 90 or 270 degrees creates a horizontal line of reflection. Other values divisible by 45 have lines of reflection that go from one corner of the target to the diagonally opposite corner (see Figure 7.12).

Fig. 7.12
Examples of Rotating
Mirror (with original
image at left).

▶ **Spiky Halo**—Just as its name implies, this creates a spiky corona
around the edge of your image or selection. The higher the setting for
Radius %, the more area of your image is included in the halo (see
Figure 7.13).

Fig. 7.13
Examples of Spiky Halo
(with original image at
left).

▶ **Twirl**—Twirls the target around its center point. Set Degree to positive values for clockwise twirling and to negative values for counterclockwise twirling (see Figure 7.14).

Fig. 7.14
Examples of Twirl (with original image at left).

▶ **Wave**—Makes your target appear to be reflected in wavy water (see Figure 7.15).

Fig. 7.15
Examples of Wave (with original image at left).

▶ **Wind**—Makes your target appear to be blurred by blowing wind (see Figure 7.16).

Fig. 7.16
Examples of Wind (with original image at left).

Take a look at an example that utilizes several of these Deformations. As you saw earlier, the Ripple Deformation by itself does a pretty good job of simulating a ripple on a reflecting pool of still water. You can also create the effect of a ripple on moving water by preceding Ripple with Wave. This example begins with the image in Figure 7.17.

Fig. 7.17
Iris image to be deformed.

1. Apply Wave to the image. In the example in Figure 7.18, Amplitude for both the Horizontal and Vertical displacement is set to 25. The Horizontal wavelength is set to 23, and the Vertical Wavelength is set to 43.

Fig. 7.18
Apply the Wave
deformation.

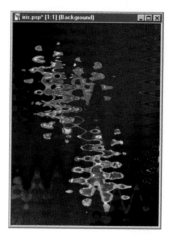

2. Apply Ripple to the image. In this example, Amplitude is set to 18 and Wavelength is set to 37. The Horizontal and Vertical centers are both set to 50 (see Figure 7.19).

Fig. 7.19
Apply the Ripple
deformation.

Here's another good combination of the special effects Deformations. Wave by itself is sometimes a bit harsh, but you can add a touch of Wind to soften the effect:

1. Apply Wave to an image just as you did in the last example: Set Amplitude for both the Horizontal and Vertical displacement to 25; set Horizontal wavelength to 23; and set Vertical Wavelength to 43.

2. Apply a small amount of Wind. Figure 7.20 shows the result with Strength set to 10.

Fig. 7.20
Wind applied after Wave.

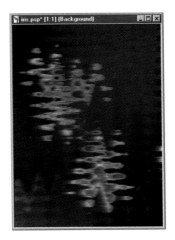

The Deformation Tool

The Deformation tool enables you to deform raster layers and selections in all sorts of controlled ways. The tool is active only if a layer or a floating selection is active; otherwise, it is greyed out on the Tool Palette.

> **NOTE**
> The Deformation tool enables you to reshape raster figures in much the same way that you can reshape a vector object with the Draw and Preset Shapes tools.

The most common way to activate the Deformation tool is to click its icon and then manipulate its handles in the image canvas to produce a deformation. Figure 7.21 shows a layered image with the Deformation tool's boundaries and handles surrounding a figure on one of the image's layers.

Fig. 7.21
Deformation tool, ready to use.

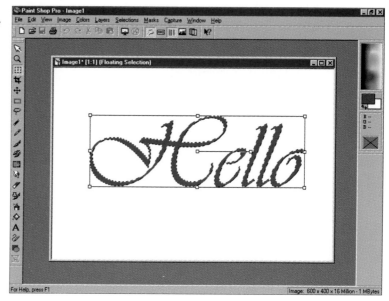

Figure 7.22 shows the Deformation tool in action. Here, the center bar was used to rotate the figure a bit. Notice how the cursor changes to a circular arrow when you position it near the outside end of the bar. When the cursor has this shape, you can rotate the figure by dragging.

Fig. 7.22
Rotating a figure with
the Deformation tool.

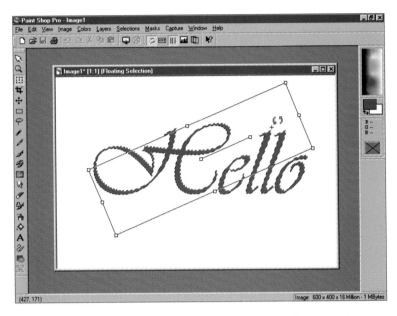

You can do several things with the Deformation tool. As you just saw, dragging the center bar rotates the figure. Dragging the handles on any of the sides of the boundary expands or contracts the figure in the direction of the drag. Finally, dragging any of the corner handles expands or shrinks the figure both horizontally and vertically all at once.

TIP
Right-drag on a corner handle to maintain the aspect ratio of the figure as it is resized.

You also can drag the figure while depressing the Ctrl key or Shift key or both keys simultaneously. When you depress either or both of these keys and position the cursor over one of the Deformation tool's handles, the shape of the cursor changes. This change in cursor shape gives you a hint as to the effect that you will produce if you drag with that particular key or key combination:

▶ Shift+drag on any of the top, bottom, or side handles to skew or shear the figure.

▶ Ctrl+drag on one of the corner handles to change the figure's perspective.

▶ Shift+Ctrl+drag on any of the corner handles to distort the figure.

You also can move the deformed figure within the image canvas by clicking anywhere inside the Deformation tool's boundaries and dragging the figure into place. When you click and drag inside the deformation boundaries, the cursor looks like the double-headed crossed arrows of the Mover tool.

After you distort the figure in the way that you want, apply the Deformation filter either by double-clicking the image and selecting Yes when asked whether you want to apply the Deformation, or by clicking the Apply button on the Tool Options palette. If you want to abandon the Deformation and return to the image as it was before you started with the Deformation tool, either click the No button in the dialog box that pops up when you double-click the image, or press the Cancel button in the Tool Options palette.

In addition to being able to use the guides and handles of the Deformation tool to apply complex Deformations to your images, you can enter deformation settings directly into the Deformation Settings dialog box, as shown in Figure 7.23.

Fig. 7.23
The Deformation Settings dialog box.

To access the Deformation Settings dialog box, double-click the Deformation tool icon. (Remember that this tool is available only if you have a floating selection or layer.) You can then enter values directly into the various textboxes to produce your desired deformation.

The dialog box equivalents of the free deform controls are summarized in Table 7.1.

TIP

Whether you use the Deformation tool or the Deformation Settings dialog box, you want to keep image distortion to a minimum. Each time a deformation is applied, some distortion of the figure is introduced. To minimize distortions of your deformed figures, try to achieve the complete effect that you want in a single application rather than applying a series of separate Deformations.

Table 7.1.
Summary of
Deform Tool
Operations and
Controls

Deformation Operations	Free Deform Controls	Dialog Box Equivalents
Resize vertically or horizontally	Center top/bottom or right/left handles	Scale
Resize both vertically and horizontally	Corner handles	Scale
Rotate	Center bar	Angle
Change perspective	Ctrl+corner handles	Perspective
Skew/shear	Shift+handles	Shear
Distort	Shift+Ctrl+corner handles	— — —

Combining Effects and Deformations

Now, take a look at a couple of examples that illustrate how you can create cool images by combining Effects (covered in Chapter 6, "PSP Effects") and Deformations. First, suppose that you want to enhance some text by slanting it and giving it some depth. Follow these steps to do so:

1. Open a new image, selecting White as the background color.
2. With the Text tool, select the font, size, and color that you want, and select Floating.
3. Click the Deformation tool icon.
4. Shift-drag on the top-center and then the bottom-center handles, as shown in Figure 7.24. Drag in one direction with the top handle and in the opposite direction with the bottom handle.

Fig. 7.24
Slanting text with the
Deformation tool.

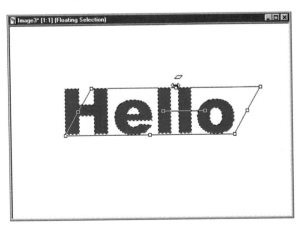

5. Click and drag inside the deformation boundary, if you need to reposition the text. Then, double-click anywhere in your image and click Yes to apply the deformation.

6. Choose **I**mage, Effects, Inner Bevel. Select the Round preset and then click OK.

7. Apply a Drop Shadow by choosing **I**mage, Effects, **D**rop Shadow. Set the following:

    Color: Black

    Opacity: 70

    Blur: 13

    Vertical and Horizontal Offsets: 15

The result will look something like Figure 7.25.

Fig. 7.25
Slanted text with shadowing, to provide depth.

For the next example, suppose you want to take the framed rose image from Chapter 6 and place it in a larger image, making the framed rose look like it is suspended in space. You can do so by following these steps:

1. Make the framed image the active image and copy it to the Clipboard with Ctrl+C.

2. Open a new image with White selected as the Background. Be sure that this image is large enough to give you room to deform the framed picture and add a shadow.

3   With the new image active, paste in the copied image as a new layer by pressing Ctrl+L. The result will look something like Figure 7.26.

Fig. 7.26
Paste in the framed
picture as a new layer.

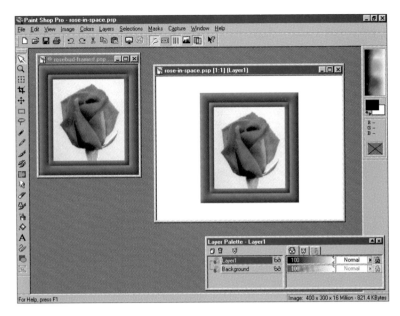

4. Click the Deformation tool's icon and Ctrl-drag the upper-right corner
handle upward. Then, Ctrl-drag the upper-left corner handle
downward (see Figure 7.27).

Fig. 7.27
Deformation of the
framed picture by
Ctrl+dragging.

5. Optionally, adjust the length of the framed picture by dragging (without the Ctrl key depressed) on one or more of the side handles.

6. Apply the deformation by double-clicking anywhere in the image and then clicking Yes.

7. Add a Drop Shadow with **I**mage, Effects, **D**rop Shadow. In this example, the following settings were used:

    Color: Black

    Opacity: 70

    Blur: 10

    Horizontal and Vertical Offsets: 10

The result should look something like Figure 7.28.

Fig. 7.28
A framed rose
suspended in space!

These are just some of the ways to use Deformations in your own graphics projects. Try using Deformations to appropriately resize a figure that you've pasted into an image. Change a pasted-in figure's perspective to match the perspective of elements that are already present in the target image. Experiment with Deformations to find other ways to use them to create convincing composites and unique effects.

8
Filters

Filters are used to apply complex modifications to your images quickly and easily. PSP includes several families of built-in filters, which you can supplement with various plug-in filters or filters that you create yourself with PSP's User Defined Filters. From correcting photos to creating textures to adding special effects, there's plenty you can do with the help of filters!

Here's what you'll be exploring in this chapter:

▶ Understanding PSP's built-in filters

▶ Exploring the power of plug-ins

▶ Taking a first look at User Defined Filters

In most of the examples in this chapter, you'll see a filter applied to a selection on only the right side of a photorealistic image. This way, you can compare the filtered area on the right with the unfiltered area on the left to get a better idea of a filter's effect.

> **NOTE**
> Filters are available only for greyscale and 24-bit color images and only on raster layers.

Getting to Know PSP's Filters

PSP6 has several sets of built-in filters: Blur, Edge, Noise, Sharpen, and Other. Each of these filter sets is located on the Image menu. To apply a built-in PSP filter, select the appropriate filter set from the Image menu, and then select the particular filter that you want to use. Some filters have controls that you can set, in which case a dialog box appears before the filter is applied to your image.

Filters that have a dialog box with settings that you can control include a window that shows a section of your original image and a window that provides a preview of the filter's effect after you set the filter's controls. You can zoom in or out on these windows by clicking the + or − Zoom buttons near the windows. Click the Mover button between one pair of Zoom buttons to bring up a window that lets you position the preview area precisely. You can also reposition the preview area by dragging in either window.

TIP

Another option available under the Image menu is the Filter Browser, which you can use to preview the effect that the various filters will have on your image, layer, or selection. Select the filter's name in the Filter Browser's dialog box and look in the dialog box's Sample Preview window.

If you see a filter that you like, click Apply in the Filter Browser dialog box. For filters that have no controls, the filter is then applied to your image. If a filter has controls, clicking Apply invokes the selected filter's dialog box so that you can set further options before the filter is applied to your image.

Keep in mind that filters can be both a blessing and a curse. If used judiciously, filters can help you to produce complex effects with minimal effort. However, filters are also very easy to overuse, producing gaudy or cliched results. Don't be afraid to try out odd combinations or apply a filter in a novel way, but be careful not to be heavy-handed with filters. After exploring PSP's filters in the next several sections, you will have an opportunity to apply a combination of these filters to images to create some interesting effects.

Blur Filters

The Blur filters are most useful for softening overly sharp images or the focus of a photo's background. Blurring can give an image a dreamy or sensual quality or can help to emphasize a central figure in an image by de-emphasizing peripheral elements.

Blur and Blur More

Blur and Blur More provide two quick ways to blur your image, layer, or selection. Neither filter has any settings that you can control—it's one-size-fits-all with these filters. As you might expect, Blur More produces a stronger blurring effect than Blur does.

You might choose to use these filters when you're in a hurry or when a precise adjustment isn't necessary. But when you need more control, the Blur filter of choice is Gaussian Blur.

Gaussian Blur

Gaussian Blur is the filter that you'll normally want to use to apply blurs to your photorealistic images. With Gaussian Blur, you can set the Radius of the blur (from 0.10 to 100 pixels) to control the intensity of the blurring effect, as shown in Figure 8.1.

Fig. 8.1
Gaussian Blur example, with Radius set to 1.0.

Among other things, Gaussian Blur also can help you create digital paintings from photos. When used in combination with Add Noise and Motion Blur (discussed later in this chapter), Gaussian Blur can be used to add a misty rain effect to an image.

Motion Blur

The Motion Blur filter produces an effect similar to using a slow shutter speed to photograph a subject speeding by you, as shown in Figure 8.2.

Fig. 8.2
Motion Blur example.

With Motion Blur you have control over both the direction of the blur and its intensity. Motion Blur is useful for producing the impression of speed, and it also can be used to create a brushstroke effect in your digital paintings.

CHAPTER 8

Soften and Soften More

The Soften and Soften More filters are another pair of one-size-fits-all filters—they have no settings that you can control. Each provides a soft blurring effect, with Soften More producing a more intense effect than Soften.

These filters, like Blur and Blur More, are good for producing a romantic or sensual effect.

Edge Filters

The Edge filters enhance or detect the edges of an image. None of these filters has any settings you can control.

Enhance and Enhance More

Enhance and Enhance More enhance the edges of an image, with Enhance More producing a stronger effect than Enhance (see Figure 8.3).

Fig. 8.3
Enhance example.

When used alone, these Edge filters usually produce overly severe effects. They're best used on a layer that's a copy of your original image, as follows:

1. On the Layer Palette, right-click on the Layer button of the original image and choose Duplicate on the resulting menu. This creates a copy of the original on a new layer above the original.
2. Apply the filter to the copied layer.
3. Adjust the layer Opacity or Blend Mode on the filtered layer to blend the filtered layer into the original.

Using the Edge filters on a copied layer enhances the edges of your image while maintaining the image's other qualities. Take a look at the filtered image in Figure 8.4a, in which the original image is on the left and a version of the same image with the Edge, Enhance filter applied is on the right. Now compare the effect to the image in Figure 8.4b, in which the Edge, Enhance filter is applied to a copied layer that is blended into the original, with Opacity set to 54 and Blend Mode set to Screen.

Fig. 8.4a
An image (left) and a version to which Edge, Enhance has been applied (right).

Fig. 8.4b
Using layers to soften the effect of the Edge, Enhance filter.

Find All, Find Horizontal, and Find Vertical

The Find All, Find Horizontal, and Find Vertical filters all darken an image, except along the edges of an image's figures. As their names imply, the filters differ only in the edges that they detect: all edges (see Figure 8.5), only horizontal edges, or only vertical edges.

Fig. 8.5
Find All example.

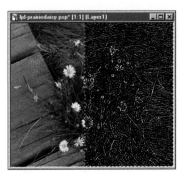

Trace Contour

Trace Contour lightens an image, except along the edges of its figures, which are darkened. You can apply Trace Contour to photorealistic images, along with the Erode filter, to produce watercolor-illustration effects or other artistic effects (see Figure 8.6).

Fig. 8.6
Trace Contour example.

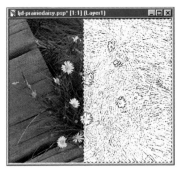

Noise Filters

All of the Noise filters are useful for editing photorealistic images. In addition, Add Noise can come in handy when used with text graphics and other digital artwork.

Add Noise

Add Noise adds "noise"—scattered bits of color—to your image. Noise can be Random, as in Figure 8.7, or Uniform, as in Figure 8.8. Random Noise is most useful as the first step in creating a texture, perhaps for a background tile or for part of a digital painting. Uniform Noise is most useful for adding texture to "flat" solid-colored areas in repaired photos.

Fig. 8.7
Add Noise, Random Noise.

Fig. 8.8
Add Noise, Uniform Noise.

Despeckle and Median Cut

Despeckle and Median Cut remove noise. You can use both filters to remove small imperfections from a photo, such as dust specks.

As the examples in Figures 8.9 and 8.10 show, although these two filters produce very similar effects, Median Cut sometimes produces an unacceptable amount of blurring. For a particular image, you might want to try each of these filters in order to see which produces the best results. Despeckle removes noise by blurring an image except along areas of contrast. Median Cut removes noise by averaging the values of adjacent pixels.

Fig. 8.9
Despeckle example.

Fig. 8.10
Median Cut example.

Sharpen Filters

All of the Sharpen filters are used to enhance detail in an image by emphasizing areas of contrast. This can make a blurry image appear to be more in focus. You also can use Sharpening to give an image a metallic look.

Sharpen and Sharpen More

Sharpen and Sharpen More are two more one-size-fits-all filters, with no settings that you can control. You usually won't use these filters on your photorealistic images, but they can be useful for creating metallic effects. As you would expect, Sharpen More produces a stronger sharpening effect than Sharpen.

When you're in a hurry, Sharp and Sharpen More might suit your purposes.

Unsharp Mask

Because it offers greater control, Unsharp Mask is the filter that you normally will use to sharpen your photorealistic images. Like the other sharpening filters, Unsharp Mask increases contrast in high-contrast areas. Unlike the other sharpening filters, however, Unsharp Mask has a dialog box with settings that enable you to control the intensity and application of the sharpening.

You can set three controls in the Unsharp Mask dialog box:

▶ **Radius**—Controls the number of pixels affected surrounding an area of contrasting brightness or color.

▶ **Strength**—Determines the amount that the contrast is increased.

▶ **Clipping**—Restricts application of the sharpening to certain pixels, depending on the amount of contrast with surrounding pixels. The higher the value for Clipping, the more contrast that must exist between the pixels to which sharpening is applied and the surrounding pixels.

Figures 8.11 and 8.12 illustrate the effects that you can create by altering the settings in the Unsharp Mask dialog box.

Fig. 8.11
Unsharp Mask, subtle sharpening (Radius: 0.50; Strength: 80%; Clipping: 15).

Fig. 8.12
Unsharp Mask, exaggerated sharpening (Radius: 2; Strength: 110%; Clipping: 5).

Other Filters

A potpourri of filters is included in PSP's Other category.

Erode and Dilate

Dilate expands the light areas of your image, layer, or selection, as shown in Figure 8.13.

Fig. 8.13
Dilate example.

Erode is like Dilate, except that the dark areas are expanded, as shown in Figure 8.14.

Fig. 8.14
Erode example.

You can use Dilate and Erode (perhaps along with the Trace Contour filter) to help create digital paintings out of your photorealistic images.

Emboss

Emboss produces an embossed or stamped effect (see Figure 8.15). Most areas of the image, layer, or selection to which you apply this filter become grey, but areas of high contrast display bright-colored edges. If you want to eliminate the bright-colored areas, desaturate the embossed area by choosing either Colors, Grey Scale or one of the operations under Colors, Adjust that let you set Saturation to 0.

NOTE

If you use Colors, Grey Scale to desaturate a 24-bit image, but you really don't want to convert the image to greyscale, then return the image to its original color depth immediately after applying Grey Scale. Simply choose Colors, Increase Color Depth and then select 16 Million Colors (24 bits).

The Emboss filter has no controls, so you have no direct way to specify the direction of the shadows for your emboss. You can easily produce the inverse of the normal Emboss results, though, by choosing Colors, Negative Image after choosing Image, Other, Emboss. Figure 8.16 shows the result of using this method on the example in Figure 8.15.

Fig. 8.15
Emboss example.

Fig. 8.16
Emboss followed by
Negative Image.

CHAPTER 8

TIP

Here's a tip from Robin Kirkey, one of the contributing authors to *Creating Paint Shop Pro Web Graphics, 2nd edition*, on how to produce even more variation in your embossings: *Before* you apply the Emboss filter, use either Image, Mirror or Image, Flip or Image, Rotate on your original image. After that, you can mirror, flip, or rotate the embossed image back to its original position. Consider a few examples of what you can create with these simple techniques. Using the same source image as the one used for the example in Figure 8.15, you can create the image shown in Figure 8.17a by applying Mirror and then Emboss and then Mirror again. Figure 8.17b shows the same image after applying Flip and then Emboss and then Flip again.

For more of Robin Kirkey's tips, head out to Robin's Nest at
http://www.annapolis.net/members/rkirkey/index.html.

Fig. 8.17a
Applying Mirror, then Emboss,
then Mirror again.

Fig. 8.17b
Applying Flip, then Emboss,
then Flip again.

Hot Wax Coating

Hot Wax Coating produces an effect that looks like you've coated your image with a melted wax in the shade of the current foreground color. You can use this filter to create several interesting effects, including 3D metallic text. An example of this is shown in Figure 8.18, in which a white, Hot Wax Coating was repeatedly applied to a text selection that was then colorized, giving the text a golden appearance.

Fig. 8.18
Hot Wax Coating
example.

TIP
Metallic effects created with repeated applications of Hot Wax Coating sometimes benefit from a little sharpening after the colorizing.

Mosaic

Mosaic makes your image look pixelated or tiled. You control the size of the "tiles" with the Block Width and Block Height controls in the Mosaic dialog box. Figure 8.19 shows both an original image and a version to which Mosaic was applied, with Block Width and Block Height both set to 5.

Fig. 8.19
Mosaic example.

Getting the Most from Filters: Real-World Examples

Now, look at a few extended examples to get a feel for what you can do just with PSP's own operations and built-in filters.

One thing that filters are useful for is creating textures, such as the sand or concrete texture shown in Figure 8.20.

Fig. 8.20
A sand or concrete texture made with PSP's filters.

CHAPTER 8

Follow these steps to create the concrete texture:

1. Open a new image with white as the background color. Then, choose **I**mage, **N**oise, **A**dd from the menubar and set % Noise to 85 and select Random.

2. Choose **I**mage, **O**ther, **E**mboss from the menubar and then soften the effect of the embossing with **I**mage, **B**lur, **G**aussian Blur set to 0.5.

3. To produce the dull, brownish color shown in the example, choose **C**olors, **C**olorize from the menubar and set Hue to 30 and Saturation to 30.

You can use the Noise filter in combination with other filters to produce all kinds of textures. Figure 8.21 shows another example, this one using Noise followed by Erode and then Hot Wax Coating.

Fig. 8.21
Textured text using Noise, Erode, and Hot Wax Coating filters and the Drop Shadow effect.

Hot Wax Coating, either alone or in combination with other filters, is quite handy for producing all kinds of interesting effects. Figure 8.22 shows a nifty variation on a standard Rectangular Gradient made with the Flood Fill tool. In this example, **I**mage, **O**ther, **M**osaic is applied to the gradient, and then **I**mage, **O**ther, **H**ot Wax Coating is applied.

Fig. 8.22
A Rectangular Gradient enhanced with Mosaic (Block Width and Block Height set to 10) and Hot Wax Coating.

Something else you might try is applying Hot Wax Coating to an image you've created with the Kaleidoscope effect (discussed in Chapter 6, "PSP Effects"). Hot Wax Coating will add depth to the kaleidoscopic image. Sometimes the result will look waxy, sometimes metallic, and sometimes brocade-like. Try it out and see what kinds of effects you can produce.

Now, let's look at a more involved filtering example. Many PSP users' talents run toward photography rather than drawing and painting, yet they like to create their own digital paintings and illustrations. If you're one of these folks, you can take a photograph and use PSP's filters to turn the photo into something that looks like a painting or illustration, as follows:

1. Start out with a photo, such as the lily that was touched up with the Clone Brush in Chapter 2, "Advanced Painting Tools." Copy the original layer of this image to a new layer by choosing **L**ayers, **Du**plicate from the menubar (or drag the Layer button of the original layer to the Add New Layer button on the Layer Palette). By working on a copied layer, you leave the original layer intact, in case you want to copy the original layer again. This also keeps the original image available to blend together with any filtered layers that you add. You will see both of these methods in this example.

2. With the new layer active, apply **I**mage, Ed**g**e, **T**race Contour, as shown in Figure 8.23.

Fig. 8.23
Trace Contour applied to the copied layer.

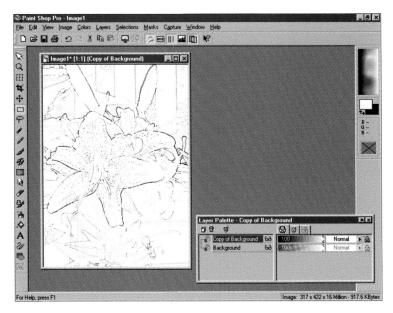

3. To emphasize the colored edges, apply **I**mage, **O**ther, **E**rode twice (see Figure 8.24).

Fig. 8.24
Erode applied, to emphasize the colored edges.

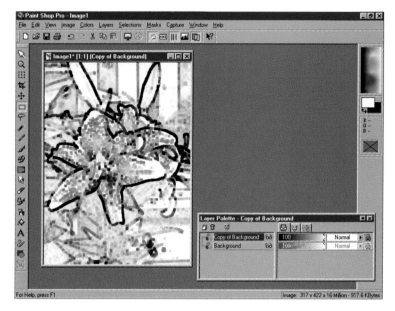

4. Let some of the original color back into the image by changing the Blend Mode of the copied layer. To darken things a bit and let the original color through, set the Blend Mode to Multiply, as shown in Figure 8.25.

Fig. 8.25
Blend Mode set to Multiply.

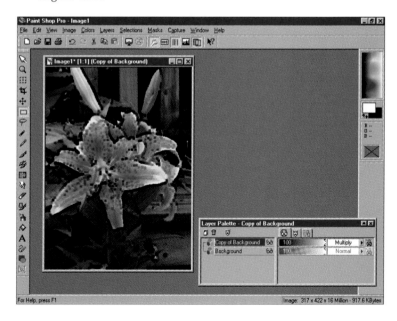

5. Copy the copied layer; with the copied layer active, choose **Layers**, **D**uplicate (or drag the Layer button of the copied layer to the Add New Layer button on the Layer Palette).

6. Use this new layer to add some texture to the image. First, change the Blend Mode of the new layer to Hard Light (see Figure 8.26). This brightens up the image quite a bit, but you'll tone that down in just a moment.

Fig. 8.26
Copy of filtered layer added.

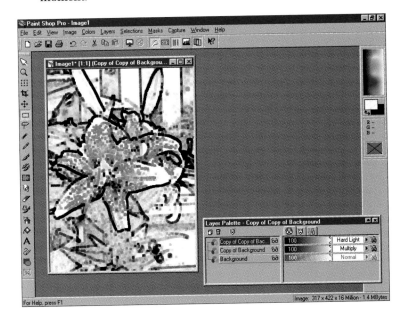

7. To add the texture, choose **I**mage, **N**oise, **A**dd. In the Add Noise dialog box, select Random and set the % Noise to 60. Then, choose **I**mage, **B**lur, **M**otion Blur, and in the Motion Blur dialog box, set Direction to 45 degrees and Intensity to 6 pixels. Then, tone down the effects of Hard Light by setting the Opacity slider for this layer to 44 (see Figure 8.27).

CHAPTER 8

Fig. 8.27
Texture added.

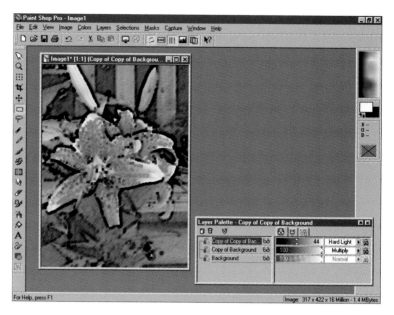

8.   At this point, you might want to use the Retouch tool on the middle layer to lightly blend the pixelated colors (see Figure 8.28). Try Retouch's Push or Smudge mode for this, varying the Opacity and Size settings in the Tool Options palette. You also can do other touch-up work with the Paintbrush and Eraser. Once again, remember to vary the Opacity and Brush Size, as needed.

Fig. 8.28
Colors can be blended together with the Retouch tool.

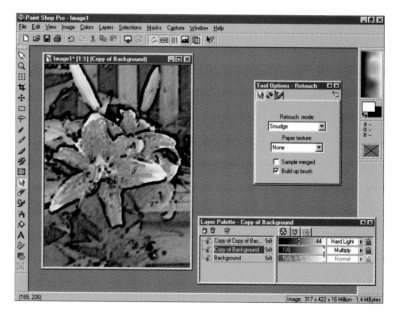

NOTE

On the Tool Controls tab of the Retouch tool's Tool Options palette, you'll see a checkbox labeled *Sample Merged*. When this box is checked, the Retouch tool blends together the pixels on the current layer with the pixels on all layers, just as if the image were flat. When this box is unchecked, the Retouch tool blends only the pixels on the currently active layer.

9.   When you feel that the image is in pretty good shape, you can flatten it. You might want to keep both the layered version and a duplicate image that you've flattened so that you have both a finished version and a layered version that you can easily fiddle with later on, enabling you to make even major changes without much trouble.

One alternative is to save your original in a format that supports layers (such as the PSP format), then flatten the image and save the flattened version. Another alternative is to save the layered version and then choose **Windows, D**uplicate to create a new copy of the image; you can then flatten the new copy and save it. In choosing which method to use, you might want to opt for the first since having two copies of your image open at once can strain your system resources.

10.   Adjust the flattened version of your painting as you would any image. Perhaps you want to tweak the brightness or contrast or add a little sharpening. Figure 8.29 shows the image after some minor adjustments were made to the brightness and contrast.

CHAPTER 8

Fig. 8.29
The finished image.

Don't think that the steps outlined here are simply a recipe that you should follow. This example is meant only to inspire you to experiment. If this wasn't enough to spark your interest, maybe Figures 8.30 and 8.31 will help show you what sorts of painting-like effects you can create with PSP's filters.

Fig. 8.30
An impressionistic landscape.

Fig. 8.31
Watercolor crocuses.

Plug-in Filters

Photoshop-compatible plug-in filters work with other graphics packages, including PSP. To install plug-in filters in PSP, simply copy the filters to whatever folder you prefer, and then select that folder as your plug-ins source by choosing **F**ile, Pre**f**erences, **G**eneral Program Preferences and selecting the Plug-in Filters tab in the Paint Shop Pro Preferences dialog box (see Figure 8.32).

Fig. 8.32
Plug-in Filters tab.

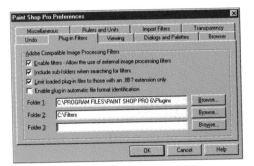

PSP finds the filters in each of the folders that you specify and in all the folders' subfolders.

Figures 8.33a-c show a few examples of what you can create by using the free, downloadable filters available at the Filter Factory Galleries (**http://www.netins.net/showcase/wolf359/plugins.htm**).

Fig. 8.33a
Pool Shadow filter by Greg Schorno, from Filter Factory Gallery A.

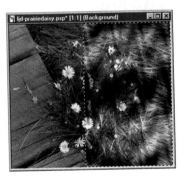

Fig. 8.33b
Difference Spirals filter
by Andy Baker, from
Filter Factory Gallery C.

Fig. 8.33c
Lead Crystal Emboss
filter by Sandy Blair,
from Filter Factory
Gallery E.

CAUTION

All plug-in filters require that MSVCRT10.DLL be in your Windows\System
folder, and some filters also need Adobe's PLUGIN.DLL (included with
Adobe's Photoshop and PhotoDeluxe).

You can download MSVCRT10.DLL at the Filter Factory Galleries and many
FTP sites, but PLUGIN.DLL is distributed only by Adobe. If you have an
Adobe product that includes PLUGIN.DLL, placing a copy of that product in
your Windows\System folder should enable you to use filters that require
PLUGIN.DLL.

Check out The Plug-in Head (**http://pluginhead.i-us.com/**) for some other
sources of downloadable plug-ins. Also take a look at Plug-in Com HQ
(**http://pico.i-us.com/**), where you can find not only some excellent filters
but also Plug-in Commander, a Filter Factory filter manager that enables
you to convert newer Filter Factory filters into a form that PSP can use
without PLUGIN.DLL. By the way, Plug-in Com HQ also has some great
masks and tubes.

If you like Filter Factory filters and don't mind spending a little money for them, look into the Filter Factory CD-ROM, available at **http://www.i-us.com/**. This affordable CD-ROM includes more than 300 fantastic filters by some of the best-known Filter Factory authors: Alfredo Mateus, Kipp McMichael, and Mario Klingemann. Also on the CD-ROM are plenty of goodies, including custom brushes and background tiles.

A moderately priced commercial plug-in package that's very popular—and for good reason—is Flaming Pear's Blade Pro (**http://www.flamingpear.com/blade.html**). This plug-in is most useful for creating textured, beveled buttons and text, like the images shown in Figure 7.34.

Fig. 8.34
Example of what you can do with Flaming Pear's Blade Pro.

Blade Pro enables you to save *presets*—reusable settings that you can load when you need them. Many, many sources of Blade Pro presets are available for download on the Web. For example, Figure 8.35 shows some of the presets available from Donna Hanson's Designs by Donna (**http://www.designsbydonna.com/presets1.html**).

Fig. 8.35
Examples of downloadable Blade Pro presets.

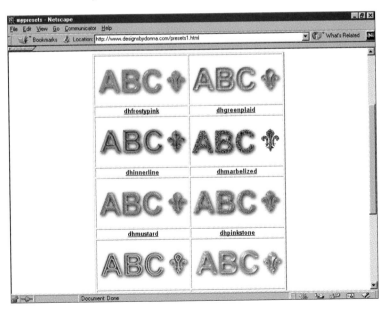

On the more expensive side are packages such as Alien Skin's Eye Candy and Xenofex (**http://www.alienskin.com/**) and MetaCreations Kai's Power Tools (**http://www.metacreations.com/**). Figures 8.36 and 8.37 show just some of the effects that you can create with these handy filter packages.

Fig. 8.36
Example of what you can do with Alien Skin's Eye Candy.

Fig. 8.37
Example of what you can do with MetaCreations Kai's Power Tools.

CAUTION

Both Kai's Power Tools 3 (KPT3) and Kai's Power Tools 5 (KPT5) work well with PSP version 5.03 and above; but if you still use version 5.00 or 5.01 of PSP, keep in mind that only KPT3 works correctly with those versions.

Plenty of other commercial plug-in filters are available, including those from Ulead (**http://www.ulead.com/**) and AutoF/X (**http://www.autofx.com/**). Although most filter packages designed for Adobe Photoshop will work with PSP, you should check with the manufacturer first. Make sure that a particular filter package is compatible with PSP before you make a purchase.

User Defined Filters

You can create your own PSP filters with User Defined Filters (abbreviated here as UDFs). You use and define these filters in the User Defined Filters dialog box by choosing Image, User Defined Filters (see Figure 8.38).

Fig. 8.38
User Defined Filters dialog box.

Even if you haven't defined any UDFs of your own, you'll see a filter supplied by Jasc Software called Sample Blur in the Filter Name list. To apply this filter to an image, select it in the list and click Apply. Figure 8.39 shows an example of the Sample Blur filter's effect.

Fig. 8.39
Example of Sample Blur UDF.

You can create entire families of your own custom filters. You'll learn how in Chapter 11, "Adding to Your Toolkit."

To whet your appetite for UDFs in the meantime, look at a couple of samples discussed in PSP's Help. The right side of the image in Figure 8.40 shows the effect of applying the Lithograph filter, the filter matrix for which is also shown in the figure. Figure 8.41 shows the effect and the matrix of the Psychedelic Distillation filter.

Fig. 8.40
Jasc's Lithograph UDF.

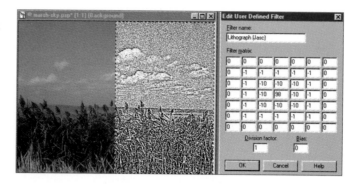

Fig. 8.41
Jasc's Psychedelic
Distillation UDF.

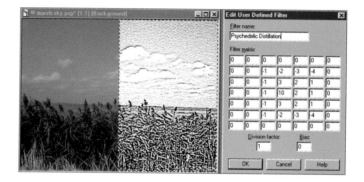

You can apply UDFs in several ways. Besides applying a filter to all color channels, as was done in the previous examples, you can apply the filter to only one or two of your image's color channels or only to the brightness levels of the image. To select separate color channels, go to the Apply To pane in the User Defined Filters dialog box and, under Color Component(s), check only the color channel(s) that you want the filter to be applied to. To apply a UDF only to the brightness levels of the image, select *Grey Values* rather than *Color Component(s)* in the Apply To pane.

Channels will be examined closely in Chapter 9, "Making Adjustments," and in Chapter 10, "Selections, Masks, and Channels," but in the meantime, you might play around with applying UDFs to individual color channels or to the brightness levels of your images. If you haven't yet looked at Chapter 11 to see how to create your own UDFs, just use Sample Blur for your explorations.

9
Making Adjustments

PSP enables you to adjust your images in many different ways. You can adjust an image's color, crop or resize it, or change its orientation. Most of the editing that you do on your photorealistic images will involve at least one of these adjustments—and probably will involve several. Likewise, most of these adjustments are useful for your drawings, too.

Using PSP, you can eliminate a color cast or broaden the brightness range in your photos, crop to a central figure, or adjust the orientation of the figures in your images. You can reduce the size of a large image or increase the canvas size. If you haven't explored these operations yet, you're missing some of the most powerful features of PSP.

Here's what you'll be exploring in this chapter:

▶ Understanding color models and color depth
▶ Understanding histograms
▶ Using adjustment layers
▶ Cropping and resizing
▶ Adjusting the position of a figure

Adjusting Colors

To understand how the color-adjusting operations in PSP work, you first need to know something about how color is represented on a video screen. Two basic color models are used to represent color on the computer: HSL (Hue/Saturation/Lightness) and RGB (Red/Green/Blue).

The HSL Model

In the HSL model, color is represented as its hue (red, yellow, magenta, and so forth), its saturation (the purity of the color), and its lightness (the amount of brightness of the color). Hue is something that everyone is familiar with, but lightness and saturation might be unfamiliar to you.

Both physical brightness and lightness involve the amount of black or white in a color. In PSP, the lightness scale varies from 0 to 255. A lightness of 0 is completely black, and a lightness of 255 is completely white. Tones and tints of a color contain various other levels in between.

Saturation, which varies from a low of 0 to a high of 255, is determined by the amount of grey in a color. A fully saturated color contains no grey, and thus is the purest form of the color. The less saturated a color is, the more grey that it includes; a totally unsaturated color is completely grey. Too much saturation can make a color look unnatural—a fully saturated red might be great for a pane in a stained glass window, for instance, but not for a rose or a brick.

The RGB Model

In the RGB model of color, colors are represented as combinations of the primary colors red, green, and blue. If you've ever specified the background color of a Web page by using hex codes, then you're already somewhat familiar with this color model.

In this model, every color has a red component, a green component, and a blue component, and the value for each color component (or channel) varies from a low of 0 to a high of 255. These values specify the amount of brightness in a color channel. If all three channels for a pixel are set at 0, for example, that pixel will be black. If all three channels are set at 255, that pixel will be white.

Whenever the three components share a value other than 0 or 255, the pixel will be some shade of grey (which shade depends on how close the shared value is to 0 or 255). Real colors are produced whenever the values in the three components aren't all equal to one another.

Take a look at an example. Figure 9.1 shows the PSP Color dialog box, which is invoked when you click the foreground or background tile on the Color Palette.

Fig. 9.1
The Color dialog box.

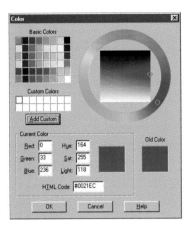

Look at the Current Color area in this dialog box. In this example, the RGB and HSL values of the medium-blue color in the color tile are displayed. The values for the RGB channels here are Red: 0, Green: 33, and Blue: 236. The values for the HSL channels are Hue: 164, Sat(uration): 255, and Light(ness): 118. (Web designers should note that the HTML code for the color is also given. For this example, the code is #0021EC.)

Colorizing and Color Adjustment

The Colors menu has eight items that you can use to adjust the color of an image. Three of these—Hue/Saturation/Lightness, Hue Map, and Red/Green/Blue—are located under Adjust. The other five are Colorize, Grey Scale, Negative Image, Posterize, and Solarize, as shown in Figure 9.2.

Fig. 9.2
The Colors menu.

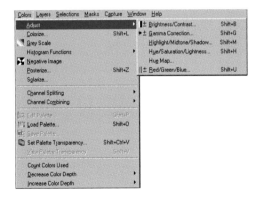

Let's begin with the three color-adjusting operations located under Colors, Adjust.

Hue/Saturation/Lightness

Hue/Saturation/Lightness uses the HSL color model. When you select this option from **C**olors, **A**djust, the Hue/Saturation/Lightness dialog box appears, as shown in Figure 9.3.

Fig. 9.3
The Hue/Saturation/
Lightness dialog box.

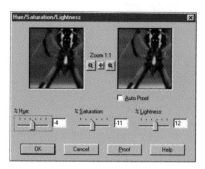

Here's a summary of the settings that you can control in the Hue/Saturation/Lightness dialog box:

▶ **Hue**—Values of 0, 100, and –100 (percent) all correspond to the original hues in the image, layer, or selection. A value of 50 corresponds to hues 180 from the original colors (180 being 50% of the 360 of the complete Color Wheel) and so on.

▶ **Saturation**—Values range from –100 for pure grey to 0 for the original saturation value to 100 for full saturation.

▶ **Lightness**—Also starts at 0 for the original lightness value. A value of –100 produces black, and a value of 100 produces white. Adjust this slider to darken or brighten the image, layer, or selection.

Hue Map

The Hue Map dialog box has controls with settings that correspond to positions on the Color Wheel, from 0 to 360. Red is at 0 and 360. The other colors represented on the top row of the Hue Map, going clockwise around the Color Wheel, go from orange to yellow to two shades of green to cyan to two shades of blue to violet to magenta. Think of the top row of the Hue Map as the Color Wheel split at red and laid out flat in a line. Figure 9.4 shows the Color Wheel as you might see it when you click the foreground or background tile on the Color Palette.

Fig. 9.4
The PSP Color Wheel.

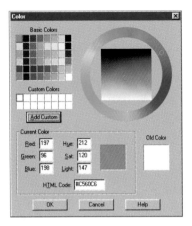

The Hue Map can seem confusing at first. One thing to keep in mind is that it's similar to Colorize (discussed later in the chapter). But whereas Colorize enables you to change all the pixels in an image, layer, or selection to one particular hue, the Hue Map enables you to adjust the hue of only certain pixels (the ones that start out as one or more of the various hues on the Hue Map sliders).

To use the Hue Map, click the Reset button in the Map Hue dialog box. You then see that the values in the row below the sliders match the values in the top row (see Figure 9.5), which leaves all the colors in your original image unchanged. You can then use the sliders to adjust the different colored pixels in your image. For instance, you can make the reds more orange by dragging the first slider down from 0 to about 25 (that is, from 0 to 25 on the Color Wheel). You can adjust each of the other sliders in a similar fashion.

Fig. 9.5
The Map Hue dialog box after clicking Reset.

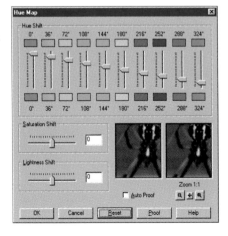

The Map Hue dialog box also has controls for adjusting saturation and lightness. Remember that saturation is color intensity or purity. The higher the saturation, the more intense or pure the colors are; the lower the saturation, the more dull and greyish the colors are. Lightness is perceived brightness. The higher the lightness, the closer to white the colors become; the lower the lightness, the closer to black the colors become.

Red/Green/Blue

Red/Green/Blue, which uses the RGB color model, affects the levels of red, green, and blue in your image, layer, or selection. Choose **C**olors, **A**djust, **R**ed/Green/Blue to access the dialog box shown in Figure 9.6.

Fig. 9.6
The Red/Green/Blue dialog box.

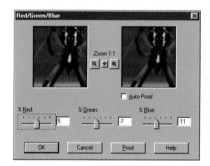

A Red setting of –10, for example, reduces the brightness in the Red channel of all the colors in the image, layer, or selection—except, of course, for those colors that already have a 0 in their Red channel.

Now, take a look at the other color-adjusting operations in the top section of the Colors menu.

Colorize

Colorize tints an image a single color. It uses the HSL model of color, with the array of colors on the Color Wheel accessed with the Hue slider in the Colorize dialog box (see Figure 9.7). Instead of referring to positions on the Color Wheel as somewhere between 0 and 360, as is done with the Hue Map, however, Colorize uses a scale of relative positions from 0 to 255, where both 0 and 255 are the values for red. Intermediate values include 43 for yellow, 85 for green, 128 for cyan, 170 for blue, and 212 for magenta.

Fig. 9.7
The Colorize dialog box.

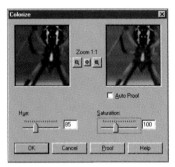

You can also set the Saturation with the Saturation slider, with values that range from 0 (completely grey) to 255 (fully saturated).

Grey Scale

Grey Scale desaturates all the colors in your image, leaving just the luminance values. If you have a multilayered image, all layers are affected, turning all the colors to shades of grey. Grey Scale also automatically reduces the color depth of any 24-bit image to 256, which means that if you begin with 16 million colors, you wind up with 256 shades of grey.

TIP
You can change a 24-bit color image—or a single layer or selection in a 24-bit image—to shades of grey without affecting the color depth. Just use any of the operations that let you adjust saturation, and set the saturation level to 0.

CHAPTER 9

Figure 9.8 shows a result of choosing Colors, Grey Scale.

Fig. 9.8
Grey Scale example,
with color original
behind.

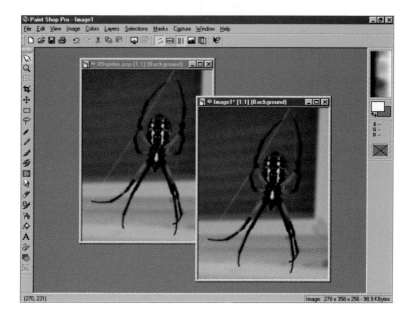

Negative Image

Negative Image does just what its name implies: It changes an image to its negative (see Figure 9.9). This operation is most useful for getting positives of scanned film negatives, but you can also use it to produce interesting effects on other images.

One such effect is embossing. Duplicate a layer by right-clicking on its Layer button and choosing Duplicate on the resulting menu. Then apply Colors, Negative Image to the duplicated layer and set the layer's opacity to 50%. At that point, everything will look completely grey. However, if you then take the Mover tool and move the top layer slightly in any direction, you'll get an embossed effect. Change the position of the top layer to adjust the depth and direction of the embossing.

Fig. 9.9
Negative Image
example, with positive
original behind.

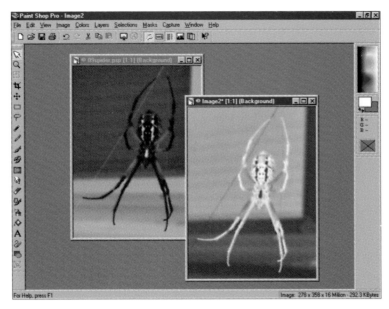

Posterize

Posterize gives your image the look of a poster. You do this in the
Posterize dialog box by decreasing the number of bits used to store color
data, thereby giving the colors a "flatter" look (see Figure 9.10).

Fig. 9.10
The Posterize dialog
box.

Normally, 24-bit color images use 8 bits per color channel to store color information. With Posterize, you can change this to 1 through 7 bits, thereby reducing the range of colors (see Figure 9.11).

NOTE

Although Posterize changes the color range of your image, the actual color depth of the image is not changed.

Fig. 9.11
Posterize example, with non-Posterized version behind.

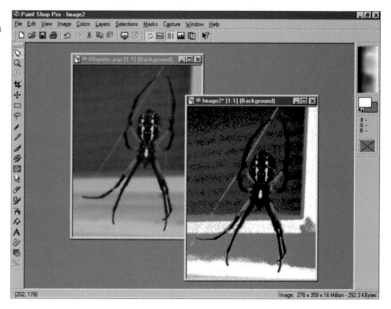

Solarize

Solarize is somewhat like Negative Image, except that you limit the range of colors that are changed with the Threshold setting in the Solarize dialog box (see Figure 9.12). Threshold restricts application to pixels above the brightness level (from 1 to 254) specified by Threshold.

Fig. 9.12
The Solarize dialog box.

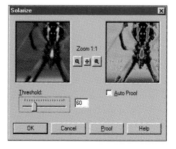

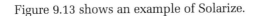

Figure 9.13 shows an example of Solarize.

Fig. 9.13
Solarize example, with
non-Solarized image
behind.

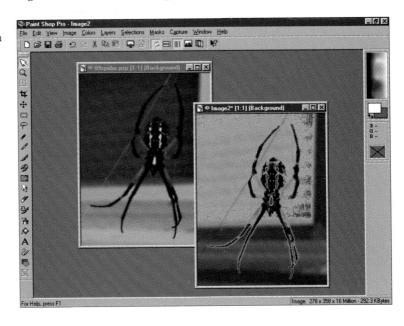

Adjusting Brightness and Contrast

The Histogram Functions under the Colors menu are used to make quick
adjustments to brightness and contrast. Additionally, three items under
Colors, Adjust can be used to adjust brightness and/or contrast:
Brightness/Contrast, Gamma Correction, and Highlight/Midtone/Shadow.
These three operations offer much more control than the Histogram
Functions do.

Histogram Functions

The Histogram Functions are Equalize and Stretch. Before discussing
these functions, take a look at the example of a histogram shown in
Figure 9.14.

Fig. 9.14
A histogram.

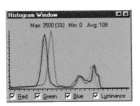

CHAPTER 9

NOTE

To view the histogram for the current image or layer, either press *H* on the keyboard; click the Histogram icon on the toolbar; or choose View, **T**oolbars and check *Histogram Window* in the Toolbars dialog box. To hide the histogram, either press *H*; click the Histogram icon again; or uncheck *Histogram Window* in the Toolbars dialog box.

A *histogram* is a graphical representation of the distribution of colors and brightness levels of an image. The colored lines in the histogram represent the distribution of red, green, and blue in an image or layer, whereas the black line represents the levels of luminance (a measure of brightness). The left side of the histogram represents the darkest areas, and the right side represents the brightest areas, with the middle part representing the midtones.

If the distribution of colors in the image is limited, the red, green, and blue lines in the histogram will be distributed unevenly. For some images, this is fine, but in many photorealistic images, this indicates an undesirable unevenness of color. In that case, you might use Colors, Histogram Functions, Equalize to even out the distribution of colors. Equalize ensures that all colors in the spectrum are included in the image or layer.

If the luminance of the image or layer is distributed across the whole horizontal axis of the histogram, then the brightness levels range from black to white. If the luminance graph covers only the middle of the horizontal axis, then the image or layer lacks deep shadows and bright highlights. You can use Colors, Histogram Functions, Stretch to stretch the luminance range so that all levels of luminance from black to white are included. This can be especially useful in enhancing greyscale, photorealistic images.

The Histogram Functions provide a quick, but often less than satisfying, means of adjusting the brightness/contrast and the color balance of an image or layer. For much more control, use the color-adjusting operations discussed earlier in this chapter to even out color distribution. And, to adjust brightness or contrast, try the group of operations discussed next.

TIP

Don't depend on your eyes alone when making color or brightness/contrast adjustments. Instead, let the histogram help you to see how colors and luminance levels are distributed.

Brightness/Contrast

Not surprisingly, the Brightness/Contrast dialog box, accessed by choosing **C**olors, **A**djust, **B**rightness/Contrast, is useful for adjusting either brightness or contrast, or both (see Figure 9.15). *Brightness* is the intensity of light, and *contrast* is the range of brightness values (which can go from black to white).

Fig. 9.15
The Brightness/Contrast dialog box.

Be careful when you change settings in the Brightness/Contrast dialog box. Severe changes in contrast can produce unwanted color shifts, and increases in brightness can wash out midtones.

Gamma Correction

The Gamma Correction dialog box, which opens when you choose **C**olors, **A**djust, **G**amma Correction, enables you to adjust the brightness of an image, layer, or selection without adversely affecting midtones (see Figure 9.16).

Fig. 9.16
The Gamma Correction dialog box.

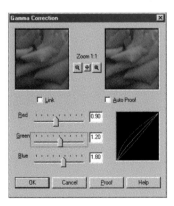

CHAPTER 9

Notice the *Link* checkbox in the Gamma Correction dialog box. If this is checked, all color channels are adjusted together, as was done with the adjusted image shown in Figure 9.17. If you uncheck this box, however, Gamma Correction lets you adjust the brightness for only one or two of your image's RGB channels, allowing you to decrease the brightness for the Blue channel, for example, while leaving the Red and Green channels as they are (see Figure 9.18). If your image needs color adjusting, not just changes to brightness, you should experiment with Gamma Correction to adjust only one or two of the color channels.

NOTE

For those of you who are familiar with Adobe Photoshop, PSP's Colors, Adjust, Gamma Correction command is very much like Photoshop's Adjust, Curves command.

Fig. 9.17
Image with Gamma Correction (0.70) applied to all channels equally; original behind.

Fig. 9.18
Image with Gamma
Correction (0.70)
applied to the Blue
channel alone; original
behind.

Highlight/Midtone/Shadow

Highlight/Midtone/Shadow is another operation that you can use to
adjust brightness without washing out midtones. As shown in Figure
9.19, the Highlight/Midtone/Shadow dialog box, accessed by choosing
Colors, **A**djust, **H**ighlight/Midtone/Shadow, enables you to control each
of these brightness ranges separately.

Fig. 9.19
The Highlight/Midtone/
Shadow dialog box.

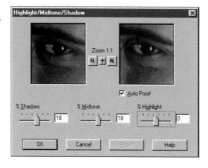

CHAPTER 9

With no adjustment, Highlight, Midtone, and Shadow are each set to 0%. Dragging any of these sliders to the left darkens the relevant tonal range, and dragging a slider to the right lightens the tonal range. For example, dragging the Highlight slider to the right increases the highlight areas, brightening the image but perhaps washing out the lighter midtone areas. Dragging the Shadow slider to the left increases the shadow areas, darkening your image by making some of the darker midtones black. Adjusting the Midtone slider to the left darkens the midtones, whereas adjusting it to the right lightens the midtones.

Figure 9.20 shows an extreme example of Highlight/Midtone/Shadow adjustment just to illustrate how powerful this operation can be.

Fig. 9.20
An extreme example of Highlight/Midtone/Shadow.

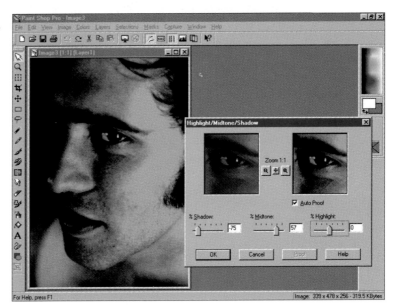

Adjustment Layers

Adjustment layers provide a nonpermanent, editable means of adjusting the color, contrast, and/or brightness of an image or layer. The operation and settings of an adjustment layer affect only layers lower in the layer stack. And, like any other layer, an adjustment layer can be toggled off and on, and its Blend Mode, Opacity, and blend ranges can be adjusted.

Add an adjustment layer by choosing **L**ayers, New **A**djustment Layer, which reveals the menu shown in Figure 9.21.

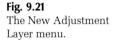

Fig. 9.21
The New Adjustment
Layer menu.

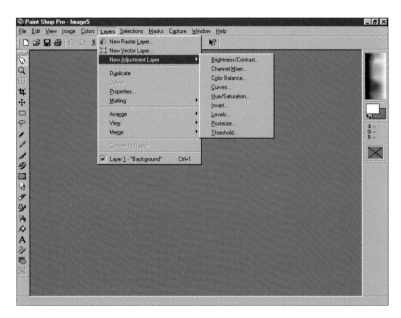

As you see, the New Adjustment Layer menu includes several adjustment operations you can choose from, including a couple that are already familiar: Brightness/Contrast and Posterize. In addition, there are several operations that are available only in the New Adjustment Layer menu: Channel Mixer, Color Balance, Curves, Hue/Saturation, Invert, Levels, Threshold. You will explore each of the latter operations in just a bit.

Before examining the adjustment operations that are unique to adjustment layers, however, try to get a feel for how adjustment layers work in general. Figure 9.22 shows the Brightness/Contrast adjustment layer dialog box.

Fig. 9.22
The Brightness/Contrast
adjustment layer dialog
box.

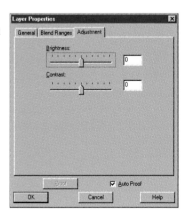

CHAPTER 9

Notice that this is a Layer Properties dialog box. In addition to the Adjustment tab, which contains the adjustment controls, there's a General tab and a Blend Ranges tab. These tabs contain the same layer controls that you find on a raster or vector layer. The adjustments that you can make with the controls available on the General tab—Opacity, Blend Mode, Group, and the various layer toggles—can also be made on the Layer Palette.

NOTE

On the Layer Palette, it's easy to tell whether a layer is an adjustment layer. An adjustment layer has a layer icon near its Layer button that looks like a square whose upper-left half is white and lower-right half is black.

When you want to edit an existing adjustment layer, double-click its Layer button on the Layer Palette. This brings up the dialog box for the adjustment layer, where you can alter the layer settings.

Channel Mixer

The Channel Mixer is most useful for adding detail to a color channel that is flat or for creating crisp greyscale images.

Figure 9.23 shows the Channel Mixer dialog box, which appears when you choose **Layers**, New **A**djustment Layer, Channel **M**ixer.

Fig. 9.23
The Channel Mixer dialog box.

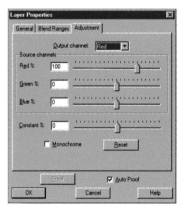

First, in the Output channel drop-down list, select the RGB channel to adjust. The initial settings will show 100 for the % for the channel itself and 0 for the % of the remaining two Source channels. You can then adjust the Source channel sliders to alter where the Output channel gets its data. Suppose, for example, that there is much more detail in your image's Green channel than in the Red channel. You can boost the detail in the Red channel by selecting Red as the Output channel, decreasing the Red %, and increasing the Green %. You can then adjust the overall brightness, if necessary, with the Constant slider.

To create a greyscale image, check the *Monochrome* checkbox under the Constant slider. Then adjust the Source channel sliders to tell PSP what proportion of the different channels to get the brightness data from. Emphasize the channel(s) that reveal the detail you want in your image, and de-emphasize the remaining channel(s). (Later, if you like, you can convert your sharp desaturated image to true greyscale by choosing Colors, Grey Scale.)

Figure 9.24 shows an interesting use of Channel Mixer.

Fig. 9.24
Using Channel Mixer to desaturate part of an image.

Here, everything but the central figure is selected. With this selection active, add a Color Mixer adjustment layer. Check *Monochrome*, and grab your greyscale data from the color channels in appropriate proportions. All areas except for the central figure are then desaturated.

CHAPTER 9

Color Balance

A Color Balance adjustment layer enables you to adjust the balance of colors in three different tonal ranges: Shadows, Midtones, and Highlights.

As Figure 9.25 shows, the Color Balance dialog box has two panels: Tone balance and Color balance.

Fig. 9.25
The Color Balance
dialog box.

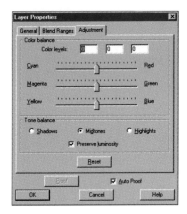

In the Tone balance pane, you choose which tonal range you want the color balancing to be applied to. In the Color balance pane, you make the adjustments, balancing colors with their opposites:

Cyan	Red
Magenta	Green
Yellow	Blue

Shifting the balance from one color to its opposite is like reducing the amount of the color. Thus, Color Balance is much like the Red/Green/Blue operation under Colors, Adjust. But, while the Red/Green/Blue operation applies across all tonal ranges, Color Balance allows you to adjust the balance of color separately in each of the three tonal ranges.

NOTE

Although you cannot make adjustments to more than one tonal range in a single step, you can make adjustments to each tonal range one at a time on a single Color Balance adjustment layer. What you'll then see on the layers below is the cumulative effect of all the adjustments.

CAUTION
Color Balance adjustments can affect overall brightness. If you want to ensure that the original overall brightness is maintained, check the *Preserve Luminosity* checkbox located at the bottom of the Tone balance pane.

Figure 9.26 shows an example of Color Balance in action, with the following settings:

Shadows = 0, −15, −25

Midtones = −50, 8, 10

Highlights = 0, 0, −10

Fig. 9.26
An example of using Color Balance, with original behind.

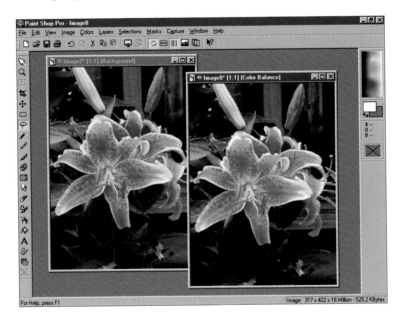

Curves

Curves is a very versatile adjustment operation, something like high-powered Gamma Correction. Use Curves to adjust overall brightness or the brightness of an individual RGB channel.

Figure 9.27 shows the Curves dialog box, which you access by choosing **L**ayers, New **A**djustment Layer, **C**urves.

Fig. 9.27

The Curves dialog box.

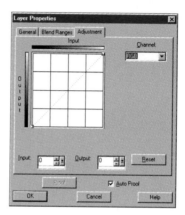

To use Curves, you manipulate control points on the curve. Notice that the curve is a graph with the horizontal axis corresponding to the Input brightness values and the vertical axis corresponding to the Output brightness values. In the Channel drop-down list, you can choose to adjust overall brightness (RGB) or one of the individual color channels (Red, Green, or Blue).

To add a control point to the curve, position the mouse cursor over the curve. When the cursor shows "+Add" beneath it, you can add a control point. Click on the curve to add a control point.

You make your adjustments by dragging control points. Drag a control point up, and you'll lighten pixels. Drag a control point down, and you'll darken pixels. Control points on the left affect pixels in the shadow range, control points on the right affect pixels in the highlight range, and control points in between affect the midtones. Figures 9.28a and 9.28b show a couple of examples.

Fig. 9.28a
Curves example:
Extreme contrast.

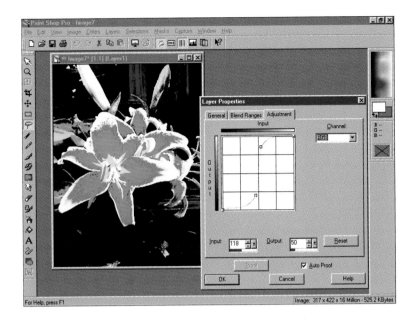

Fig. 9.28b
Curves example:
Brightness correction.

CHAPTER 9

Figure 9.28a shows an example where extreme contrast has been introduced. Notice how the curve is almost straight up and down in the midtone range. Whenever you have a steep slope like this, you'll get a high degree of contrast. To decrease contrast, decrease the slope of the curve.

Figure 9.28b shows a more everyday use of Curves. Here, the shadows have been brightened, with the highlights and upper midtones left pretty much alone.

NOTE

You can use Curves to create an effect similar to Invert (discussed later in this chapter) by reversing the slope of the line in the graph: Drag the leftmost control point to the top left of the graph and drag the rightmost control point to the bottom right of the graph. (Normally, however, you want the overall direction of the curve to go from the lower left to the upper right.)

NOTE

You can use a single Curves adjustment layer to make adjustments to both the RGB master channel and to individual channels. The combined result is what you'll see on lower layers.

Be careful with Reset if you've made adjustments to multiple channels. For any adjustment layer that has a Reset button, hitting the Reset button resets all the adjustments made on that adjustment layer.

Hue/Saturation

Similar to the **C**olors, **A**djust operation Hue/Saturation/Lightness, a Hue/Saturation adjustment layer can be used to manipulate hue, saturation, and luminance. The controls for Hue/Saturation are not like any you've explored yet in this chapter, though, as you can see in Figures 9.29a and 9.29b.

Fig. 9.29a
Dialog box for
Hue/Saturation, with
Master selected for Edit.

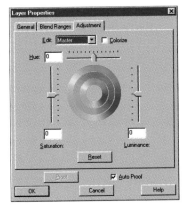

Fig. 9.29b
Dialog box for
Hue/Saturation, with
one of the color ranges
selected for Edit.

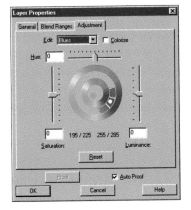

When Master is selected for Edit (see Figure 9.29a), you see three
concentric rings in the middle of the dialog box:

▶ The outer ring displays all the colors on the color wheel and
represents the color ranges for the original image, with the colors
fully saturated.

▶ The inner ring displays changes brought about by any adjustments
that are made, although increases to saturation aren't represented
here because the ring starts out with the colors fully saturated.

▶ The middle ring is the control ring. When Master is selected, you
make adjustments by entering data in the Hue, Saturation, and/or
Luminance textboxes or by moving the Hue, Saturation, and/or
Luminance sliders. The results of these adjustments are represented
on the control ring.

CHAPTER 9

When Edit is set to a color range instead of to Master (see Figure 9.29b), you'll see the complete inner and outer rings, but in place of the complete control ring you'll see a partial ring that represents the color range to be adjusted. On the control ring, you'll also see three sets of controls: two triangular controls at either end of the partial ring, a circle in the middle of the range, and two bars flanking the circle.

▶ Drag the *triangular* controls to broaden or narrow the range of the colors to be adjusted.

▶ Drag the *circular* control to change which hues on the original are affected.

▶ Drag the *bars* to set the point at which the effect is applied full-strength: Any area in the range that is between the two bars is applied full-strength, whereas areas in the range, but outside the bars, are applied at increasingly reduced strength, as they fall away from the bars.

You can make independent adjustments on several color ranges. The result will be the cumulative effect of those adjustments. For example, Figure 9.30 shows an image that has the default Red range with Saturation increased, and the default Blue range with Saturation and Luminance both decreased.

Fig. 9.30
Example of
Hue/Saturation.

NOTE

You can use a Hue/Saturation adjustment layer to colorize lower layers. Check the *Colorize* checkbox in the Hue/Saturation dialog box and then make your adjustments.

Remember that when you want to colorize a greyscale image, you first need to increase its color depth to 16 million colors (24 bit).

Invert

Invert produces a result much like **C**olors, **N**egative Image, in which an image is converted to its negative. An even closer analogy would be putting a solid pure white layer above the target layer and setting the white layer's Blend Mode to Difference.

NOTE

There are no settings for the Invert adjustment. The Layer Properties dialog box for this adjustment has controls only on the General and Blend Range tabs.

You can get some very interesting effects by combining a white Difference layer and Invert:

1. Add a new layer above the original image layer. On the new layer, paint with white on the areas covering the central figure on the image layer below.

2. Set the Blend Mode of the layer with the white paint to Difference. You'll then get an effect like the one in Figure 9.31. This image has one layer containing a photo of lilies and a layer above that which has nothing but white painted on top of one of the lilies and Difference selected as its Blend Mode.

Fig. 9.31
Difference Blend Mode applied to a layer containing a white area.

CHAPTER 9

3. Now add an Invert adjustment layer above the layer that contains the white area (see Figure 9.32).

Fig. 9.32
Invert adjustment layer added above the layer containing the white area.

The areas that had been affected by the Difference layer now take on their natural color, while the areas outside those affected by the Difference layer are inverted.

Levels

Levels is one of the most useful and versatile color adjustment operations included with PSP. Use Levels to adjust overall brightness range or contrast or to fine-tune individual color channels.

Figure 9.33 shows the Levels dialog box, accessed by choosing **Layers**, New **A**djustment Layer, **L**evels.

Fig. 9.33
The Levels dialog box.

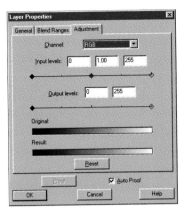

You use the Channel drop-down list to adjust overall brightness (Master) or one of the RGB color channels (Red, Green, or Blue).

Use the Input levels slider to adjust brightness and contrast:

▶ Slide the black diamond right to darken dark pixels.

▶ Slide the empty diamond left to lighten light pixels.

▶ Slide the grey diamond left to lighten midtones or right to lighten midtones.

TIP

Drag the black and empty diamonds of the Input levels slider closer and closer together to increase the contrast.

Use the Output levels slider to lighten dark pixels and to darken light pixels:

▶ Slide the black diamond right to lighten dark pixels.

▶ Slide the empty diamond left to darken light pixels.

TIP

To create an effect that is similar to Invert, drag the Output levels black diamond to the right, and drag the empty diamond to the left of the black diamond. The farther apart the two Output levels diamonds are, the greater the contrast.

CHAPTER 9

NOTE

When you make adjustments with Levels, notice how the Result bar changes as you make adjustments, indicating how the original brightness levels are affected by the adjustments.

Figures 9.34a and 9.34b show a couple of examples of the types of effects that you can create with Levels.

Fig. 9.34a
Example of Levels:
Input levels = 38, 2.00, 224.

Fig. 9.34b
Example of Levels:
Output levels = 192, 63.

Threshold

You can use the final operation on the New Adjustment Layer menu, Threshold, to change all pixels in lower layers to pure black or pure white. Which pixels become black and which ones become white is determined by the Threshold setting, the only control available in the dialog box for this operation.

With Threshold set to 128, as in Figure 9.35, all pixels with brightness values below 128 become black and all other pixels become white.

Fig. 9.35
Threshold set to 128.

Figure 9.36 shows the same image with Threshold set to 200. In this case, all pixels with brightness values below 200 become black, and all other pixels become white.

Fig. 9.36
Threshold set to 200.

Cropping and Resizing

There are two ways to alter the size of your image. You can crop the image to cut away extraneous areas, or you can resize the image to retain all areas of the image intact while changing its dimensions.

PSP provides a lot of flexibility when it comes to cropping and resizing images. You can crop with the Cropping tool—either by hand or via the Crop Area dialog box—or crop to a selection. You can resize an image by using any of three algorithms, or let PSP choose the best of the three for you for a particular image.

Cropping

Crop an image to eliminate elements that detract from the area that you want to focus on. One of the easiest ways to crop is to choose the Crop tool and drag it around the part of the image you want to keep. The Crop tool defines a rectangular area, from one corner to its diagonally opposite corner.

After you define the crop area, you can move it by clicking and dragging inside the crop area with the Crop tool (but not with the Mover tool—if you choose the Mover tool or any other tool, the crop area is deselected). You also can adjust the boundaries of the crop area by positioning the mouse on any of the sides or corners of the boundary and dragging to enlarge or shrink the area. To crop to the boundaries of the crop area, either double-click within your image or click the Crop Image button on the Tool Controls tab of the Crop tool's Tool Options palette.

NOTE

If you decide that you don't want to crop to an area after you have defined it, right-click the image, which turns off the crop area. You then can redefine the crop area or select a different tool or operation.

Another easy way to crop is to crop to a selection. This method is especially handy if you already have a selection (particularly a nonrectangular selection) and simply want to crop to the edges of the selection. To use this method, with a selection active, choose Image, Crop to Selection. PSP defines a rectangular crop area that includes the entire selection and then crops to that area. Figure 9.37 shows an irregularly shaped selection, and Figure 9.38 shows the result of applying Image, Crop to Selection to that selection.

Fig. 9.37
An irregularly shaped
selection to crop to.

Fig. 9.38
The resulting cropped
image.

Notice that cropping to an irregular selection replaces any remaining
areas outside the selection with the current background color, as set in
the Color Palette (on a Background layer) or with transparency (on a
real layer).

CAUTION

In general, you want to be sure that *Antialias* is unchecked and that *Feather*
is set to 0 before you make a selection you want to crop to. If you accidentally
have *Antialias* or *Feather* set for your selection and then crop to that
selection, you'll get an edge of pixels (in the current background color)
surrounding your cropped image.

CHAPTER 9

Another cropping method—one that perhaps is used less often, but can really be very handy—is to double-click the Crop tool icon to bring up the Crop Area dialog box, as shown in Figure 9.39.

Fig. 9.39
The Crop Area dialog box.

In the Crop Area dialog box, you can select the following:

▶ **Custom size and position**—Enables you to specify the coordinates of two corners of the crop area.

▶ **Surround current selection**—Enables you to crop to a selection.

▶ **Select opaque area – current layer**—Enables you to crop to a rectangular area that surrounds all the nontransparent pixels on the current layer.

▶ **Select opaque area – merged**—Enables you to crop to a rectangular area that surrounds all the nontransparent pixels on all visible layers (as if the layers were merged into a single layer).

NOTE

Unlike the Image, Crop To Selection operation, the Surround current selection setting of the Crop Area dialog box does not replace areas outside the selection with the current background color or transparency. Instead, with this setting, a rectangular crop area is defined that includes the selection and immediately surrounding areas.

Also note that when the Crop tool is active, Crop To Selection is not available in the Image menu.

You'll probably find the Crop Area dialog box very useful, especially if you have several images that you want to crop in the same way. In that case, you simply need to set the coordinates in the dialog box once and then apply the crop to each of the images one after the other. You don't need to carefully measure and position the crop area for each image.

Resizing Images and Layers

You can either resize an entire image, whether that image is flat or layered, or resize a single layer in a layered image. In either case, choose Image, Resize (or press Shift+S) to access the Resize dialog box, as shown in Figure 9.40.

Fig. 9.40
The Resize dialog box.

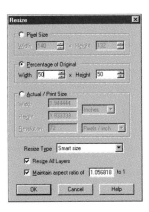

Begin by looking at the bottom of the Resize dialog box, starting with the Resize Type drop-down list box, which includes four types from which you can choose:

▶ **Smart size**—Allows PSP to choose which type of resizing to use.

▶ **Bilinear resample**—Makes interpolations based on the colors of adjacent pixels along the horizontal axis. This method is best for *reducing* the size of 24-bit and greyscale images, such as digital photos.

▶ **Bicubic resample**—Makes interpolations based on the colors of all pixels surrounding a pixel. This method is best for *increasing* the size of 24-bit and greyscale images, such as digital photos.

▶ **Pixel resize**—Adjusts the size of the pixels in the image. This is the best method for line art. It's the only resizing type available for color images with color depths less than 24-bit.

TIP

If you want to use a resizing method other than Pixel resize on a color image that has a color depth less than 24-bit (such as a GIF), temporarily increase the color depth by choosing **C**olors, Increase Color Depth, **16** Million Colors (24 bit).

CHAPTER 9

Two other options located at the bottom of the Resize dialog box are *Resize All Layers* and *Maintain aspect ratio of.* Check *Resize All Layers* if you want to resize your entire image; leave this checkbox unchecked if you want to resize only the currently active layer. Check *Maintain aspect ratio of* if you want to restrict the relative dimensions of your resized image to the width-to-height ratio of the original image. This is almost always what you'll want, because altering the aspect ratio distorts your image.

Now, examine the three upper panes in the Resize dialog box:

▶ **Pixel Size**—Specify the new Width or Height, or both, in terms of pixels. If you have the *Maintain aspect ratio of* checkbox checked, then you should change only one of the dimensions—the other dimension will be calculated appropriately by PSP.

▶ **Percentage of Original**—Specify the new dimension(s) as a percentage of the original. Again, if you have the *Maintain aspect ratio of* checkbox checked, you should change only one of the dimensions, and PSP will calculate the other one for you.

▶ **Actual/Print Size**—Choose units for the dimensions (either inches or centimeters) and for the resolution (either pixels/inch or pixels/cm). Then, change either the dimensions or the resolution. The options in this pane are most useful if you're going to print your image.

TIP

Instead of using Resize's Actual/Print Size setting to adjust the size of an image that you want to print, try choosing **File, Page Setup** to adjust the size of the printed image. That way, the image file itself remains unchanged because you're only making your printer do the resampling.

Resizing the Image Canvas

You also can resize your image canvas. If you make the image canvas larger than it was originally, the dimensions of your original figure will not change; you simply add extra background area to your image. If you make the image smaller than it was originally, however, the canvas shrinks, and your figure will be cropped.

To resize the image canvas, choose Image, Canvas Size to access the Change Canvas Size dialog box, as shown in Figure 9.41.

Fig. 9.41
The Change Canvas Size dialog box.

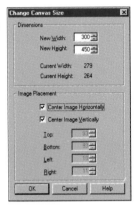

Set the dimensions you want for the resized canvas with New Width and New Height. (PSP helps you by displaying the original Width and Height below the New Width and New Height controls.)

Determine the placement of the original image relative to the resized canvas's dimensions by using the controls in the pane labeled Image Placement. You can choose to center the original image in the new canvas horizontally, vertically, or both, or you can specify other positioning.

CAUTION

When you resize the canvas to a size smaller than its original dimensions, your image is cut off, and the areas of the image falling outside the canvas are lost.

CHAPTER 9

Reorienting Figures

PSP provides three operations for reorienting figures in your images, all three of which are available on the Image menu. Two of these operations, Flip and Mirror, are quite simple: Flip flips an image, layer, or selection vertically, making the top become the bottom and the bottom become the top, as shown in Figure 9.42; Mirror gives you the mirror-image of the original, as shown in Figure 9.43.

Fig. 9.42
Flip example, with copy of original image behind.

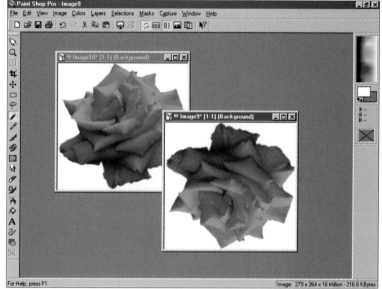

Fig. 9.43
Mirror example, with copy of original image behind.

The third operation for reorienting figures in your images, Image, Rotate, enables you to rotate a figure any number of degrees to the left or right. This operation is only slightly more complex than Flip and Mirror. Figure 9.44 shows the controls that you can set in the Rotate dialog box.

Fig. 9.44
The Rotate dialog box.

Figure 9.45 shows an image along with a version that has been rotated 45 degrees to the left.

Fig. 9.45
Rotate example, with original image behind.

TIP

To minimize distortion, rotate your figure fully in a single step. The fewer rotations you apply to a figure, the less distortion occurs.

Also, if you're editing an 8-bit image (such as a GIF), you can minimize distortion by temporarily increasing the color depth to 24-bit before using Rotate. To increase the color depth, choose **C**olors, **I**ncrease Color Depth, **16** Million Colors (24 bit).

Editing Images:
Some Real-World Examples

Now take a look at some actual digital photos that need adjusting, beginning with the color photo in Figure 9.46.

Fig. 9.46
A photo that could use some color adjustment.

This photo was taken without a flash in a combination of daylight and artificial light. You might like the orangish cast that it has, but if you prefer more natural tones, PSP has what you need.

Display the histogram by pressing the *H* key on the keyboard (see Figure 9.47). As you can see, the histogram shows that the image has a lot of red but very little blue. The lack of anything at the right end of the histogram also shows that the photo has very few bright pixels.

Fig. 9.47
Use the histogram to diagnose the problem.

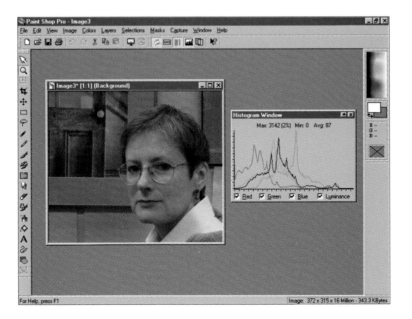

Because this image needs both broad color adjustment and brightening, either Gamma Correction followed by a brightening operation or Hue/Saturation/Brightness would be helpful. To use the Gamma Correction method, follow these steps:

1. Choose **C**olors, **A**djust, **G**amma Correction and uncheck *Link*.

2. To decrease the red and increase the blue, move the Red slider to the left and the Blue slider to the right. Figure 9.48 shows the result with Red set to 0.80 and Blue set to 1.30.

Fig. 9.48
Gamma Correction used to reduce red and increase blue.

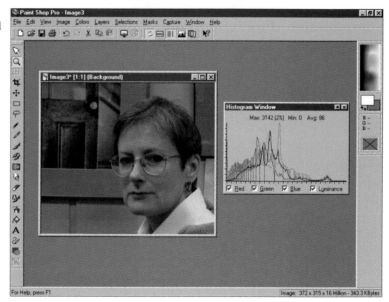

3. To increase the brightness range of the image, choose **C**olors, Hist**o**gram Functions, **S**tretch. As Figure 9.49 shows, this adjustment adds just the right amount of brightness to this example.

Fig. 9.49
Stretch used to increase the brightness range of the image.

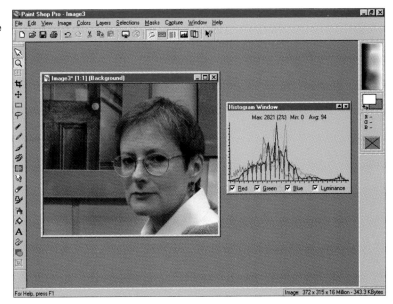

4. You might still want to push the curve of the histogram over to the bright end a bit. To do this, choose **C**olors, **A**djust, **H**ighlight/Midtone/Shadow. The midtones and shadows are already fine, so leave Midtone and Shadow set to 0. Pull the Highlight slider over just a bit to the right. Figure 9.50 shows the result of setting Highlight to 10.

Fig. 9.50
Brightness curve of the histogram adjusted with Highlight/ Midtone/Shadow.

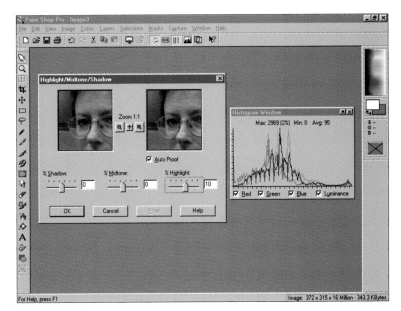

CHAPTER 9

The finished, color-corrected photo is shown in Figure 9.51.

Fig. 9.51
The color-corrected
photo.

TIP

You can take an alternative approach to color-correcting this photo. Instead of using Gamma Correction and Stretch, you can add a solid-blue layer above the original, setting the Opacity rather low (around 20-30%) and perhaps adjusting the Blend Mode to Color, Dodge, Overlay, or Soft Light.

To check the histogram at that point, you need to flatten the layers (because the histogram inspects only a single layer at a time). You can then decide what further adjustments, if any, are needed.

Another alternative is to use adjustment layers rather than color adjustment operations. The advantage to this is that the changes made are editable, and remain so unless the adjustment layers are merged with the photo's layer.

Now, try correcting a black-and-white photo, such as the one in Figure 9.52. As you can see and as the histogram shows, this image is overly dark, with almost no highlights and with detail lost in the shadows.

Fig. 9.52
A black-and-white photo in need of adjustment.

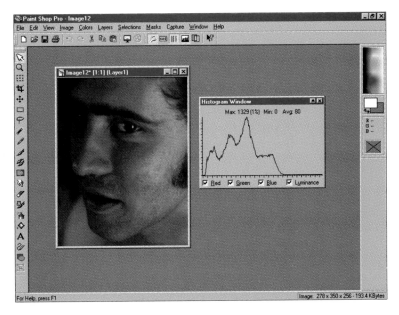

As Figure 9.53 shows, you can begin to lighten up the photo a bit, without losing detail, by using Gamma Correction.

Fig. 9.53
Using Gamma Correction to lighten the photo.

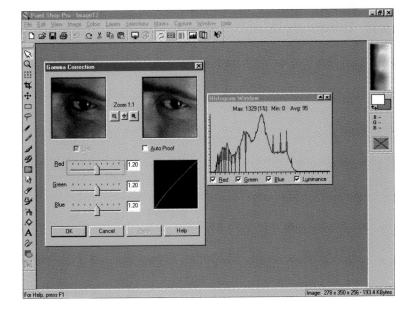

NOTE

In greyscale images, Link is greyed out, because a greyscale image has no color channels. Gamma Correction affects any or all of the color channels in a color image, but affects only the brightness levels in a greyscale image.

This is a big improvement. The brightness range is shifted away from the dark end of the histogram without washing out the shadows. But a few highlights remain and some of the detail is still lost in shadow (see Figure 9.54).

Fig. 9.54
The brightness range has improved, but more adjustment is needed.

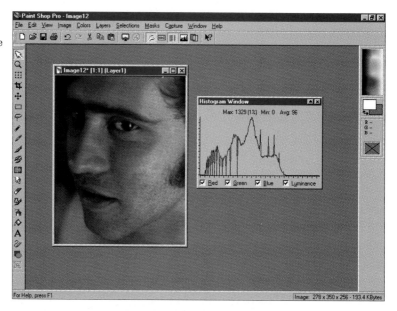

At this point you can try either Colors, Adjust, Brightness/Contrast or Colors, Adjust, Highlight/Midtone/Shadow. Because you want just a little more lightening, along with a subtle tweaking of the contrast, choose Brightness/Contrast.

Brightness/Contrast can be a rather clumsy tool, so start with small changes, and be sure to make liberal use of the Brightness/Contrast dialog box's Preview window. For the example image, all that's needed is a Brightness setting of 5% and a Contrast setting of 10% (see Figure 9.55).

Fig. 9.55
Small adjustments to
Brightness and Contrast
can make a big
difference.

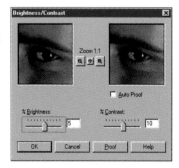

Take a look at the adjusted photo and its histogram in Figure 9.56. You
now have a good brightness range, and the details that were hiding in the
shadows are now revealed.

Fig. 9.56
The corrected photo and
its histogram.

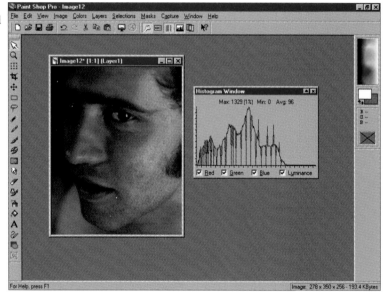

CHAPTER 9

At this point, you might want to start considering composition. The current composition of this image isn't bad, but suppose that you want to emphasize this fellow's eyes. You can focus in on the eyes by cropping away areas at the top and bottom of the photo. Choose the Crop tool and drag to make a crop selection, as in Figure 9.57.

Fig. 9.57
Cropping the photo.

If you're not satisfied with the crop selection defined when you release the mouse button, position the cursor over the crop selection border and drag to adjust the selection. When you have the crop selection as you want it, double-click anywhere in the image canvas. The result is shown in Figure 9.58.

Fig. 9.58
The cropped photo.

Tinting is something else that you might want to try with a black-and-white photo. Let's tint the example photo a sepia color.

1. Increase the color depth to 24 bit by choosing **C**olors, **I**ncrease Color Depth, **16** Million Colors (24 bit).

2. Choose **C**olors, **C**olorize to access the Colorize dialog box.

3. Adjust the Hue and Saturation settings to tint the photo. For a sepia tint, you want a desaturated, yellowish color. Figure 9.59 shows the example photo colorized with Hue set to 30 and Saturation set to 34.

Fig. 9.59
A tinted version of the photo.

To produce similar results using adjustment layers, you might want to crop the image first. Then add an adjustment layer that uses one of the more powerful brightness/contrast controls: Curves or Levels. Figure 9.60 shows a cropped version of the greyscale photo example with a Levels adjustment layer added above the photo layer. Input levels here are set to 0, 1.19, 242, and Output levels to 20 and 255.

Fig. 9.60
A cropped version of the original photo, with a Levels adjustment layer.

CHAPTER 9

To tint the image, increase the color depth to 16 million colors (24 bit) and then add a Hue/Saturation adjustment layer with *Colorize* checked (see Figure 9.61). Hue here is set to 30, Saturation to 34, and Luminance to 0.

Fig. 9.61
The photo tinted with a Hue/Saturation adjustment layer.

Notice how the Saturation level of this image is higher than the example image with Colorize, even though both are set to 34. That's because Colorize uses a Saturation scale of 0 to 255, whereas Hue/Saturation uses a Saturation scale of 100 to –100. To produce an effect with Hue/Saturation that is more like the one produced earlier with Colorize, set Saturation to about 20 or less.

NOTE

To get histogram information for layers affected by adjustment layers, make the uppermost of the relevant adjustment layers the active layer. The histogram then shows the composite brightness data for the adjusted layers.

These examples give you just a hint of what can be done with the adjustment operations available in PSP. Try them yourself on your own images, especially your digital photos. You might be surprised—even small adjustments can yield incredible improvements.

10

Selections, Masks, and Channels

To have real control over your images, you need a firm understanding of selections, masks, and channels. Used in combination, selections, masks, and channels can make many image-editing tasks relatively easy, especially those that involve isolating particular areas of an image.

Here's what you'll be exploring in this chapter:

▶ Understanding the relationship between selections, masks, and channels

▶ Using selections, masks, and channels to isolate image areas and produce special effects

▶ Editing, saving, and loading selections and masks

Selections

In Chapter 3, "Being Selective," you already explored how to use the selection tools and how to add to and subtract from a selection. In this section, you'll take a closer look at how a selection is represented in PSP and how you can save and load selections.

A selection can be represented as a greyscale bitmap, which enables it to be saved to a special channel called an *alpha channel*. The purpose of an alpha channel is to store non-color information so that you can reuse it or edit it later, either in the original image or in another image. To save a selection to an alpha channel, choose **S**elections, Sa**v**e To Alpha Channel. The Save To Alpha dialog box appears, as shown in Figure 10.1.

Fig. 10.1
The Save To Alpha
dialog box.

In the dialog box's Preview window, you see a black-and-white representation of the selection. If you have New Channel selected in the Available Alpha list and then click the OK button, you are prompted to enter a name for the selection. Name the selection, if you want to, and then click OK.

A selection also can be saved to disk by choosing **S**elections, **S**ave To Disk. In the Save Selection Area dialog box, navigate to the folder in which you want to save the selection and enter a name for the selection file (which will be given an extension of .SEL).

NOTE

Why save a selection to disk? You save a selection so that you can reuse it later, either in its original source image or in another image.

To load a selection from an alpha channel, choose **S**elections, **L**oad From Alpha Channel to access the Load From Alpha dialog box (see Figure 10.2).

Fig. 10.2
The Load From Alpha
dialog box.

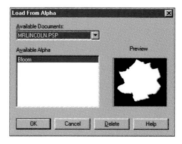

In the Load From Alpha dialog box, you can choose any open image that has an alpha channel as the source image. A black-and-white representation of the alpha channel is displayed in the Preview window. If the image has more than one alpha channel, you can select the channel that you want from the Available Alpha list. When you select an alpha channel and click OK, the alpha channel is loaded in the active image as a selection.

NOTE

When a loaded selection is added to the active image, the loaded selection has the same dimensions as the original selection.

Suppose that you then want to reposition the selection marquee in the active image. Choose the Mover tool, right-click within the selection area, and right-drag until the selection area is where you want it.

To load a selection from disk, choose **S**elections, **L**oad From Disk. In the Load Selection Area dialog box, navigate to the folder that contains the selection file you want to use, select the file, and then click Open. As with a selection loaded from an alpha channel, the selection is loaded into the active image in the same dimensions of the original selection. If you want to reposition the selection marquee in the active image, just right-drag with the Mover tool.

CAUTION

When you load a selection that is larger than the image you're loading to, portions of the selection that don't fit in the image canvas are lost.

Mask Basics

People new to PSP sometimes shy away from masks, thinking that masks are too complicated for mere mortals to deal with. Actually, masks are quite simple to understand and use.

What Is a Mask?

Think of a mask as something like either masking tape or acid, because masks can be used either to keep paint off certain parts of a layer or to eat away paint that is already there. A mask is more versatile than masking tape or acid, though. A mask not only can *completely* mask out areas of layers but also can *partially* mask out some areas, letting the paint show through, but at a lower opacity.

A mask is a greyscale bitmap. Black areas on the mask completely mask out paint. In contrast, white areas on the mask allow all the paint to show through, and grey areas on the mask partially let the paint show through. The darker the grey, the less paint shows through.

A mask both keeps new paint off a layer and strips existing paint from the layer. To see what this means, consider a layer filled with paint, as shown in Figure 10.3.

Fig. 10.3
A single-layered image.

NOTE

Masks work only on layers, so when you add a mask to a Background—in either a flat image or a layered image—the Background is automatically promoted to a layer.

Now, suppose that you apply one of the sample masks included with PSP, RECTANGLE 1.MSK, (see Figure 10.4) to the layer shown in Figure 10.3. RECTANGLE 1.MSK can be found in the Edges folder on the PSP CD. (You'll see how to load a mask from disk in just a little while.) The result of applying this mask to the image in Figure 10.3 is shown in Figure 10.5.

Fig. 10.4
RECTANGLE 1.MSK
sample mask from PSP.

Fig. 10.5
The masked layer.

As you see in Figure 10.5, the area covered by the dark part of the mask becomes transparent. The mask has replaced the paint on that part of the layer with transparency.

Now, return to the unmasked, layered image of Figure 10.3 and apply the sample mask to a new, empty layer above the painted layer. If you then Flood Fill the masked layer with bright-yellow paint, the result looks something like Figure 10.6a.

Fig. 10.6a
The flooded masked layer.

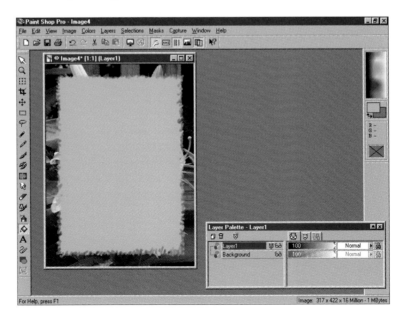

The light area of the mask allows that part of the layer to take on the yellow paint, whereas the dark part of the mask blocks the paint.

This probably isn't the effect that you normally want from an edge mask, though. Instead you probably want the solid paint to show around the edge and the central part of the masked layer to be transparent (to let the content of the lower layer show through). You can easily create this effect by inverting the mask. Just choose **Masks, Invert**. The result is shown in Figure 10.6b.

Fig. 10.6b
The same image with the mask inverted.

Creating and Editing Masks

You can create masks in a variety of ways. One method you can use to produce quite interesting results is to create a mask from an image. To do so, open both the image that will serve as the basis of the mask and the image that you want to apply the mask to. Then, choose **Masks, New, From Image** to open the Add Mask From Image dialog box, shown in Figure 10.7.

Fig. 10.7
The Add Mask From Image dialog box.

In the Source window drop-down list, select the image that you want to use as the basis of your mask. In the Create Mask From section of the dialog box, you have three choices:

▶ **Source luminance**—Creates a mask based on the luminance levels in the source image. Dark colors in the source produce transparency on the masked layer—the darker the color in the source, the less opaque the pixels on the masked layer become.

▶ **Any non-zero value**—Black areas in the source image create complete transparency on the masked layer, leaving all other areas fully opaque.

▶ **Source Opacity**—Transparent areas in the source produce transparency on the masked layer, opaque areas maintain the opacity of the masked layer, and semi-transparent areas produce partial masking.

The last control in the Add Mask From Image dialog box is the *Invert mask data* checkbox. When this box is checked, the mask is inverted. For example, when you've selected Source luminance and have checked the *Invert mask* checkbox, lighter colors in the source produce more transparency than darker colors.

Figure 10.8 shows a simple image that has been added as a mask to the topmost layer of a two-layered image, converting some of the areas of the gradient-layer to transparency, thereby allowing the solid color of the lower layer to show through. (The masked image is shown in front of the image that was used as the basis for the mask.)

Fig. 10.8
Example of a mask created from an image.

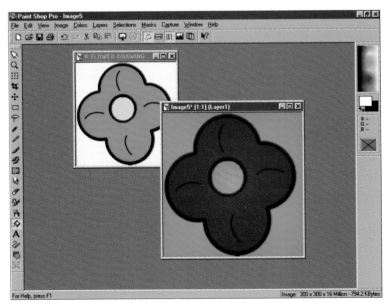

In this example, Source luminance is selected and *Invert mask data* is not checked.

You also can create a mask by hand. To do so, choose either **M**asks, **N**ew, **H**ide All (to start with a mask that completely masks out the paint on the active layer) or **M**asks, **N**ew, **S**how All (to start with a mask that lets all the paint on the active layer show through).

> **TIP**
>
> Click the Mask button on the Layer Palette to create a new mask on the active layer. Or right-click on the Mask button to bring up a menu with options to Show All, Hide All, or From Image.

To edit the mask rather than the image itself, choose **M**asks, **E**dit. This is a toggle, so when you want to go back to editing the image instead of the mask, simply choose this menu option again. When the toggle is on and you're editing the mask, a checkmark appears next to the menu option. When the toggle is off and you're editing the image itself, no checkmark appears near this menu option. You can also tell whether you're in Mask Edit mode or not by examining your image's title bar: In Mask Edit, the title bar displays **(*MASK*)**.

When you're editing a mask, it's sometimes helpful to show a representation of the mask. If you choose **M**asks, View **M**ask, the mask displays as a reddish, semitransparent gel covering the active layer. Those parts of the mask that completely mask out the layer's paint appear dark red, whereas those areas that let the paint show through don't show any red at all. Partially masked areas appear as various shades of red, with the degree of semitransparency over the underlying image varying with the level of masking.

Figure 10.9 shows an example of a mask being edited, with View Mask on.

Fig. 10.9
Editing a mask with
View Mask on.

CHAPTER 10

You use black, white, and shades of grey to paint on a mask. Black creates total masking, whereas white allows all of the layer's paint to show through. Greys allow various levels of masking—the darker the grey, the higher the degree of masking.

You can use just about any of PSP's tools and operations to edit a mask, including all the drawing and painting tools, the selection tools, filters and effects, and the color adjustment operations that affect brightness and contrast.

That just about covers mask editing. Before leaving this section, though, take a look at a couple of the controls on the Layer Palette that affect masks: the Enable Layer Mask and Link Mask toggles, both found on the Mask tab on the righthand side of the Layer Palette (see Figure 10.10):

▶ **Enable Layer Mask**—You can use this toggle to turn off a mask temporarily. Click the toggle once and the mask is turned off. Click the toggle again and the mask is turned on. The Enable Layer Mask toggle does not add or remove a mask; it only temporarily disables and re-enables the effects of the mask.

▶ **Link Mask**—This toggle is useful when you want to move a mask or a layer independently of the other. When the Link Mask toggle is on, moving a layer also moves its mask, and vice versa. When the Link Mask toggle is off, if you edit the layer, the Mover tool moves the contents of the layer without moving the mask. And, if you edit the mask, the Mover tool moves the mask without moving the contents of the layer.

Fig. 10.10
The Enable Layer Mask and Link Mask toggles on the Layer Palette.

NOTE
When a layer has a mask, a mask icon appears on the layer's Layer button on the Layer Palette.

Loading and Saving Masks

To load a mask from disk, choose **M**asks, **L**oad from Disk and then choose the filename of the mask you want. To load RECTANGLE 1.MSK, for example, navigate to your Edges subfolder in your PSP folder and select RECTANGLE 1.MSK, as shown in Figure 10.11.

Fig. 10.11
Loading a mask from disk.

Click Open, and your mask is loaded onto the current active layer.

To save a mask to disk, choose **M**asks, **S**ave To Disk and save the mask as an .MSK file in whatever folder you select.

You also can save a mask to an alpha channel, an option that offers several advantages. For example, you might want to save a mask to an alpha channel so that you can reuse it in another image. Or maybe you want to end your current editing session, but you also want to be able to edit the mask later. Saving the mask to an alpha channel sometimes is a good alternative to merging the mask with your image. After you merge a mask with an image, you can't get the mask back. But a mask saved to an alpha channel gives you both the effect of the mask and the option of modifying the mask later.

Saving a mask to an alpha channel is very similar to saving a selection to an alpha channel. First, choose **M**asks, **Sa**ve To Alpha Channel. Then, in the Save To Alpha dialog box, you'll see a black-and-white representation of the mask in the Preview window. Click OK, and you'll be prompted to name the new channel.

You also load a mask from an alpha channel much as you would load a selection. Choose **M**asks, **L**oad From Alpha Channel, and then choose the alpha channel from the Load From Alpha dialog box.

> **NOTE**
>
> When you load any saved selection or a mask saved to an alpha channel, the loaded selection or mask will have the same dimensions as the original. However, a mask loaded from disk will stretch or shrink to fit the dimensions of the image it is loaded to.

Deleting Masks

Masks are saved along with an image (as long as the file format used supports alpha channels, as does the PSP format). However, you can also either permanently remove a mask or permanently merge a layer's mask with the layer itself. In either case, you first choose **M**asks, **D**elete, which presents you with a prompt that asks whether you want to merge the mask into the current layer. If you just want to get rid of the mask, select No. If you want to permanently merge the mask with the layer, select Yes.

There are several reasons why you might choose to merge a mask. One is that masks take up space in your image, in terms of both file size and the amount of resources required during editing sessions. So, for example, if you're low on disk space, you should merge masks where you can rather than save them with your images. Another reason for merging a mask is to remove paint permanently. A mask itself doesn't really *remove* paint— it only makes it look like the paint is removed. If you want to remove paint entirely and permanently, merge your mask.

Color Channels

Like selections and masks, color channels are represented as greyscale bitmaps. White pixels in one of the channels represent full intensity in the channel; for example, a white pixel in the Red channel's bitmap represents full-intensity red. Black pixels represent no intensity—a black pixel in the Red channel's bitmap represents no red at all. Colors in digital images are produced by combining the greyscale bitmaps that make up the separate color channels.

The RGB Color Model

The RGB color model is the one typically used for images for display on a video screen, such as Web graphics. You might remember from the previous chapter that under the RGB color model, a 24-bit image is a composite of three channels: one Red channel, one Green channel, and one Blue channel. You can take a look at each of the three channels of an image separately by choosing **C**olors, **C**hannel Splitting, **S**plit to RGB to split the image into its RGB channels. Figure 10.12 shows an image along with its three RGB channels.

Fig. 10.12
An image and its RGB channels.

NOTE
A 24-bit image has 8 bits for each of its channels. These 8 bits allow for 256 levels of brightness for each pixel in each channel, from black (0) to white (255). This is why each channel of a 24-bit image can be represented as a 256-shade greyscale image.

When the individual channels are split apart like this, they can be edited separately. You can recombine them later by using Colors, Channel Combining, Combine from RGB.

The HSL Color Model

The HSL color model is an alternative to RGB and, like RGB, is used primarily for images for display on a video screen. Under the HSL color model, a 24-bit color image is also represented as a composite of three greyscale bitmaps, with one bitmap for the Hue channel, one for the Saturation channel, and another for the Lightness channel.

You can split an image into its HSL channels by using Colors, Channel Splitting, Split to HSL. You also can edit each of these channels separately and then recombine them with Colors, Channel Combining, Combine from HSL.

TIP

You can create color images from greyscale images by combining the separate greyscale images as either RGB or HSL channels. This probably isn't a technique you'll use very often, but you might have fun trying it out, just to see how it works.

You can make plaid or gingham patterns, for example, by using three greyscale images with differently shaded horizontal and vertical stripes as the three channels of an RGB image.

The CMYK Color Model

One other color model exists that we haven't explored yet: the CMYK color model. "CMYK" stands for Cyan, Magenta, Yellow, and Black, which are the basic colors used in printing. PSP provides limited support for CMYK, and part of this support is the capability to split an image into the four color channels for CMYK. You do this by selecting Colors, Channel Splitting, Split to CMYK.

For more information on CMYK, see the *PSP Users Guide*. And be sure to consult your print shop to find out specifically what it needs from you for your print jobs. If you're doing all of your printing on an inkjet printer at your home or office, you don't need to know anything about CMYK, because your printer driver will take care of translating your RGB image for printing.

Advanced Techniques for Isolating Areas

This section shows you how you can really make the most of selections, masks, and channels to isolate areas in an image.

Converting Selections and Masks

As you saw earlier, both selections and masks can be represented as greyscale bitmaps, and both can be saved to alpha channels. Because selections and masks are such close cousins, a selection can be converted to a mask, and a mask can be converted to a selection.

You can create a mask from a selection in the active image by choosing either **M**asks, **N**ew, **H**ide Selection (to mask out the area of the selection) or **M**asks, **N**ew, Sho**w** Selection (to mask out everything except the selection). You can then edit the mask, if you like, or save it to disk or an alpha channel. You can load a saved mask to any image.

To create a selection from a mask that you have on the active layer of the active image, choose **S**elections, **F**rom Mask. You can then use the selection on that or any other layer of the image, or save the selection to disk or to an alpha channel. You can load a saved selection to any image.

NOTE

A selection saved to an alpha channel also can be loaded as a mask. And a mask saved to an alpha channel also can be loaded as a selection.

Combining Masks and Selections

Although PSP provides no *direct* way to combine two masks or two selections, some *indirect* ways are available. For example, you can use two or more masks or selections in a separate greyscale image to get the effect of a combined mask or selection. You can then use this image to create a mask or selection and load it to another image.

One way to do this is to create an image with a white background and a few transparent layers, one layer for each of the masks or selections that you want to combine. Load each mask or selection on its own layer, invert it if necessary, and then fill the layer (or the selection on the layer) with black. Merge any masks with their layers. You can then use this image as the basis of a mask that you can add to another image.

Using Channels to Make Selections

It's time to bring channels into the picture. Sometimes, making a good selection on your image by using the Magic Wand or other selection tools is just about impossible. You might find, though, that making your selection on one of the image's RGB, HSL, or CMYK channels is much easier. A hazy, brown object on a green background might be hard to select in the complete image, for example, but might be a piece of cake to isolate from the Red color channel. And because a split channel is an image, and a selection or mask can be loaded from one image to another, you can save a selection made in one of the image's channels and then load it into the original image itself.

Take a look at a very simple example. The leftmost image in Figure 10.13 shows a green, glossy figure against a speckled, multicolored background. The foreground figure isn't a good candidate for the Magic Wand, and the background would be nearly impossible to select directly. You might be able to do a passable job of selecting the foreground figure with the Freehand tool set to Smart Edge, but you have an easier route available here:

1. Split this image into its HSL channels (using **C**olors, **C**hannel Splitting, **Sp**lit to HSL). You'll see that, in the Saturation channel, the glossy figure is quite distinct from the background (see Figure 10.13).

Fig. 10.13
Saturation channel of the example image, with original image behind.

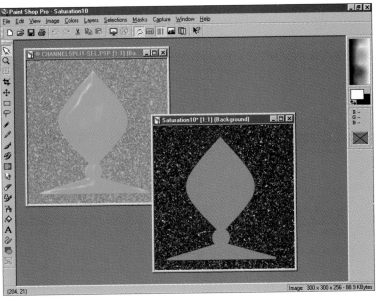

2. Click the Magic Wand on the dark figure in the Saturation channel to make the selection.

TIP

You can use the operations under Colors, Adjust to make the contrast in a split channel even sharper.

3. Save the selection to an alpha channel with **S**elections, Sa**v**e to Alpha Channel.

4. Make the original image the active image by clicking its title bar, and then load the selection to this image with **S**elections, L**o**ad from Alpha Channel.

5. In the Load From Alpha dialog box, choose the Saturation channel from the Available Documents drop-down list and choose your saved selection from the Available Alpha list (see Figure 10.14).

Fig. 10.14
Choosing settings in the Load From Alpha dialog box.

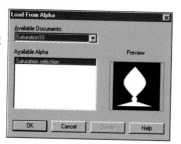

You can then make any adjustments to the selection that you still need to make (such as contracting, expanding, or feathering the selection). You're ready to use the selection in any way that you wish: Copy the selected area to the Clipboard and paste it as a new image, invert the selection and press the Delete key to delete the background, convert the selection to a mask, or whatever you like. For example, Figure 10.15 shows the selected figure in the example after it has been copied to the Clipboard and then pasted into an image with a gradient background.

Fig. 10.15
Selected figure pasted on a new background.

NOTE

In real graphics projects, you'll probably need to do more work than in this simple example to get your selection right, but this method can bring seemingly impossible-to-make selections into the realm of the possible.

Editing and Recombining Channels

You just looked at channel splitting as a means of making selections. Earlier in the chapter, you explored splitting an image into its CMYK channels for professional print jobs. Now you are going to see that splitting an image into separate channels also can be useful for color correction and for creating odd effects.

For example, you can reduce a reddish cast in an image by splitting the image into its RGB channels and darkening the Red channel. Then, recombine the channels with Colors, Channel Combine, Combine From RGB. See Figures 10.16 and 10.17 for a comparison of a reddish image and its modified Red channel counterpart.

Fig. 10.16
Image with a reddish cast.

Fig. 10.17
Image corrected by darkening the Red channel.

You also can adjust an image by using filters on one or two split channels. For instance, sharpening sometimes introduces unwanted noise. But try one of the Sharpen filters on only one or two channels and then recombine the channels. The result will probably be subtle sharpening without noise.

To create effects, try using other filters on a channel, such as Emboss, Hot Wax Coating, or Mosaic. Also try applying one of the Histogram functions to a channel. Combine the modified channel with the other channels and see what results! Also try shuffling the channels (for instance, using the Red channel as the Blue channel, the Blue channel as the Green, and the Green as the Red) or splitting into RGB channels and then recombining as HSL channels. Much of the time, the result will be positively hideous, but sometimes, you'll be in for a pleasant surprise (see Figure 10.18).

Fig. 10.18
Examples of images
with modified channels.

Artistic Edges

Before leaving this chapter, take a look at a favorite use for masks: making artistic edges. You already looked at a simple edge mask earlier in this chapter, RECTANGLE 1.MSK, which is included with PSP6. You also can find collections of artistic edges commercially or for free download on the Web. In addition, Photo/Graphic Edges by AutoF/X (**http://www.autofx.com/**) is a very sophisticated—and rather expensive—edge package. Another great edge package—this one in just about everyone's price range—is Harry Heim's Edge & Frame Galaxy (available at **http://pico.i-us.com/**). As you'll see in just a bit, it's also easy to make your own edges.

The simplest way to use an edge mask is to load the mask, as you did earlier in the chapter with RECTANGLE 1.MSK. Edged graphics also can be enhanced with drop shadows or glows, as the example in Figure 10.19 shows. You also can use multiple edges in a single image, loading them one at a time and perhaps enhancing each with filters or other effects, as shown in Figure 10.20.

Fig. 10.19
Example of enhanced edged image.

Fig. 10.20
Example of image with multiple edges.

Here's how to create your own edge mask:

1. Open a largish, new image (in the range of 300-1000 pixels high and wide) and give it a white background. Make the image a greyscale image by using Colors, Grey Scale, or open it initially as a greyscale (8-bit) image.

2. Paint the areas that should be masked out. Use black for complete masking and shades of grey for partial masking; the transparent parts of the mask should be kept white.

3. Apply filters or effects, if you like.

Figure 10.21 shows an edge image that was created in this way.

Fig. 10.21
Handmade edge image.

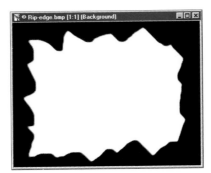

You can save your edge image as a PSP mask in either of two ways:

▶ Save the image as a Windows or OS/2 bitmap (*.BMP) file. In the Save As or Save Copy As dialog box, be sure to select this file type and then click the Options button. Set Compression to Run Length Encoding. Save the BMP file to the folder where you want to keep your edge masks.

To use a BMP file as a mask, you have to open the mask file and load it to your image with **M**asks, **N**ew, **F**rom Image. To make loading the mask easier, go to your Edges folder, using Windows Explorer, and change the extension of your BMP file to .MSK. This way, you won't have to open the mask file to load it. Instead, just load the mask with **M**asks, **L**oad From Disk.

▶ Save the mask to disk. With the edge image active, choose **M**asks, **N**ew, **F**rom Image. Select This Window as the source window and select Source Luminance under Create mask from.

Your image will look a little strange at this point. But don't worry, you're going to throw away that image when you're done. Choose **M**asks, **S**ave To Disk. In the Save Mask Channel dialog box, navigate to the folder where you want to store your edge mask, give your mask a name, and click Save. Then close the image you were working from, without saving it.

Now you can use your edge mask just as you would any other mask available on disk (see Figure 10.22). Choose **M**asks, **L**oad From Disk and navigate to the folder that holds your mask. Select the mask you want from the file list, click Open, and there you are!

Fig. 10.22
Handmade edge mask
applied to a photo.

11

Adding to Your Toolkit

The standard Paint Shop Pro tools can take you far, but you're not limited to these tools. PSP6 lets you expand your toolkit by enabling you to create your own Paper textures, Sculpture patterns, brushes, Picture Tubes, picture frames, and filters. In this chapter, you'll learn how to add to your toolkit and what kinds of effects you can achieve.

Here's what you'll be exploring in this chapter:

► Making your own Paper textures, Texture Effect textures, and Sculpture Effect patterns

► Creating your own brushes and Picture Tubes and exploring how the two differ

► Making your own picture frames

► Rules of thumb for creating your own User Defined Filters

Making Your Own Textures

Any 256-shade greyscale image can be saved as a BMP for use as a Paper texture or as a texture for use with the Texture Effect. For best results, the greyscale should be a seamless tile and should be rather dark with relatively high contrast. The image must be saved as a BMP and located in PSP's Textures folder (usually C:\Paint Shop Pro 6\Textures). (See Figure 11.1.)

TIP

To create a seamless tile in PSP, make a selection in your textured image and then select Selections, Convert To Seamless Pattern. (If you get an error message that your selection is too close to the edges of your image, make a new selection and try again.)

Fig. 11.1
Save your greyscale
image as a BMP file.

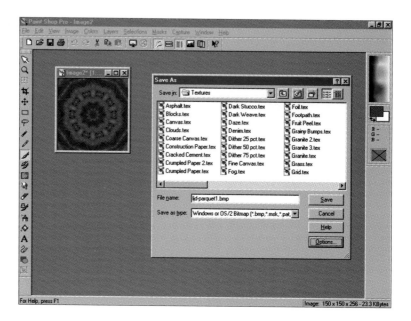

NOTE

In PSP5, textures had to have an extension of TEX, but PSP6 will also recognize files with the BMP extension as texture files.

PSP5 users also should note that there no longer is a PaperNam.idx file that needs to be modified in order for your texture to be recognized. PSP6 will recognize any BMP or TEX file in your Textures folder as a texture.

After you create your new texture file and save it to the Textures folder, the new texture will be available as a Paper texture the next time you select a painting tool, as shown in Figure 11.2.

Fig. 11.2
The new texture
appears in the Paper
texture list.

You use the new Paper texture just as you would use one of PSP's own textures. After you select a painting tool, such as the Paintbrush or Airbrush, go to the tool's Options tab in the Tool Options palette and select your new paper from the Paper texture drop-down list. Go to the tool's main tab, if you need to, and make any other setting adjustments. You can then paint by using your paper texture, as shown in Figure 11.3.

Fig. 11.3
Using the new texture.

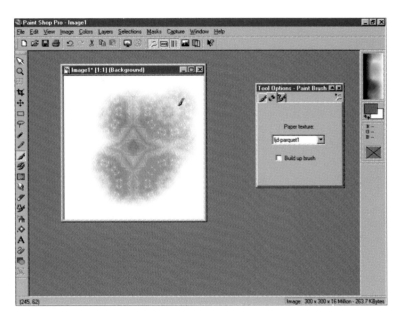

Any greyscale image that is saved as a Paper texture can also be used as a Texture Effect texture. Figure 11.6 shows the example texture from Figure 11.4 in use with the Texture Effect.

Fig. 11.4
The new texture in use.

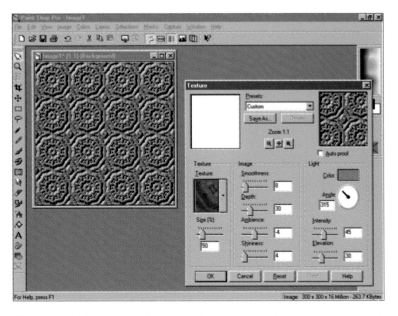

Keep in mind that not all images that make good Paper textures make good Texture Effect textures (and vice versa). You need to use your discretion when selecting a texture.

Making Your Own Sculpture Effect Patterns

Just as you can make your own textures for use with the Texture Effect, you can make your own patterns for use with the Sculpture Effect. Any 24-bit color image can be used as a pattern, but for best results, the image should be a seamless tile.

Here's an easy method for making your own simple patterns:

1. Create a seamless pattern with PSP's Kaleidoscope Effect (discussed in Chapter 6, "PSP Effects") or make a seamless pattern from a texture image by making a selection in the image and using **S**elections, **C**onvert to Seamless Pattern (discussed in Chapter 3, "Being Selective").

2. Save your pattern image as an OS/2 or Windows Bitmap [BMP] file, selecting these options:

    > Format = Windows

    > Encoding = RGB

    Save the pattern file to your Patterns folder (normally, C:\Program Files\Paint Shop Pro 6\Patterns). Any RGB Bitmap file in the Patterns folder that has an extension of BMP or PAT will be recognized as a pattern.

Figure 11.5 shows an example of Sculpture with a kaleidoscope pattern and Figure 11.6 shows an example with a seamless pattern made from a selection.

Fig. 11.5
The Sculpture Effect using a kaleidoscope pattern.

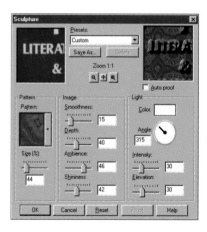

Fig. 11.6
The Scultpure Effect
using a seamless pattern
made from a selection.

Creating Your Own Brushes

You also can create your own brushes for use in PSP. To use a custom
brush, select one of the painting tools, such as the Paintbrush or
Airbrush. Then, go to the Tool Options palette and click the Brush
Options button in the upper-right area of the tool's main tab, which opens
a drop-down list; choose Custom from the list, which opens the Custom
Brush dialog box shown in Figure 11.7.

Fig. 11.7
The Custom Brush
dialog box.

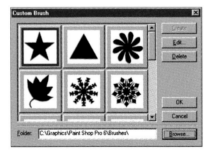

You can create your own custom brush out of any selection. As an
example, open one of PSP's tube files and create a brush out of one of the
tube elements, as follows:

1. Apply one of the coins from the Coins tube file to a new image with
   a Transparent background.

2. Select the coin by clicking with the Magic Wand in the transparent
   area surrounding it and then by inverting the selection by choosing
   Selections, Invert.

3. With the inverted selection active, choose one of the painting tools
   (to have access to the proper Tool Options palette).

CHAPTER 11

4.   Click the Brush Options button on the Tool Options palette and choose Custom, as shown in Figure 11.8.

Fig. 11.8
Create a new brush from a selection.

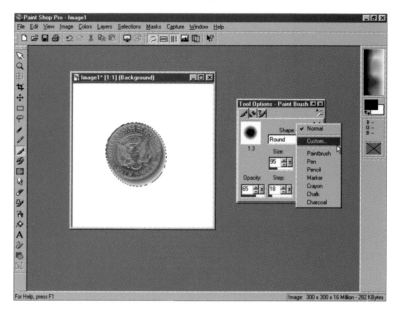

5.   In the Custom Brush dialog box, click the Create button (see Figure 11.9). (If the Create button is greyed out, you don't have an active selection in your image.) The current selection is then added immediately to the available custom brushes.

Fig. 11.9
Click the Create button to make a new brush from the selection.

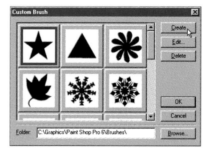

6.   To use a custom brush, select the brush from the Preview window in the Custom Brush dialog box by clicking the brush and then clicking OK.

TIP

If you want to change the default Step of a custom brush, double-click the brush instead of single-clicking. A dialog box with a Step control slider will pop up. Select your Step setting, click OK, and then click OK in the Custom Brush dialog box.

Now compare the difference between the results produced with the custom brush created from a tube element and the results produced with the tube itself. The custom brush paints with a single color—either the current foreground color, if you paint with the left mouse button depressed or the current background color, if you paint with the right mouse button depressed. The opacity of the paint is determined by the Opacity setting selected in the Tool Options palette.

Figure 11.10 shows an example of the half-dollar custom brush in use, with Opacity set to 75.

Fig. 11.10
The coin brush in use.

Compare the results shown in Figure 11.10 with the results that you get when you use the tube, as shown in Figure 11.11. With a tube, you paint with a fully opaque, full-color image. Which to choose—the brush or the tube—will depend on what effect you want to achieve.

Fig. 11.11
The coin tube in comparison.

CHAPTER 11

Try creating another brush, using a dingbat character as the selection:

1.   Set the foreground color to Black, and then select the Text tool and click inside an empty image.

2.   In the Add Text dialog box, select the dingbat font you want to use, in the style and size you want, and check *Floating*.

3.   In the text box, add the dingbat character you want to use for your brush and click OK.

4.   Choose one of the painting tools. Click the Brush Options button on the tool's main tab of the Tool Options palette and choose Custom. When the Custom Brush dialog box appears, click the Create button, as shown in Figure 11.12. The dingbat character is now added to your available custom brushes.

Fig. 11.12
Using a dingbat character to make a brush.

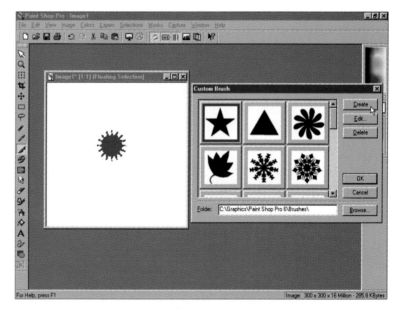

Figure 11.13 shows an example of the dingbat character in use, with Opacity set to 15.

Fig. 11.13
The dingbat brush in
use.

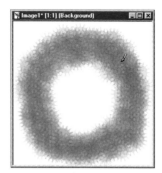

NOTE

You aren't restricted to using only one character when you create a custom brush from a text selection. If you want to use a word or phrase or other string of characters as a brush, that works just as well as a single character.

Keep in mind, though, that the maximum size for a brush is 255×255 pixels.

NOTE

Want to find out more about creating and managing custom brushes? Would you like to find brushes available for download? Then head out to Deborah "MomJ" Jacobs's Mousehold Creations at **http://www.capecodmouse.com/ moushold/psp/**. MomJ has everything that a brush fanatic could ask for.

There are lots of places from which to download PSP custom brushes. And, as Mom would tell you, PSP also recognizes Adobe Photoshop brushes!

Creating Your Own Picture Tubes

Using PSP's File, Export, Picture Tube command, adding a new tube that you've created is easy. To create your own tube, start by opening a new image and selecting Transparent as the image's background color. The dimensions of this tube canvas should be large enough to hold all of your tube elements in a series of regularly spaced columns and rows.

As an example, suppose that you want to make a tube based on the rose image in Figure 11.14, which has been isolated from a photograph of a French Lace rose.

Fig. 11.14
Image used to create the
example tube.

You'll create the tube by using this image and three other images that are different flipped and/or mirrored versions of the original.

Each of the four images for the French Lace tube is 100×100 pixels, so to accommodate the four tube elements, the tube canvas needs to be either 400×100—four columns and one row—or 200×200—two columns and two rows. For this example, a 200×200 canvas is used, as shown in Figure 11.15.

Fig. 11.15
Open a new canvas for positioning your tube elements.

TIP

Although the size of Picture Tube elements can be scaled either up or down when you select a particular tube to paint with, the results are much better when you scale down than when you scale up. For this reason, it's best to make your tube elements as large as you're likely to want to use them.

For example, suppose that you usually want to paint with the roses displayed at about 50×50 pixels, but occasionally you want them to be about 100×100 pixels. In that case, create the tube with elements that are 100×100 pixels.

Before you place the Picture Tube elements on your newly opened canvas, turn on PSP's grid—which makes aligning objects easier—by selecting **View**, **Grid**. You can adjust the spacing of the gridlines by selecting **File**, Preferences, **General** Program Preferences (on the Rulers and Units tab).

Follow these steps to place the Picture Tube elements on the tube canvas:

1. Copy a selection from a source image to the Clipboard and then paste the copied selection to the tube canvas as a new selection.

2. Position the selection, centering it within the first cell area of your tube canvas. In the rose example, the first pasted-in selection is positioned in the upper-left 100×100 pixel area of the tube canvas, as shown in Figure 11.16. After you position the selection correctly, click with the right mouse button outside the selection to anchor the selection and turn off the selection marquee.

Fig. 11.16
Position each tube
element.

CAUTION

All opaque areas on the tube canvas will appear as opaque paint when you use your tube. You normally will want each tube element to be a figure surrounded by transparency. When the figure that you want for your tube element is only part of an opaque area of the source image, be sure to select only the part of the image that you want for your tube before using Edit, Copy.

3. Continue in the same way to copy, paste, and position the next tube element. Do the same with all the tube elements, positioning each in an appropriate area of the tube canvas.

TIP

If you want to add a drop shadow to each of your tube elements, you don't need to make a selection before you apply the effect. The Drop Shadow (available under Image, Effects) works without a selection on a layer any time that the layer contains transparency. Just apply Drop Shadow to the layer, and drop shadows will be added around each opaque figure on the layer.

CHAPTER 11

4. When all of your tube elements are positioned correctly, you're ready to export the image as a tube. Make sure that the tube canvas image is the active image by clicking its title bar. Then, choose **F**ile, Expor**t**, **P**icture Tube. The Export Picture Tube dialog box, shown in Figure 11.17, is then displayed.

Fig. 11.17
Exporting a Picture Tube.

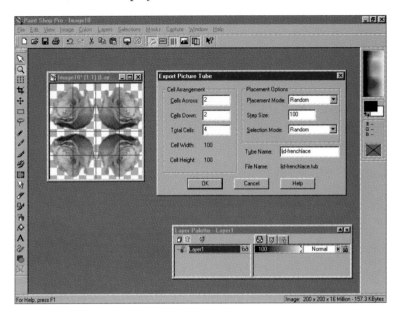

CAUTION

Before you export your image as a Picture Tube, be sure that it has exactly one layer and no floating selection. If it has more than one layer, or you've flattened the image, or a floating selection is active, PSP will refuse to export the image as a tube. Instead, you'll receive this rather confusing error message: "To save the image as a Picture Tube, the image must be 24 bit and have only one layer with a transparency."

5. In the Export Picture Tube dialog box, fill in the number of Cells Across and the number of Cells Down. The field for Total Cells updates automatically. This example has two Cells Across and two Cells Down, for a total of four cells.

6. Fill in the settings you want for the Placement Options (see Chapter 1, "Basic Drawing and Painting Tools," for details on these options) and in the Tube Name field, enter the name of the new tube as you want it to appear in the Tube drop-down list on the Picture Tube tool's Tool Options palette. (*ljd-frenchlace* was entered as the name of the example tube.) After you choose all the settings and enter the name of the tube, click OK.

After you click OK in the Export Picture Tube dialog box, PSP creates the new tube file and adds its name to the list of available tubes.

The new tube is ready to use. Choose the Picture Tube tool and select the new tube from the Tube drop-down list in the Tool Options palette. Then, paint away with your new creation!

Making Your Own Picture Frames

Picture Frames are a new addition to PSP6. To add a frame to your image, choose **I**mage, **P**icture Frame to start the Picture Frame Wizard (see Figure 11.18).

Fig. 11.18
The Picture Frame
Wizard.

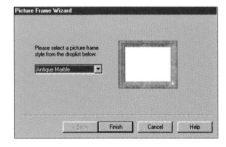

In the Wizard, select the frame you want to use. If you select a rectangular frame with no transparent areas outside the frame, just press Finish to apply the frame. If there are transparent areas around the edges of the frame (as there are for any nonrectangular frame), press Next and you'll be presented with another Picture Frame Wizard dialog box, as shown in Figure 11.19. In this second dialog box, you tell PSP how to fill in the transparent outer areas.

Fig. 11.19
Second window of
Picture Frame Wizard.

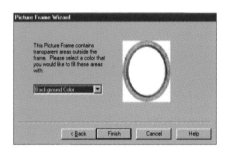

To apply the frame, click Finish.

It's very easy to make your own rectangular Picture Frames. Create a new 24-bit image on a transparent layer, as in Figure 11.20. Here, the Texture and Inner Bevel Effects are applied to a frame-shaped selection, and then the selection is turned off.

Fig. 11.20
Creating a new Picture
Frame.

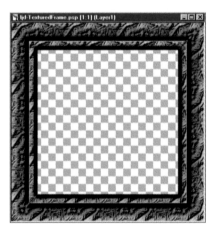

Save this file as a PSP file and put it in your Frames folder (normally
C:\Program Files\Paint Shop Pro 6\Frames). Change the extension to
PFR, and the next time you use the Picture Frame Wizard you'll see your
new frame in the list.

NOTE

You can skip the renaming step by adding PFR to the list of extensions for
PSP files. To add the extension, choose File, Preferences, File Format
Associations. Highlight the entry for Paint Shop Pro Image (*.psp) and click
the Extensions button. Then, click the Add button, type in PFR, and click the
OK button. Notice that the PSP entry now says this: Paint Shop Pro Image
(*.psp, *.pfr). Click OK again to make the change and exit the File Format
Associations dialog box.

Then, when you save a picture frame file, you can just type in the PFR
extension after the filename.

Creating a nonrectangular frame is almost as easy as creating a
rectangular one. Before saving the file, select the picture frame and the
internal "hole," as shown in Figure 11.21. (An easy way to make such a
selection is to select the outer transparent areas and then choose
Selections, Invert.)

Fig. 11.21

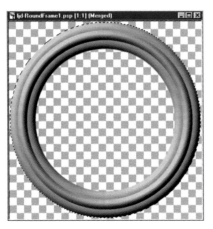

CHAPTER 11

Selecting the frame of a new nonrectangular Picture Frame. Next, save the selection to an alpha channel by choosing **S**elections, Sa**v**e to Alpha Channel. Then, save the picture frame file as you do a rectangular picture frame. Figure 11.22 shows the nonrectangular frame with the areas outside the frame set to White.

Fig. 11.22
Picture Frame applied to a photo, with outside areas set to White.

TIP

Picture Frames stretch or shrink to fit the image that they're applied to. When the aspect ratio of the frame is quite different from the aspect ratio of the image, the frame will be distorted. So you might want to create several versions of your frame, each with a different aspect ratio. For example, you might have one that's 1-to-1 (a square), one that's 2-to-3 and one that's 3-to-2.

Keep in mind, too, that the image quality of the frame is maintained best when the frame is shrunk rather than stretched. So try to create your frames about as large as you're likely to use them.

User Defined Filters

Many PSP users find User Defined Filters baffling. The PSP documentation does a good job of covering the technical aspects of User Defined Filters, but if you don't know anything about matrix arithmetic, or if you think of a "summation" as something a lawyer presents in court, then you might not even know where to begin with User Defined Filters.

This section leaves most of the technical details aside and concentrates on a few rules of thumb that will help you to make your own Blur, Emboss, Sharpen, and Edge Detect filters. These filters can be used on any 256-greyscale or 16-million color image.

The Technical Stuff

Let's begin by getting some of the technical stuff out of the way. Open the User Defined Filter matrix by choosing Image, User Defined Filters. In the User Defined Filters dialog box, click New (leaving all the settings at their default values). The Define New Filter dialog box appears, as shown in Figure 11.23.

Fig. 11.23
A new User Defined Filter matrix.

The cells of the matrix represent pixels in an image. The center cell represents the target pixel, and the surrounding cells represent the pixels surrounding the target. The numbers that you place in the cells determine brightness changes in the pixels. A positive number in the center cell increases the target pixel's brightness, and a negative number decreases the target's brightness. Numbers in the surrounding cells combine to affect the target pixel further. The filter examines each pixel in an image separately, calculates how to change each target, and then applies all the results to the image.

In general, you want to keep the overall brightness of the image the same as the original. The total of all the values in the cells helps determine the brightness of the filtered image. If the total equals 1, the filtered image will have the same overall brightness as the original (provided the Division factor is kept at 1 and the Bias is kept at 0). If the total value is greater than 1, the overall brightness increases; if the total value is less than 1, the overall brightness decreases.

NOTE

If you experiment with User Defined Filters without understanding how the total of the cell values affects brightness, you might very well end up with filters that do nothing more than turn your image solid white or solid black.

You can maintain the original brightness of your image even if the values of the cells don't total 1. You do this by adjusting the Division factor. If the total of your cells equals 5, setting the Division factor to 5 will maintain the image brightness (because 5 divided by 5 equals 1). Your Division factor doesn't have to be equal to the total of the cell values, but other values will change the image's brightness—not always to good effect.

As you'll see when you look at a few examples, the Bias is most useful for embossing filters. The Bias value is added to the modified pixel's brightness, and thus has a big effect on the filtered image's contrast.

UDFs for the Rest of Us

Okay, now you're ready to look at a few examples. Throughout this section, the sample filters are applied to the library image in Figure 11.24.

Fig. 11.24
Base image to be filtered.

First, open the Sample Blur filter that comes with PSP. To see the matrix for this filter, select Sample Blur in the User Defined Filter dialog box and click Edit. Figure 11.25 shows the matrix for this filter, along with the results of applying the filter to the library image. To apply a User Defined Filter, select the filter from the list in the User Defined Filters dialog box and click Apply.

Fig. 11.25
PSP's Sample Blur filter.

Notice in this filter that the center cell is set to a positive value and that a symmetric pattern of cells surrounding the center cell also contains positive values. The Division factor is set to the total of the cell values. These are the basic characteristics of any blurring filter.

Now we'll make our own Blur filter. Figure 11.26 shows the matrix values and Division factor for a more severe Blur filter, along with the effect of applying this filter to the library image.

Fig. 11.26
More severe Blur filter.

CHAPTER 11

Notice that, again, the center pixel is set to a positive number, and a symmetric pattern of positive cell values is set in the surrounding cells. The total of all the cell values is 57, so to maintain the overall brightness of the original image, the Division factor is set to 57.

Emboss Filters Galore

A color Emboss filter makes an image look embossed while generally maintaining the colors of the original image. The matrix values of such a filter, and its effect on the library image, are shown in Figure 11.27.

Fig. 11.27
A color Emboss filter.

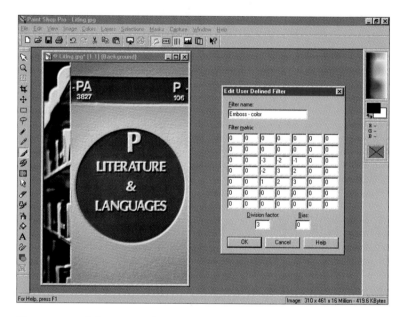

The matrix of this example shows the basic characteristics of color-embossing filters. The center cell value can be either positive or negative. The crucial factor is that cells to one side of the center cell have positive values, and the cells to the other side of the center cell have negative values. The relative position of the positive and negative values determines where the highlights and shadows appear in the embossed image.

Now look at a few embossing filters that more closely resemble PSP's Emboss filter (discussed in Chapter 8, "Filters").

You can create an embossing effect without much color by putting positive values in some of the cells to one side of the center cell and adjusting the Bias. Figure 11.28 shows one such filter and its effects.

Fig. 11.28
A basic embossing filter.

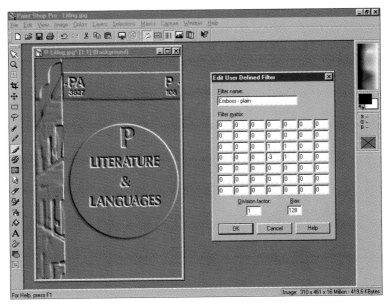

TIP

You can use Bias in any User Defined Filter to affect the contrast of your filtered image. For high-contrast effects, enter grid values that yield a relatively large sum, and enter very large positive or very low negative values for Bias.

In your embossing filters, you can change where the highlights and shadows appear (and thus change which areas appear raised and which appear recessed) by changing the relative position of the positive and negative cell values. Figure 11.29 shows the result of switching the relative position of the cells of the basic embossing filter in Figure 11.28.

Fig. 11.29
The basic embossing
filter reversed.

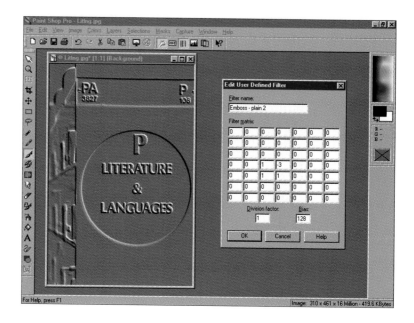

TIP

If you want your embossed image to have no hint of color, apply the filter
only to your image's grey values. In the User Defined Filter dialog box, select
Grey Values rather than Color Component(s) for Apply To.

Sharpen Filters

Now it's time to explore Sharpen filters, which sharpen the focus of a
blurry image. For Sharpen, enter a relatively large positive value for the
center cell, and enter negative numbers (such as -2 or -1) in a symmetrical
pattern in some of the surrounding cells. The smaller the value in the
surrounding cells, the more severe the sharpening effect will be. Figure
11.30 displays a basic Sharpen filter.

Fig. 11.30
A Sharpen filter.

To soften the sharpening effect, increase the value in the center cell and compensate for the increase with the Division factor.

TIP

You can make any User Defined Filter effect more subtle by increasing the value of the center cell and compensating for the increase with the Division factor.

Edge Detect Filters

The Edge Detect filter enhances the areas of an image in which there are contrasts in brightness or color. For edge detection, the values entered for any cells surrounding the center cell should be positive, and the value of the center cell should be a negative number equal in magnitude to the sum of the values of the surrounding cells. Figure 11.31 shows an example.

CHAPTER 11

Fig. 11.31
An Edge Detect filter.

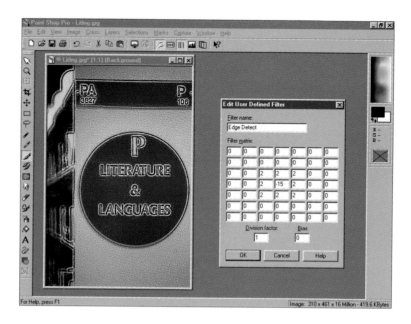

Infinite Filter Possibilities

Experiment with variations on the sample filters covered here. For example, the Electric filter, shown in Figure 11.32, is a variation of a basic Sharpen filter, with some added peripheral values and a fairly high Bias.

Fig. 11.32
The Electric filter.

Other variations to try in your own filters include using 0 as your center cell value and/or using Division factors that don't completely compensate for grid sums that aren't equal to 1. Figures 11.33 and 11.34 are examples of such filters.

Fig. 11.33
A filter with a center cell value of 0, a Division Factor that doesn't equal the grid sum, and an extreme Bias.

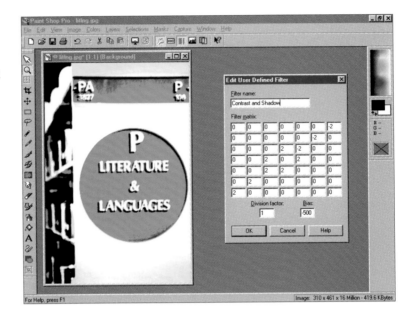

Fig. 11.34
A filter with an extreme Bias and a Division Factor that doesn't equal the grid sum.

If you prefer to keep to the basics, Table 11.1 summarizes the rules of thumb for simple User Defined Filters.

<table>
<tr><td>Table 11.1.
Rules of Thumb for
User Defined
Filters*</td><td></td><td></td></tr>
</table>

	Center Cell Value	**Surrounding Cell Values**
Blur	Positive	Positive
Sharpen	Positive	Negative
Edges	Negative	Positive
Emboss	Positive	Symmetric positive and/or negative

*Compensate for sums not equal to 1 with the Division Factor.

12
Animation Shop

Bundled with PSP is Jasc Software's GIF animator, Animation Shop.
Although a separate piece of software that functions fully without PSP,
Animation Shop is designed to work together with PSP to help you create
GIF animations that can be displayed in a Web browser or other GIF-
animation player. You also can save your files as Autodesk animations or
AVI movies.

Here's what you'll be exploring in this chapter:

▶ Understanding animation

▶ Getting acquainted with Animation Shop

▶ Adding transitions and effects to animations

▶ Editing and optimizing your animations

▶ PSP and Animation Shop integration

Animation Basics

Animation produces the illusion of movement from a series of still
images. By making slight changes from one image to the next in the series
and then rapidly displaying one after the other, you create a dynamic
whole from a collection of static pieces.

If you're old enough to remember the days before videotape, you've
probably seen a section of movie film. Each frame of the film displays a
snapshot of a scene that is gradually progressing. Play those snapshots
one after another at just the right speed, and you seem to see the scene as
it actually unfolded. With animation software, you can make your own
short "films," putting together a series of digital drawings or
photorealistic images to make a moving picture.

CHAPTER 12

To understand animation, you should first learn to distinguish between two related—but quite distinct—elements of any animation: the *frame* and the *cel*. (*Cel* is short for *celluloid*, the material that film used to be made of.) A frame is something like a container for a particular image. A frame "holds" the still image in position relative to the other still images in a sort of filmstrip.

A cel is the content of a particular frame. The image that comprises one cel might be used at different points in the animation, in several different frames. So, for example, you might have a five-frame animation that uses only three cels. The animation's first frame might contain a cel showing a cat with closed eyes. The second frame might contain a cel showing the cat with half-opened eyes, and the third frame might contain a cel showing the cat with its eyes wide open. The fourth frame might contain the cel that shows the cat with half-opened eyes (the same cel as in the second frame), and the fifth might contain the cel that shows the cat with its eyes closed (the same cel as in the first frame). Play this animation, and you see a sleeping cat that opens its eyes for a moment and then goes back to sleep. Figure 12.1 shows the three cels that you could use to produce such an animation.

Fig. 12.1
Three cels for a simple five-frame animation.

Another important point to understand about animation is the role played by a frame's *display time*. Unlike a real film, in which all the frames are displayed at a constant rate, in a computer animation, you can control the display time for each individual frame. This helps you to create illusions of movement with a minimal number of frames, which in turn greatly helps to keep the file sizes of your animations in check.

TIP

Some folks think that you need to add more frames to smooth out the movement in a choppy animation. Often, this is just the opposite of what is needed. Instead, you might get better results by *reducing* the number of frames and adjusting the display times of the remaining frames.

Working in Animation Shop

Animation Shop makes obvious use of the filmstrip metaphor. To see this, open Animation Shop and begin a new animation by choosing **F**ile, **N**ew or by clicking the New icon on the toolbar. This opens the Create New Animation dialog box, where you enter the Width and Height of your new animation and select whether the Canvas Color for your animation is transparent or opaque. When you click OK, you'll then see something like Figure 12.2.

Fig. 12.2
The Animation Shop "filmstrip."

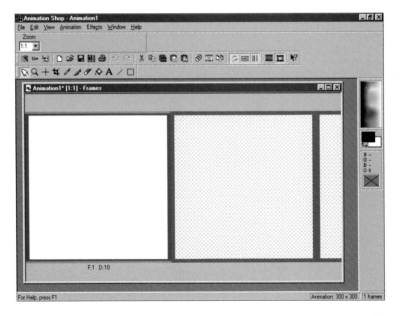

You'll first see a window showing a strip waiting to receive some frames and content. At this point, you can add some empty frames or frames filled with cels. To add empty frames, choose **A**nimation, **I**nsert Frames, **E**mpty and fill in choices in the resulting dialog box. You can use the drawing tools later to create content for empty frames or paste the content of the Clipboard into a frame.

CHAPTER 12

To add frames and their cels to the filmstrip simultaneously, choose **A**nimation, **I**nsert Frames, From **F**ile and fill in choices in the resulting dialog box. The image files that you select will be imported into new frames in your animation.

Figure 12.3 shows a three-frame version of the sleepy-cat animation described in the previous section. The closed-eyed cel was added first, and then the half-open-eyed cel, and then the open-eyed cel. To create the five-frame version, the half-open-eyed cel would be added again, followed by the closed-eyed cel.

Fig. 12.3
A simple animation.

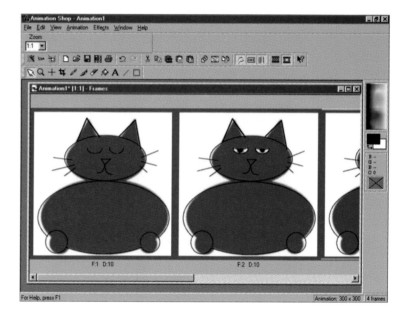

Animation Wizard

You've been briefly introduced to constructing an animation by opening a new file with File, New. However, it is recommended that you *not* create animations this way—at least not until you've become experienced in using Animation Shop. Instead, you should use Animation Shop's Animation Wizard. Unlike a lot of wizards, you'll find the Animation Wizard intuitive and easy to use. Let's build an animation , such as the three-frame sleepy-cat animation, by using the Animation Wizard.

1. To begin a new animation, select **F**ile, **A**nimation Wizard or click the Animation Wizard button on the toolbar. You'll then see the first dialog box for the Animation Wizard (see Figure 12.4). For the dimensions of your animation, select Same size as the first image frame, and then click Next.

Fig. 12.4
Step one in the
Animation Wizard:
choosing the
dimensions.

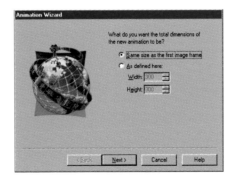

2. The next step is to set the default canvas color for your frames (see Figure 12.5). The canvas color is the default color for any otherwise-empty areas of a frame. You have two choices: Transparent or Opaque.

    For this example, select Opaque and choose White. After you select the canvas color, click Next.

Fig. 12.5
Step two: picking a
canvas color.

3. The next dialog box (see Figure 12.6) asks how to position images in the frames and how to fill in any areas of a frame that aren't filled completely by an image that you add to your animation. All the cels used in this example are the same size, and each cel entirely fills its frame, so you really don't have to worry about this. Click Next to accept the defaults and continue.

Fig. 12.6
Step three: positioning
and filling in extra
space.

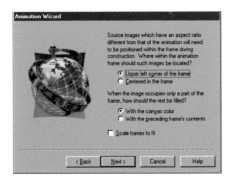

CHAPTER 12

4. In the next dialog box, you're asked how you want your animation to loop (see Figure 12.7). You can have the animation loop either indefinitely or only a specific number of times. For this animation, choose Play it _ times and fill in the blank with 1.

NOTE

As you'll see later in this chapter, you can change the looping setting after your animation is built.

You also can set the display time in this dialog box, which is the length of time between the point at which a frame in an animation is first displayed and the point at which the next frame in the animation is displayed. The default display time is 10/100 second. As with the looping setting, you can change display-time settings later on.

Choose whatever length of time you want for the default display time, and then click Next (50/100th of a second is selected in this example).

Fig. 12.7
Step four: setting the looping and the display time.

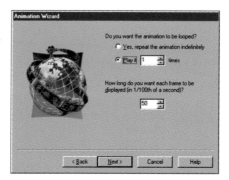

5. The next dialog box is where you add the component files to your animation. Figure 12.8 shows this Animation Wizard box and the Open dialog box that displays when you click the Add Image button.

Fig. 12.8
Step five: adding frames to your animation.

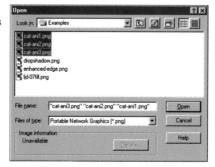

You can add the first file by clicking the **A**dd Image button and then selecting and opening the file from the selection list. You can then repeat this step for each component file. Alternatively, you can add all the files at once by using Shift+click or Ctrl+click in the Open dialog box, to select multiple files (just as you would in Windows Explorer or other Windows applications). An example of the resulting list of files to be added as your new frames is shown in Figure 12.9.

Fig. 12.9
Step five, continued: the list of files to add.

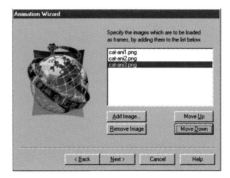

If you accidentally insert an incorrect file, just select that file and click the Remove Image button. You also can reposition a file in the file order by selecting the file and clicking the Move Up or Move Down button.

6. After you add all of your component files and have them in the proper order, click Next and then click Finish. You'll then see the new filmstrip, consisting of each of the frames for your animation. As in the handmade example, each frame has a label that indicates its frame number and display time.

7. For this example, save your animation as a GIF by using Save As and choosing CompuServe Graphics Interchange (*.gif). When you then give your animation a name and click Save, the Animation Optimization Wizard is invoked. For now, accept the default settings for the Optimization Wizard by clicking the Next button in each of the Optimization Wizard's windows.

In your own animation projects, if you want to save the project for later editing, you might want to use the MNG file format for your work-in-progress. MNG is Animation Shop's native format. Unlike GIF, MNG supports 24-bit color depth with lossless compression, just as the PSP file format does in PSP itself. Later, after you finish work on the project, you can use Save As to create the GIF version of your animation.

NOTE
You can view your animation in action within Animation Shop by selecting View, Animation or by clicking the View Animation button on the toolbar.

CHAPTER 12

Transitions and Effects

Animation Shop includes image transitions and two types of effects: image effects and text effects. Effects and transitions are automated dynamic transformations of an image or text. *Transitions* do simple morphing of two images, and *effects* transform an image in a fixed way, such as fading it to grey or exploding it into pieces.

Image Transitions

As its name implies, image transitions create a gradual transition between a start image and an end image. One example of this is the Dissolve transition, shown in Figure 12.10.

Fig. 12.10
The Dissolve image transition.

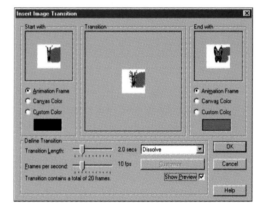

To use this transition, follow these steps:

1. To begin the transition, start with an animation that contains at least two frames: one frame that contains the start image and another that immediately follows the start image and contains the end image.

2. Select the start image by clicking the appropriate frame in the filmstrip with the Arrow tool.

3. Choose Effects, Insert Image Transition and in the Insert Image Transition dialog box, select Dissolve in the drop-down list.

4. Set the length of the transition with the Transition Length slider and the number of frames per second with the Frames Per Second slider. These two settings determine the number of frames that are added for the transition. Keep an eye on that number, because the more frames in your animation, the larger the file size will be.

In addition to transitioning between two images, you can have a transition that goes from an image to a solid color or vice versa. Figure 12.11 shows an example of this with the Blinds transition.

Fig. 12.11
Transitioning from an image to a solid color with the Blinds transition.

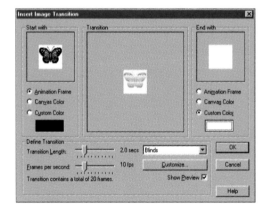

In this example, an image is chosen for Start With, but End With is solid white. Notice that there are three options you can choose from for Start With and End With: Animation Frame, Canvas Color, and Custom Color. To transition from an image to white, choose Animation Frame for Start With. For End With, you can choose Canvas Color if the animation's default canvas color is white. Otherwise, you need to select Custom Color and set the custom color to white.

Notice that, unlike Dissolve, the Blinds transition has an active Customize button. Some transitions (like Dissolve) work only one way, but others (like Blinds) can be adjusted in various ways. Click the Customize button for Blinds and you get the dialog box shown in Figure 12.12.

Fig. 12.12
Blinds Transition customization dialog box.

Different transitions have different customization controls. When you explore the many image transitions, be sure to check out the customization features, where available.

Image Effects

Image effects are somewhat like transitions, but when you apply an effect (such as Motion Blur), you add the effect to an existing selected frame or series of selected frames. Effects are much more like transitions when you insert them rather than apply them. When you insert an effect, new frames containing the effect are inserted between the selected frame and the next frame in the filmstrip.

To apply an effect, select the frames that you want the effect applied to and then choose Effects, Apply Image Effect. Figure 12.13 shows the Apply Image Effect dialog box with Motion Blur selected.

Fig. 12.13
Applying the Motion Blur Image Effect.

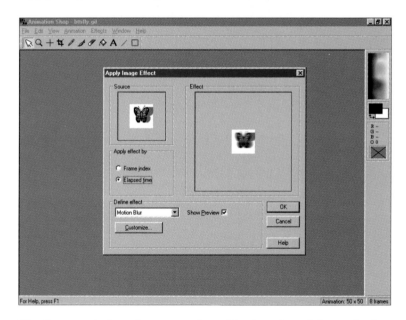

The Source window shows you the cel in the selected frame. In the Define Effect drop-down list, you select the effect you want to apply. If you have Show Preview selected, the results of applying the effect are shown in the Effect window.

You also have two options for how to apply the effect—either by Frame index or by Elapsed time. The effect increases in intensity over time, and the Apply effect by options determine how to distribute the increase. With Frame Index, the increase is distributed evenly across affected frames. With Elapsed Time, frames with longer display times show a steeper increase than shorter frames do.

To insert an effect rather than apply it, select the frame that the effect should be inserted after. Then, choose **E**ffects, Insert Image Effect. You'll see the Insert Image Effect dialog box, shown in Figure 12.14.

Fig. 12.14
Inserting the Motion Blur Image Effect.

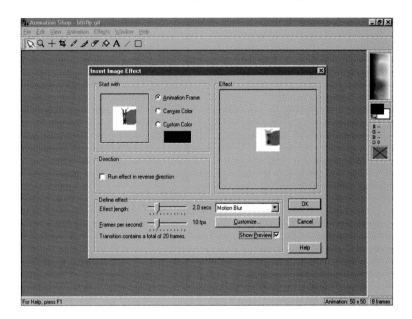

The controls available in the Insert Image Effect dialog box are like the ones for Apply Image Effect. Notice that there are two additional controls, though: Effect length and Frames per second. Just as with the analogous Image Transition controls, you set the length of the transition with Effect length and the number of frames per second with the Frames per second slider. Also like the Image Transition controls, these two settings determine the number of frames that are added for the transition, which affects the size of your file.

Text Effects

Text effects are like Image effects. You begin with a frame or series of frames to which you add some text. To apply a Text effect, select the frame(s) to which the effect should be added, and choose Effects, Apply Text Effect.

CHAPTER 12

Figure 12.15 shows the Apply Text Effect dialog box, with Define Effect set to Highlight and text Appearance set to Canvas Color.

Fig. 12.15
Applying a Text effect.

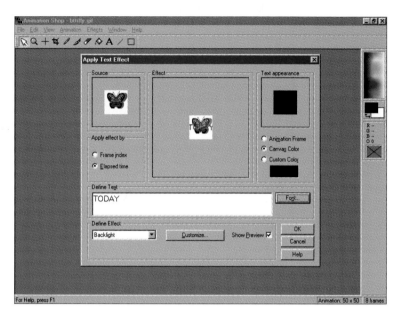

You add your text in the Define Text box. To select the font and other text characteristics, click the Font button, which brings up Animation Shop's Add Text dialog box.

As with Image effects, you also can insert a Text effect between a selected frame and the following frame (see Figure 12.16).

Fig. 12.16
Inserting a Text effect.

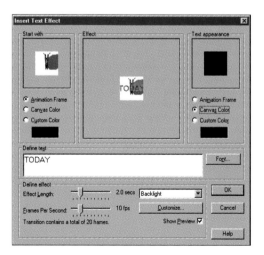

You control the number of frames that are inserted by setting Effect length and Frames per second. And each of the Text effects has its own customization controls accessed with the Customization button.

TIP
You also can create animated banners with text by using the Banner Wizard. To begin a banner, choose **F**ile, **B**anner Wizard. Then, follow the Wizard's prompts to create your banner and add text.

Editing Animations

Don't think that you're stuck with the images that you've imported into Animation Shop. You can do plenty to alter the cels in your animation frames or reorganize the frames themselves.

The Tool Palette

Most of the tools on the Tool Palette (see Figure 12.17) can be used to edit cels; you're already familiar with these tools because they all appear in PSP as well.

Fig. 12.17
The Tool Palette.

The following tools are available on the Tool Palette:

▶ **Arrow**—The neutral cursor that is used in Animation Shop to select frames.

▶ **Zoom**—Use to zoom in and out on your animation.

▶ **Registration Mark**—Adds registration marks to each frame in your animation to help you position figures or images in the frames. Add a registration to a single frame; analogous marks will appear in all of the frames of your animation.

▶ **Crop tool**—Works like the PSP Crop tool. When you crop a single frame in an animation, all of the frames are cropped to the same size.

▶ **Dropper**—Used to pick up foreground and background colors for the Color Palette.

▶ **Paintbrush**—The primary drawing tool in Animation Shop. You paint with the Color Palette foreground color by dragging with this tool, and you paint with the Color Palette background color by right-dragging with this tool.

▶ **Eraser**—The other drawing tool available in Animation Shop. This
tool works a little differently from the Eraser in PSP. In Animation
Shop, dragging or right-dragging with this tool paints with whatever
the default canvas color is set to, whether opaque or transparent.

▶ **Flood Fill**—Except under special circumstances that are discussed in
a bit, clicking with this tool fills an area with the current foreground
color, as set in the Color Palette. Right-clicking fills an area with the
current background color, as set in the Color Palette.

▶ **Text**—Useful for adding static text to a frame. This works like a
simplified version of the PSP Text tool. If you want dynamic text that
changes across a series of frames, you'll probably want to use Text
effects rather than this tool.

▶ **Line**—Enables you to draw either a Normal line or a Bézier curve.
You can set the width of the line and choose to make it antialiased.

▶ **Shape**—Enables you to draw a rectangle, square, ellipse, or circle.
The shape can be either outlined or filled and either antialiased or
not.

One thing to keep in mind when using the Tool Palette tools in
Animation Shop is that Animation Shop has no Tool Options palette.
Instead, you control a tool's settings with the controls in the Style Bar, as
shown in Figure 12.18. (Users of PSP versions 3 and 4 will be familiar
with the Style Bar.)

Fig. 12.18
The Style Bar when the
Paintbrush or Eraser is
active.

TIP

The Style Bar is floatable. If you like, you can reposition it—just click in an
empty area of the Style Bar and drag it to a new position.

When the active tool is either the Arrow tool, Zoom, Dropper, or Text
tool, the only control available on the Style Bar is Zoom. When the
Paintbrush or the Eraser is active, controls for both Zoom and Width are
available. Line and Shape also have controls for width and antialias,
and Shape has a control for Style.

Be sure to examine the controls for the Flood Fill tool, shown in
Figure 12.19.

Fig. 12.19
Style Bar when Flood
Fill is active.

This Style Bar has two controls that are like those on PSP's Flood Fill tool
Tool Options palette—Match mode and Tolerance—which work just as
they do in PSP. The third control, however, is relevant only to
animations: the *To Canvas Color* checkbox.

To Canvas Color overrides the normal fill colors. Either clicking or right-
clicking when this box is checked fills the area with the default canvas
color, whether it's set to an opaque color or to transparency. This setting
is very useful, for example, if you want your animation to have a
transparent background, but the cel in the current frame has an opaque
background; if the default canvas color is set to transparent, just check
the *To Canvas Color* box and fill the background with transparency. (That
sure beats trying to eliminate the opaque background with the Eraser!)

Reorienting a Frame

Just like images in PSP, in Animation Shop, you can Flip or Mirror a cel
in a frame. (Rotate isn't available, though.)

To flip a cel, first select its frame with the Arrow tool. Then, choose
Animation, **F**lip. To apply Flip to a series of frames, select a frame at one
end of the series and then Shift+click the frame at the other end of the
series. Choose **A**nimation, **F**lip, and all the cels in all the selected frames
will be flipped.

To mirror a cel, select its frame and then choose **A**nimation, **M**irror. To
mirror the cels in a series of frames, select the frames and then choose
Animation, **M**irror.

Adding and Deleting Frames

If you decide to add frames to your animation, you have a few methods
from which to choose. You've already seen one way, earlier in this
chapter: choose **A**nimation, Insert **F**rames (and choose either From **F**ile or
Empty). Two even easier methods are available, though: Right-click an
existing frame and choose either **A**dd, From **F**iles to open the Insert
Frames from Files dialog box or choose **A**dd, **E**mpty Frames to open the
Insert Empty Frames dialog box.

CHAPTER 12

Let's first look at the Insert Frames from Files dialog box, shown in Figure 12.20.

Fig. 12.20
Insert Frames from
Files dialog box.

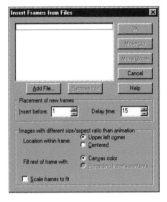

You can select the image (or series of images) that you want to add, much as you did earlier with the Animation Wizard. Set the Insert before option to the frame number of the frame that should follow the newly inserted one. (For example, if your animation is composed of three frames and you want to add a new frame between the first and second frames, set the Insert before option to 2.) If you want your new frame to be the last frame in the animation, set this number to one more than the frame number of the current final frame. Set the Delay time as you like. (Delay time is just another name for display time.) Adjust any of the other settings as needed, and click OK.

Now take a look at the Insert Empty Frames dialog box, shown in Figure 12.21.

Fig. 12.21
Insert Empty Frames
dialog box.

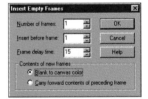

To add a frame to an animation with the Insert Empty Frames dialog box, set the Number of frames that you want to insert, and set Insert before frame and Frame delay time as appropriate. Choose whether you want the added frames to be filled only with the default canvas color or to carry over the contents of the frame that precedes the added frames.

If you decide to delete frames from your animation, you can either select the frame and choose **Edit**, **D**elete or simply right-click the frame and choose Delete. You can delete a series of frames simultaneously by selecting the frame at one end of the series, Shift+clicking on the frame at the other end, and then deleting.

Copying, Pasting, and Reversing Frames

To copy, move, or reverse the order of a series of frames, begin by selecting the frames in the series: Click with the Arrow tool on the frame at one end of the series and then Shift+click with the Arrow tool on the frame at the other end of the series. (If you want to copy or move only a single frame, select that one frame only.)

After frames are selected, you can do any of the following to copy the frames to the Clipboard:

▶ Choose **Edit**, **C**opy

▶ Press Ctrl+C

▶ Click the Copy button on the toolbar

▶ Right-click one of the selected frames and choose **C**opy

To paste copied frames, you can take any of these actions:

▶ Choose **Edit**, **P**aste, As **N**ew Frames

▶ Press Ctrl+V

▶ Click the Paste As New Frames button on the toolbar

▶ Right-click the frame in front of which you want to paste the copied frames, and then choose **P**aste, As **N**ew Frames

When you choose Edit, Paste (either on the menubar or after right-clicking a frame), you also have the option to Paste Into Selected Frame. You also can paste into a selected frame by pressing Ctrl+E or by clicking the Paste Into Selected Frame button on the toolbar.

> **TIP**
>
> To accomplish the equivalent of the Copy and Paste operations in one step, use Edit, Duplicate Selected. Duplicate Selected copies the selected frames and pastes them after the last frame in the selected series of frames.

You move a frame by cutting the selected frames before pasting them. You can cut the frames by using any of the following methods:

▶ Choose **Edit**, **C**ut

▶ Press Ctrl+X

▶ Click the Cut button on the toolbar

▶ Right-click one of the selected frames and choose Cut

CHAPTER 12

Another way to move a frame is to select the frame and then drag and drop it into another frame.

One of the most useful operations for making animations is reversing the order of a series of selected frames. To do this, select the frames in the series and then choose **A**nimation, Re**v**erse Frames. Let's look at a couple of examples.

First, let's return to the three-frame sleepy-cat animation. Suppose that you want to use this animation as the basis of a five-frame animation that has the cat opening and then closing its eyes. To do so, you need to add the cel that has the cat with half-opened eyes and then the cel that has the cat with closed eyes. You can simply add those images to the animation again as new frames, but you can get the same result by copying existing frames:

1.   Select frames 1 and 2 in the original animation and then copy those selected frames, as shown in Figure 12.22.

Fig. 12.22
Copying frames 1 and 2 from original cat animation.

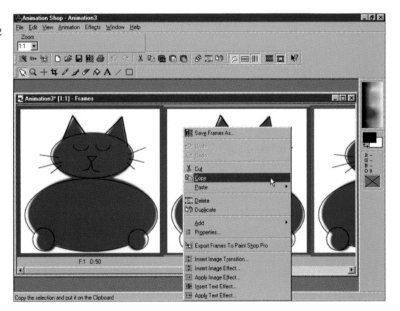

2.   Select frame 3 and paste the copied frames in front of this frame, as shown in Figure 12.23.

Fig. 12.23
Pasting frames in front
of frame 3.

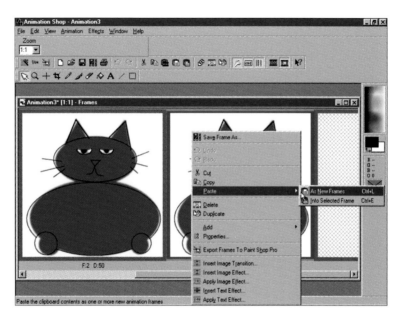

3. Add the old frame 3 (now frame 5) to the selection and then reverse
    the frames, as shown in Figure 12.24.

Fig. 12.24
Reversing frames 3
through 5.

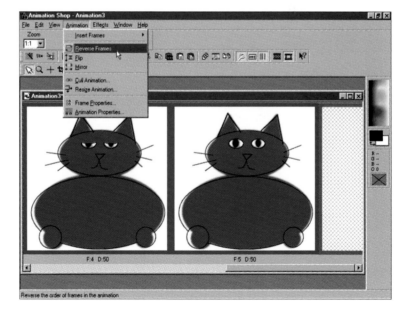

CHAPTER 12

That does it! The new five-frame animation is shown in Figure 12.25.

Fig. 12.25
The finished animation.

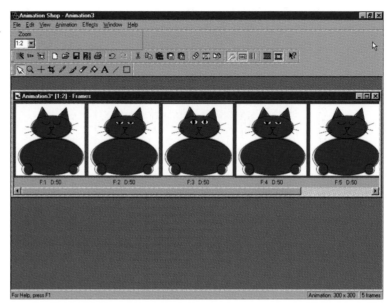

You can do the same sort of thing with an image transition or inserted effect. Suppose that you want to create an animation of a flower image fading to grey and then returning to full color:

1. Begin with a single frame that contains the flower image, and then choose Effect, Insert Image Effect and choose Fade To Grey. Choose settings for Length of Effect and Frames Per Second to get the five-frame animation shown in Figure 12.26. Select frames 2 through 4 from this animation and copy those frames to the Clipboard.

Fig. 12.26
Copying frames 2
through 4 after inserting
the effect.

2. Select frame 5 and paste the copied frames in front of this frame
    (see Figure 12.27).

Fig. 12.27
Pasting frames in front
of frame 5.

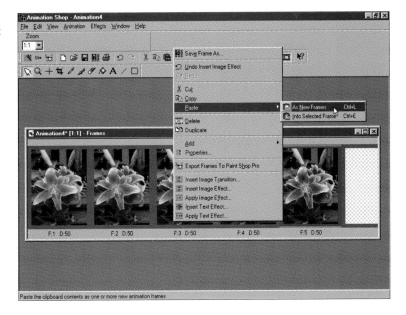

3. Add old frame 5 (now frame 8) to the selection and reverse the selected frames (see Figure 12.28).

Fig. 12.28
Reversing frames 5 through 8.

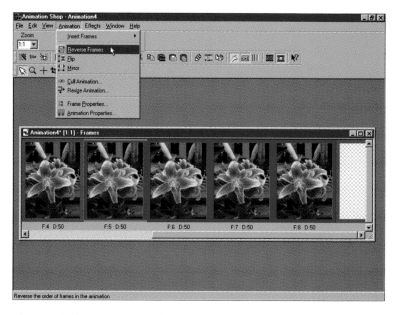

The finished animation is shown in Figure 12.29.

Fig. 12.29
The finished animation.

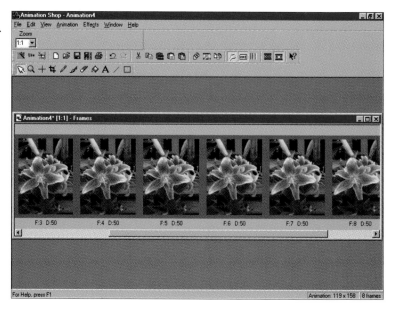

NOTE

If you paste when no frames are selected, the contents of the Clipboard are added *after* the last frame in an animation. If this is what you want, you can ensure that no frames are selected by choosing **E**dit, Select **N**one or by clicking with the Arrow tool in any area of the filmstrip that doesn't contain a frame.

Modifying Frame and Animation Properties

It's easy to modify the properties of a frame (or series of selected frames) or the animation properties.

To modify the *properties of a frame*, right-click the frame and choose Pr**o**perties from the menu that appears. The properties that you can then change are the frame's Display Time and any comments that you want to add about the frame. If you've selected a series of frames, then the changes you make will apply to all the selected frames.

To change the *animation properties*, right-click any part of the filmstrip that doesn't contain a frame, and then choose **A**nimation Properties. You then can change the looping of your animation or the default canvas color. You can also add comments, if you like.

TIP

Go To Frame is the other option available on the menu that displays when you right-click in an area of the filmstrip that doesn't contain a frame. If you choose Go To Frame, you can specify a frame number, and PSP will take you to that frame (without selecting the frame).

Cropping and Optimizing Animations

Animation file sizes can get quite large, but you should try for a file size that is as small as possible without compromising quality too much. You can do a few things to help achieve this goal. You can crop your animation, because (all else being equal) the smaller the physical dimensions of your file, the smaller the file size. You also can run Animation Shop's Optimization Wizard, which enables you to take several steps to optimize the file size of your animations.

Cropping

To crop your animation, choose the Crop tool. There are two ways to define the crop selection area:

▶ In one frame, drag to define the crop selection.

▶ Click the Options button on the Style Bar. This opens the Crop Options dialog box, where you can define the coordinates for the crop area. You can set absolute coordinates, or you can choose to select the opaque area or the animated area (the area that changes from frame to frame).

In either case, the crop selection border will appear in each frame of your animation. If the crop area is not positioned correctly, you can reposition it by dragging inside the crop area in one of the frames. If you want to abort the crop completely, click the Clear button on the Style Bar. Or, if you're satisfied that the crop area is defined correctly, click the Crop button on the Style Bar to crop all the frames of your animation.

TIP

You can resize your animation with **Animation, Resize Animation**. This brings up the Resize dialog box, which is just like the one in PSP.

With Resize, all areas of your animation are retained—nothing is cropped away—but the animation cels and frames are shrunk or stretched.

Culling Frames

One of the simplest ways to optimize an animation is to cull (that is, remove) some of the frames. This can be particularly useful when you have an AVI file that you want to convert to an animated GIF. Subtle differences from frame to frame might not be missed if you remove a few frames, but the change in file size can be substantial.

To cull frames, choose Animation, Cull Animation. The Cull Animation dialog box is then displayed. In the textbox, type a value n to tell Animation Shop to remove a frame every n frames.

NOTE

Cull Animation will cull frames from your entire animation if you have either no frames selected or all frames selected. To restrict the culling to a smaller series of frames, just select the frames before choosing Cull Animation.

The Optimization Wizard

The Optimization Wizard runs automatically the first time that you save your animation in any format except AVI; you also can run the Wizard at any time by choosing File, Optimization Wizard.

Let's run the Optimization Wizard on the five-frame sleepy-cat animation, saving the animation as a GIF. The Wizard first presents the Optimized Output window (see Figure 12.30). Here, you select whether to overwrite the existing animation or make the optimized version a new file. In this example, the optimized version will be created as a new file.

Fig. 12.30
The Optimization Wizard's Optimized Output window.

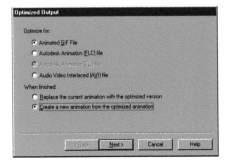

CHAPTER 12

When you click Next, the Animation Quality Versus Output Size window appears (see Figure 12.31). The pane on the right presents a summary of the currently selected optimization settings. The slider on the left provides a quick way to adjust the number of colors to use in generating the palette for the animation. If you move the slider up toward Better Image Quality, more colors are used in the palette. Move the slider down toward Smaller File Size, and fewer colors are used.

Fig. 12.31
The Optimization Wizard's Animation Quality Versus Output Size window.

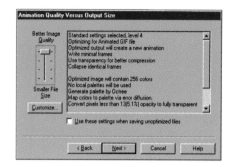

Before clicking Next, click the Customize button below the slider. You'll then see the Colors tab of the Customize Optimization Settings window, as shown in Figure 12.32. Here, you can select not only the number of colors to use for the animation palette, but also the palette-creation and color-reduction methods.

Fig. 12.32
The Colors tab of the Optimization Wizard's Customize Optimization Settings window.

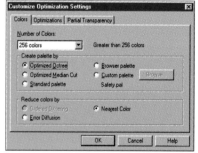

For the Palette, Optimized Octree will be fine. And because this animation consists of simple drawings with solid colors, choosing Nearest Color will produce good results.

NOTE

For complex images, such as photorealistic images, one of the adaptive palettes and Error diffusion will probably yield better-quality results than will Nearest color and either the Standard palette or the Browser-safe palette.

Now, click the Optimizations tab, in which you can select five optimization settings (see Figure 12.33):

▶ **Remove Non Visible Animation Elements**—Removes comments.

▶ **Write Minimal Frames**—Saves only the parts of the frames in which pixels have changed.

▶ **Collapse Identical Frames**—Deletes duplicate consecutive frames and increases the Display time for the remaining frame to compensate for the deletions.

▶ **Map Identical Pixels To Transparent**—Pixels that haven't changed from the previous frame are made transparent.

▶ **Enable Browser-Specific Optimizations**—Enables other optimizations that aren't supported by all Web browsers. Be careful with this one, because it can introduce unsightly artifacts when the animation is viewed in a browser that doesn't support these optimizations.

Each of these will make the file size smaller without adversely affecting the image quality of your animation.

Fig. 12.33
The Optimizations tab of the Optimization Wizard's Customize Optimization Settings window.

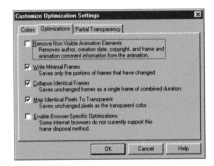

When you save an animation as a GIF, the third tab on the Customize Optimization Settings window is Partial Transparency (see Figure 12.34).

Fig. 12.34
The Partial Transparency tab of the Optimization Wizard's Customize Optimization Settings window.

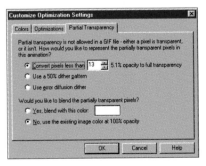

CHAPTER 12

This is where you tell PSP how to handle semi-transparent pixels. GIF supports only full transparency or full opacity, so semi-transparent pixels must be converted to one or the other. The controls on this tab let you specify what level of opacity should be treated as fully opaque and what level as fully transparent. You also specify whether semi-transparent pixels should be blended with the background color or simply maintain their own color.

After you click OK in the Customize Optimization Settings window, you are returned to the Animation Quality Versus Output Size window, and the information in the right pane will be updated to show what settings you selected. Click Next, and you'll see the Optimization Progress window and its progress bars, as shown in Figure 12.35. When the bars are filled, the optimization is complete.

Fig. 12.35
The Optimization Wizard's Optimization Progress window.

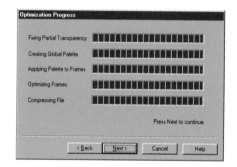

Click Next, and you'll be taken to the Optimization Results window, where Animation Shop provides you with information on your optimized animation (see Figure 12.36). It shows not only the file size, but also the estimated download times at various baud rates. If you're satisfied with the results, click Finish. If not, click Cancel and start over again, if you like.

Fig. 12.36
The Optimization Wizard's Optimization Results window.

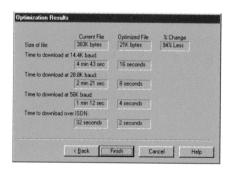

For this example, the file size of 21K is pretty good, but to see what you can get by reducing the number of colors, run Optimization Wizard again on this animation, with the number of colors reduced from 256 to 16. The result will be a file of about 7K. A 14K difference is pretty substantial, and a proportional reduction for a larger original could really amount to something!

Animation Shop and PSP

With PSP5 and Animation Shop 1, there was very little integration of the two programs. PSP6 and Animation Shop 2, however, are much more tightly connected. As a result, when the editing tools in Animation Shop aren't quite enough to fill your needs, you can temporarily export animation frames to PSP and later send the edited frames back to Animation Shop.

To begin, select the frame(s) that you want to export from Animation Shop to PSP. Then, choose **F**ile, Export Frames to Paint S**h**op Pro. Or, right-click in a frame and choose Export Frames to Paint Shop Pro. PSP then loads automatically and each frame is opened as a separate file. You can then edit the frames as you would any image.

When you want to update the frames in Animation Shop but keep working in PSP, choose **E**dit, Update **B**ack to Animation Shop. When you're finished and are ready to close PSP and return to Animation Shop, choose **F**ile, Exit & Return to *animation_name* (where *animation_name* is the name of your animation).

You can then continue in Animation Shop with your updated animation.

Using Layers to Create Cels

PSP offers two ways to use layers to create animation cels. The first method is outlined at **http://loriweb.pair.com/l-anim.html**. With this method, you use selective display of the layers in a PSP file along with Save Copy As to save individual animation cel files. The second method is outlined at Jasc Software's Design Studio at **http://www.jasc.com/anishop.html**. In this method, you create the content of each frame of your animation as a separate layer in your PSP file. Let's look at an example of each.

CHAPTER 12

Save Copy As Method

This is the method I usually use to create animation cels from layers. Begin with a Background layer that contains image elements that remain the same in each cel. The Background used to make the cels for the three-frame sleepy-cat animation is shown in Figure 12.37.

Fig. 12.37
Background layer of the sleepy-cat PSP file.

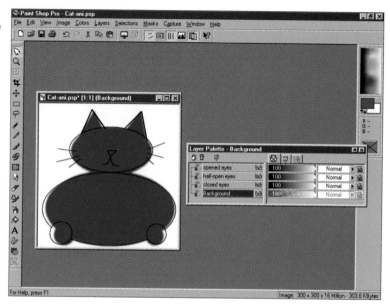

On higher layers, you need only the parts of the image that change; the rest of the layer should be transparent. For the sleepy cat, three layers were created above the Background, each containing only one of the three different versions of the cat's eyes. The Visibility toggles on the Layer Palette were then used to selectively display only the Background and each of the higher layers, one at a time, using Save Copy As to save each cel. Figure 12.38 shows the Layer Palette and what is displayed to make the opened eyes cel.

Fig. 12.38
Background and
opened eyes layers
visible, ready for
Save Copy As.

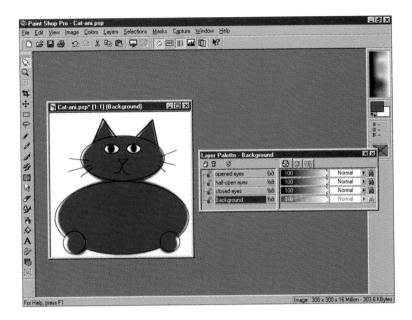

TIP

Give your cel images names that will help you to select the files in the right
order in Animation Shop. For the cels for the three-frame sleepy-cat
animation, for example, the file for the first cel is named CAT-ANI1.PNG, the
second CAT-ANI2.PNG, and the third CAT-ANI3.PNG.

After you create all the cel files, you can construct your animation in
Animation Shop.

TIP

If you're in PSP, you can easily load Animation Shop by choosing **F**ile, Run
Animation Shop. And if you start out in Animation Shop, you can easily load
PSP by choosing **F**ile, Run Paint Shop Pro.

CHAPTER 12

Layer/Frame Method

To create animation cels by using the Layer/Frame method, go into PSP and create a file with separate layers for each frame. You must save the layered file in PSP format. If you then open this PSP file in Animation Shop, and if you've made the proper preference settings, Animation Shop will automatically convert each of the file's layers to separate frames in a new animation.

1. In PSP, build your animation from the bottom up: the first layer for the content of the first frame, the second layer for the second frame, and so on. Figure 12.39 shows the first layer for a version of the three-frame sleepy-cat animation created by using this method.

Fig. 12.39
The lowermost layer is the first frame.

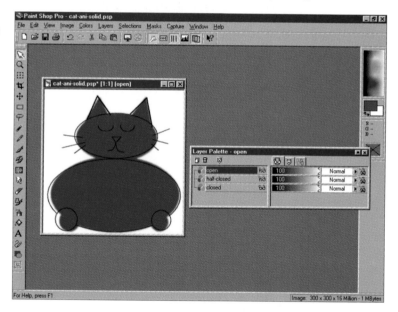

2. After you finish making all the layers, be sure to turn on the Visibility toggles for each of the layers. Animation Shop will only be able to "see" layers that have their Visibility toggle turned on (see Figure 12.40).

Fig. 12.40
The PSP file with all layers visible (topmost layer overlays all other layers here).

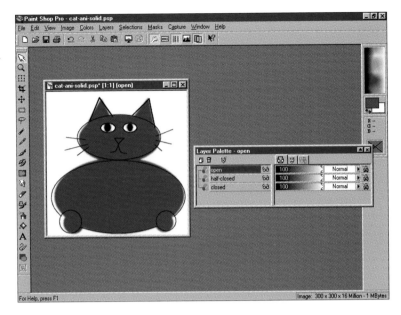

3. Save the file in PSP format, and then load Animation Shop.

4. In Animation Shop choose **F**ile, Preferences, **G**eneral Program Preferences. Click the Layered Files tab (see Figure 12.41). Select Keep each layer as a separate frame, and click OK. (Once you select this setting, it stays in effect until you change it, but it's not a bad idea to check first anyway.)

Fig. 12.41
The Layered Files tab of the Preferences dialog box.

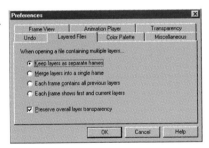

5. Open the PSP file that contains your animation. Animation Shop builds the new animation, with one frame for each layer, beginning with the lowermost layer and continuing up until there are no more layers.

There's also a variation of the Save Copy As method that is similar to the Layer/Frame method. It doesn't involve saving the individual cels, but rather utilizes another one of Animation Shop's preference settings for layered files:

1.   Create the PSP image as described in the Save Copy As Method section: Put the unchanging portion of the animation on the Background, and create layers that contain nothing but the parts of the animation that change.

2.   Make sure that all the layers are visible, and save the file in PSP format.

3.   Run Animation Shop. Choose **File**, Preferences, **G**eneral Program Preferences. Click the Layered Files tab and select *Each frame shows first and current layers*. Click OK.

4.   Open the PSP file. Animation Shop then builds your animation automatically, combining the Background with each of the file's layers, one layer per frame, from the bottom layer up.

You're now ready to create your own animations with Animation Shop. Begin with something simple, such as a banner with moviing text. Then go on to more complex projects, using PSP to create your animation cels. There are plenty of uses for animations, from attention-grabbing banners for Web pages, to polished business presentations, to artistic short films. Have some fun and see what other uses you can find for animations. You may discover that computer animation opens up a new outlet for your creativity.

Appendix A
Acquiring Images into PSP

There are three means of importing images into PSP: You can scan images directly into PSP, you can load images from your digital camera into PSP, and you can use PSP to do screen captures. Each of these methods imports images directly to PSP, enabling you to begin editing an image without going through any extra steps.

Scanning

If you have a TWAIN-compliant scanner installed, you can import images directly into PSP from your scanner. In PSP, choose File, Import, TWAIN, Select Source and select the appropriate TWAIN-compliant device. Figure A.1 shows the Select Source dialog box with the 32-bit driver for a Microtek scanner selected.

Fig. A.1
The Select Source dialog box with Microtek 32-bit driver selected.

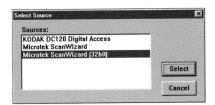

Next, choose File, Import, TWAIN, Acquire to open your scanner's software. Figure A.2 shows Microtek's ScanWizard software opened in PSP.

Fig. A.2
ScanWizard opened in PSP.

You can then scan an image or object according to the directions for your scanner. When you perform a scan, the scanned image appears in PSP. Close your scanner's software when you're done with the scan, and then you can edit and save the scanned image with PSP.

Figure A.3 shows a scanned photo, and Figure A.4 shows a group of buttons that was scanned.

Fig. A.3
A scanned photograph.

Fig. A.4
Scanned objects.

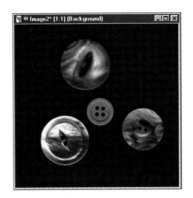

TIP

To scan objects, open your scanner lid fully, or remove it if possible. Place the object(s) carefully on the scanner bed and cover the object(s) and scanner bed with a piece of felt or cardboard. The color of your cover should contrast well with your object—having white, black, and neutral-grey pieces handy prepares you for just about anything.

Keep in mind that the depth of field of a scanner is not very great, so it's best to stick with objects that are relatively thin. Buttons, watches, beads, cookies, nuts, and other small objects are good candidates for scanning.

Experiment with other types of objects, though. Some folks have had good luck scanning balls, dolls, and even telephones!

Using Digital Cameras

PSP directly supports many different brands and models of digital cameras and is compatible with any camera with a TWAIN-compliant driver. After you install the driver for your camera and connect the camera to your computer, open PSP and choose File, Import, TWAIN, Select Source, and then select the appropriate device. Figure A.5 shows the Select Source dialog box with the driver for a Kodak DC120 selected.

Fig. A.5
The Select Source
dialog box with camera
driver selected.

NOTE

If your digital camera is your only TWAIN-compatible device, you won't need to use Select Source, since your camera's TWAIN driver will be the only driver available.

What you do next depends on whether your camera is one of the supported cameras or another type of camera. If you have a supported camera, choose **F**ile, **I**mport, **D**igital Camera, **A**ccess. The Digital Camera dialog box appears, as shown in Figure A.6.

Fig. A.6
The Digital Camera dialog box.

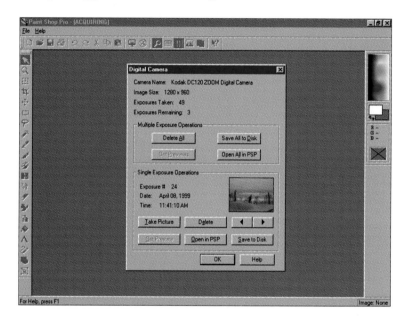

NOTE

The very first time you use your supported camera, you'll probably need to configure it. Choose **F**ile, **I**mport, **D**igital Camera, **C**onfigure and select the appropriate COM port and speed. If you're unsure about the COM port or speed, leave the entry set to Auto Detect.

If you have another type of camera, after you select the driver for your camera, choose **F**ile, **I**mport, **T**WAIN, Ac**q**uire. Your camera's software then opens, and you can use it as you normally would.

PSP provides built-in support for the following digital cameras:

Agfa ePhoto 1280	Epson PhotoPC 600	Olympus C-1000L	Pretec DC-800
Agfa ePhoto 1680	Epson PhotoPC 700	Olympus C-1400L	RELISYS Dimera 2000
Agfa ePhoto 307	Fuji DS-10	Olympus C-1400XL	RELISYS Dimera 3500
Agfa ePhoto 780	Fuji DS-20	Olympus C-400	Ricoh DC-1
Apple QuickTake 200	Fuji DS-250HD	Olympus C-400L	Ricoh DC-2
Canon PowerShot 350	Fuji DS-7	Olympus C-410	Ricoh DC-2E
Canon PowerShot A5	Fuji DS-8	Olympus C-410L	Ricoh DC-2L
Canon PowerShot A5 Zoom	Fuji DX-5	Olympus C-420	Ricoh DC-3
	Fuji DX-7	Olympus C-420L	Ricoh DC-4
Casio QV-10	Fuji FinePix 500	Olympus C-800	Ricoh DC-4T
Casio QV-100	Fuji FinePix 700	Olympus C-800L	Ricoh DC-4U
Casio QV-10A	Fuji MX-500	Olympus C-820	Ricoh RDC-2
Casio QV-11	Fuji MX-700	Olympus C-820L	Ricoh RDC-2E
Casio QV-120	HP Photo Smart	Olympus C-830L	Ricoh RDC-300
Casio QV-200	Kodak DC120	Olympus C-840L	Ricoh RDC-300Z
Casio QV-30	Kodak DC20	Olympus C-900 Zoom	Ricoh RDC-4300
Casio QV-300	Kodak DC200	Olympus D-200L	Sanyo DSC-1
Casio QV-5000SX	Kodak DC210	Olympus D-220L	Sanyo DSC-V1
Casio QV-70	Kodak DC220	Olympus D-300L	Sanyo DSC-X1
Casio QV-700	Kodak DC25	Olympus D-320L	Sanyo Image-PC
Casio QV-7000SX	Kodak DC260	Olympus D-340L	Sanyo VPC-G1
Casio QV-770	Kodak DC40	Olympus D-400 Zoom	Sanyo VPC-G200E
Casio QV-780	Kodak DC50	Olympus D-500L	Sanyo VPC-X300
Chinon ES1000	Konica Q-EZ	Olympus D-600L	Sharp VE-LC1
Epson CP-100	Leica Digilux	Olympus D-600XL	Sharp VE-LC2
Epson CP-200	Mustek VDC-200	Olympus D-620L	Sharp VE-LS5
Epson CP-500	NEC PC-DC200 Picona	Panasonic CoolShot	Sharp VL-DX1
Epson CP-600	NEC PC-DC401	Panasonic KXL-600A-N	Sharp VR-SU1
Epson CP-700Z	Nikon CoolPix 300	Phillips ESP2	Toshiba Allegretto M1
Epson Colario	Nikon CoolPix 900	Phillips ESP80	Trust PhotoCam
Epson PhotoPC	Nikon CoolPix 900S	Polaroid PDC640	Trust PhotoCam Plus
Epson PhotoPC 500	Nikon CoolPix 910	Pretec DC-600	
Epson PhotoPC 550			

Performing Screen Captures

You also can use PSP to perform screen captures. To set the capture
options, choose Capture, Setup. This opens the Capture Setup dialog box,
shown in Figure A.7.

Fig. A.7
The Capture Setup
dialog box.

In the leftmost pane of this dialog box, you can choose what to capture on
the screen. The following lists the options and the results of choosing each:

▶ **Area**—Your cursor turns into a cross when your capture begins. Click
this cursor at one corner of the rectangular area that you want to
capture, and then position the mouse cursor at the diagonally
opposite corner. Click again to complete the capture.

▶ **Object**—When your capture begins, the Windows object under the
mouse cursor will be highlighted with black. Move the cursor to the
object that you want to capture and then click. The object will then
be captured.

▶ **Client area**—The active client will be captured.

▶ **Window**—The active window will be captured.

▶ **Full screen**—The entire screen will be captured.

In the middle pane of the Capture Setup dialog box, you can select when
the capture takes place. You can direct PSP to wait until you right-click,
or you can direct PSP to wait until you press a hotkey, which can be any
of the function keys, perhaps in combination with Shift, Alt, or Ctrl.
Alternatively, you can set the Delay timer anywhere from 1 to 60 seconds
so that the capture occurs automatically after a set time.

The Capture Setup dialog box also enables you to set a few options in the
right pane. For all Capture types in the left pane, except Area, you can
choose whether to include the mouse cursor. You also can choose to
make multiple copies, which keeps PSP in Capture mode until you
maximize PSP again.

To make a capture, follow these steps:

1. Open the application in which you want to make a screen print. Then open PSP and set the Capture Setup options.

2. Choose **C**apture, **S**tart or press Shift+C to begin the capture. PSP automatically minimizes itself.

3. Position the cursor in the application, if appropriate, and then either right-click, hit the hotkey, or wait for the delay timer to run out—whatever you set to activate the capture. When you're done, PSP automatically maximizes, unless you've chosen multiple captures (maximize PSP yourself in that case).

4. In PSP, edit the captured image(s) as you like.

TIP

You might wonder, "How can I make screen prints for my PSP tutorials? Every time I start a capture, PSP minimizes itself!"

Keep in mind that PSP is getting out of the way so that you can capture a screen in an application. So, you simply need to open two copies of PSP; one to display the application screens you want to capture and another to do the capturing.

NOTE

For screen captures of the *entire* screen and *without* the cursor showing, you don't need any type of screen capture program, not even PSP. Just press the PrtScrn key, and the current screen will be placed on the Windows Clipboard. You can then use **E**dit, Paste As **N**ew Image in PSP to create a new image from what's on the Clipboard, and then crop the image or edit it as you choose.

Appendix B
Adjusting Color Depth

Color depth is the amount of color data—and thus the maximum number of colors—that an image can accommodate. Color depth is determined by the number of bits used to store the color information of a pixel in an image.

The lowest color depth is 1-bit, which accommodates only two colors: black and white. The highest color depth in PSP is 24-bit, which can accommodate up to 16.7 million colors.

> **TIP**
>
> If a PSP operation you want to use is greyed out, chances are that the color depth of your image is too low. Many of PSP's operations and filters work only on greyscale images and 24-bit color images.
>
> If you want to apply one of these operations to an image with a lower color depth, you can temporarily increase the color depth to 24-bit. Choose **Colors**, **Increase Color Depth**, **16** Million Colors (24-bit). Later, you can return the image to its original color depth by choosing **Colors**, **Decrease Color Depth**.

A 24-bit image has three 8-bit color channels, each channel having 256 levels of brightness. A pixel that has 0 as the value of each channel is black, and a pixel that has 255 as the value of each channel is white. Using other values results in colors and shades of grey. Altogether, $256 \times 256 \times 256$ (16.7 million) different values can be stored in those 24 bits.

Two basic types of images use a single 8-bit channel: 256-color images and greyscale images. These images are "paletted"—256 fixed colors or shades of grey are used to represent all the colors or brightness levels in the image. The colors or shades of grey are arranged in a palette, with each color assigned a palette index (depending on the color's order in the palette). Figure B.1 shows the Web graphics Safety Palette included with PSP. Notice that the tile with Palette index 215 is highlighted and that this tile has color channel values of R:255, G:255, and B:255.

Fig. B.1
Safety Palette
(Safety.pal).

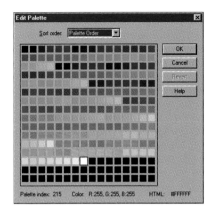

TIP

To display the palette of an 8-bit image, choose **C**olors, **E**dit Palette. You can replace colors in the palette by double-clicking a color tile in the palette and then using the Color dialog box to replace the original color of that tile.

To view an image's color depth, choose **V**iew, **I**mage Information, and look at Pixel Depth/Colors in the Image pane. An 8-bit color image will show 8/256, whereas a 24-bit color image will show 24/16 Million.

To increase an image's color depth, choose **C**olors, **I**ncrease Color Depth, and then choose the color depth you want. Decreasing an image's color depth is a little more involved, however.

NOTE

Typically, the reason you decrease an image's color depth is to optimize its file size. Another frequent use is the obligatory color reduction that occurs when you edit a 24-bit image and then save it in GIF format, which is an 8-bit file format.

To decrease an image's color depth, choose **C**olors, **D**ecrease Color Depth. After selecting the color depth you want, you will then see one of the Decrease Color Depth dialog boxes shown in Figures B.2a-d, depending on which color depth you chose.

Fig. B.2a
Decrease Color Depth -
64K Colors (24 bit)
dialog box (the 32K
Colors dialog box is
similar).

Fig. B.2b
Decrease Color Depth -
256 Colors (8 bit) dialog
box (the 16 Colors
dialog box is similar).

Fig. B.2c
Decrease Color Depth -
2 Colors (1 bit) dialog
box.

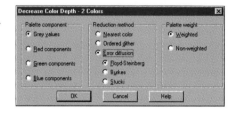

Fig. B.2d
Decrease Color Depth -
X Colors (4/8 bit) dialog
box.

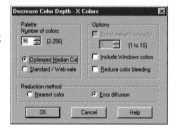

If you choose to decrease color depth to 64K or 32K, you must choose a reduction method: either Nearest color or Error diffusion. With Nearest color, a pixel's color is replaced with the color closest to it that appears in the reduced Color Palette. Error diffusion also replaces a pixel's color with the closest color in the reduced palette, but the difference from the original color (the error) is passed on to the next pixel, and so on. This method spreads the error in the color replacement across all the pixels in the image. Typically, the Error diffusion method produces an image whose colors approximate those of the original image more closely than the Nearest color method.

CAUTION

64K-color (16-bit) and 32K-color (15-bit) images are handled in memory as 24-bit images. As a result, their color depth might be inadvertently set to 16 million colors (24-bit) if you perform any operation on these images other than Save, Save As, or Save Copy As. If you want color depth reductions to 64K or 32K colors, your best bet is to perform the reduction immediately before saving the image.

If you choose to reduce color depth to 256 colors, you have a third option for a color reduction method—Ordered dither. *Dithering* is the mixing together of pixels with two different colors to create the illusion of a third color. Ordered dither uses dithering from a set palette, to approximate the colors in the original image. (This method sometimes makes your image look like a color picture on newsprint.)

When you reduce to either 256 colors or 16 colors, you must choose a palette and a reduction method. The following are the two palette-generation methods to choose from:

▶ **Optimized Median Cut and Optimized Octree**—Both methods produce adaptive palettes based on the number and distribution of colors in the original image. They use different algorithms, however, and so can yield noticeably different results. In general, Optimized Median Cut produces results that are closer to the original (although plenty of exceptions exist), whereas Optimized Octree takes less time.

▶ **Standard/Web-safe Palette**—Uses a standard palette that includes colors from across the spectrum.

The following are three other options that you can set when reducing to 256 or 16 colors:

▶ If you choose one of the adaptive palettes—Optimized Median Cut or Optimized Octree—you have the option of including the standard Windows colors in the palette.

▶ If you choose Error diffusion as the reduction method, you then have the option to Reduce Color Bleeding, which minimizes the "bleeding" of colors from left to right that the Error diffusion method produces.

▶ You can use the third option, Boost marked colors by, to emphasize colors in a selection that you made before initiating the color reduction. If you choose this option, you also can set a value for the degree of the color boost, from 1 (least effect) to 10 (greatest effect).

With Decrease Color Depth - X Colors, you can reduce the color depth of an image to any number between 2 and 256. You can choose the number of colors to be included in the palette and either the Nearest color or the Error diffusion reduction method. If you have a selection in your image, you also can choose Boost marked colors by. And, if you selected Error diffusion as the Reduction method, you have the option to Include Windows' colors and/or Reduce color bleeding. (When Include Windows' colors is selected, the smallest number of colors you can specify is 20.)

TIP

Because you can't reduce color depth to 8-bit (17 to 255 colors) if your image already has a color depth of 8 bits, Decrease Color Depth - X Colors can't be used directly on a 256-color image, such as a GIF. To reduce the number of colors in the palette of a 256-color image to a value between 17 and 255, you first need to *increase* the color depth to 16-million colors (24 bit).

You also can reduce the color depth of an image to two colors (black and white). Among other things, this can be useful for simulating halftones and other print-like effects. Ordered dither and the various Error diffusion methods are fun to experiment with here, and don't forget to try both the Weighted and Non-weighted options under Palette weight.

NOTE

PSP enables you to edit the palette of a 1-bit image. For example, you can change the white palette entry to blue and change the black palette entry to yellow. To try it yourself, choose **C**olors, **E**dit Palette (or press Shift+P) when you have a 1-bit image open. In the Edit Palette dialog box, click one of the two palette entries. Then, select a new color as you normally would in the Color dialog box.

NOTE

You can increase or decrease the color depth of an image only if the image has a single layer. If you try to adjust the color depth of a multilayered image, PSP asks whether you want to flatten the image. If you choose Yes, the image will be flattened and then the color depth will be adjusted. If you choose No, the image will be left alone and the color-depth adjustment will be aborted.

Appendix C
Web Graphics

Images are used on Web sites for a variety of purposes—as background tiles, buttons, bars, banners, and other accents. To be effective, however, Web graphics must be both well-designed and have file sizes that are compact enough to load quickly.

> **NOTE**
>
> The topic of Web graphics is more than enough to fill a book of its own, and there are quite a few good books on Web graphics. For more information on Web graphics issues, you might also want to head out to the Basics section of Lori's Web Graphics at **http://loriweb.pair.com/basics.html**.

GIF, JPEG, and PNG

Three file formats generally are supported for display in Web browsers: GIF, JPEG, and PNG. (Even now, however, you might find that your browser or Web host supports only GIF and JPEG.)

▶ GIF images are 8-bit, and thus can have a maximum of 256 colors. The compression method used for GIF is *lossless*, which means that GIF compression does not involve loss of data. GIF compression favors solid blocks of colors (especially horizontal blocks) and therefore is best for images with sharp edges and few colors, such as line art and other simple drawings.

▶ JPEG images are 24-bit, and thus can have up to 16.7 million colors. JPEG compression is *lossy*—when you compress a JPEG, you lose data. JPEG compression is best for images with many colors and subtle color shifts, such as photorealistic images.

NOTE

Some folks make the mistake of thinking that JPEG is always the best format for any Web graphic. But the JPEG versions of images that are best suited for GIF compression usually have larger file sizes and generally show degraded image quality when compared to their GIF counterparts.

If you're unsure which format to use to save a particular Web graphic, begin by saving the image in PSP format. Then you can use Save Copy As to save both a JPEG version and a GIF version of your image, allowing you to compare the two to see which is best in terms of file size and/or quality.

▶ PNG is many people's idea of an ideal format for digital images. PNGs can have up to 16.7 million colors, and the PNG compression method is lossless. However, universal standards for handling PNGs have not yet been established.

Transparent GIFs and PNGs

One of the reasons that GIFs and PNGs are so useful for Web graphics is that they allow transparency in your images. GIF lets you translate a single color to transparency. The PNG specification allows more than one color to be translated to transparency, and semitransparency is also allowed.

Reducing Color Depth

When you start working on a transparent GIF or PNG, you'll likely begin with a 24-bit color depth, because this makes all of PSP's filters and other operations available to you. When it comes time to set your transparent color, however, you need to reduce your color depth to 256 colors.

CAUTION

Although PNGs normally have 24-bit color depth, PSP reduces the color depth to 8-bit if you set a transparent color with Colors, Set Palette Transparency. And, as with GIFs, you can set only a single, completely transparent color in an 8-bit PNG.

You can maintain 24-bit color and still get transparency (and semi-transparency) with PNG by adding an alpha channel. Be aware, though, that not all browsers properly display PNGs that have an alpha channel. For now, the safest way to get transparency with PNGs is to use 8-bit paletted color.

NOTE

If your image's color depth isn't set to 256 colors (8-bit) before you start to set a transparent color, PSP prompts you to reduce the image's color depth, and then sends you to the Decrease Color Depth - 256 Colors dialog box. You are strongly advised *not* to depend on this method, though. Instead, reduce the color depth yourself before you start to set the transparent color. That way, if you need to clean up your image after the color-depth reduction, you can do so right away, and then you'll be ready to set the transparent color.

To reduce the color depth, choose **C**olors, **D**ecrease Color Depth, **256** Colors (8 bit). When the Decrease Color Depth - 256 Colors dialog box opens, choose the Palette and Reduction method (and other relevant options, if any). See Appendix B, "Adjusting Color Depth," for details on color-depth adjustment.

Eliminating Dithering

If you use one of the reduction methods that produces dithering, you should then check whether the color that you want to translate to transparency has become dithered. Keep in mind that only a single color can be translated to transparency, so if you have dithering where you want transparency, you need to eliminate the dithering. Use the Zoom tool (the "magnifying glass") to zoom in on your image to look for dithering. Figure C.1 shows an example of an image with a dithered background.

NOTE

Dithering is the process of mixing together two different colors that occur in a color palette to approximate a third color that doesn't occur on that palette.

Fig. C.1
Image with a dithered
background.

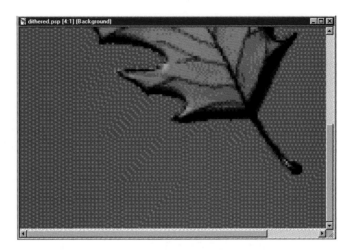

If you want to eliminate dithering, use the Color Replacer tool (discussed in Chapter 2, "Advanced Painting Tools"). For the image in Figure C.1, most of the dithered background is a medium blue, which is sprinkled with dots that are light blue, dark blue, and aqua.

To eliminate the dithering, take the following steps:

1. Set the foreground color in the Color Palette to one of these colors (for example, medium blue) by clicking with the Eye Dropper on a pixel of that color in the image.

2. Right-click one of the other pixel colors in the background to set the background color in the Color Palette. Choose the Color Replacer.

3. If the background color set in the Color Palette isn't present in the image except where you want to eliminate that color, just double-click in the image.

4. If, however, the color that you want to eliminate from some areas in your image also appears in other areas where you'd like to keep the color, you need to carefully paint with the Color Replacer to eliminate only the dithering in the area that you want to translate to transparency. Repeat this process with the other dithering colors until you've cleaned up the whole area so that it is only a single, solid color.

Figure C.2 shows a cleaned-up version of the image shown in Figure C.1.

Fig. C.2
Cleaned-up version of
the dithered image.

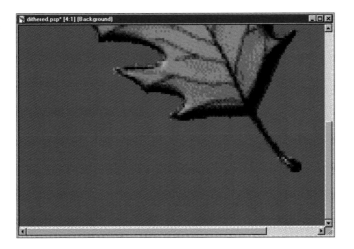

Setting Transparency

After you have a version of your image with a single, solid color in the
area that you want to make transparent, you're ready to set transparency.

CAUTION
Be sure that the color used for transparency occurs in your image *only* where
you want transparency. *All* occurrences of the color will be translated to
transparency, so you need to be careful.

PSP provides three ways to set transparency. One makes use of the
Transparent GIF export facility, discussed later in "Transparent GIF
Export." The other two methods—setting the background color and
setting the palette index—make use of the **C**olors, Set Palette
Transparency operation.

The first method that makes use of **C**olors, Set Palette **T**ransparency
enables you to set transparency based on the current background color as
set in the Color Palette.

1. Set the Color Palette's background color to the color that you want to translate to transparency by choosing the Dropper tool and right-clicking the appropriate color in your image.

2. Choose **C**olors, Set Palette **T**ransparency. You'll then see the Set Palette Transparency dialog box, shown in Figure C.3.

Fig. C.3

Set Palette Transparency dialog box, with transparency set to current background color.

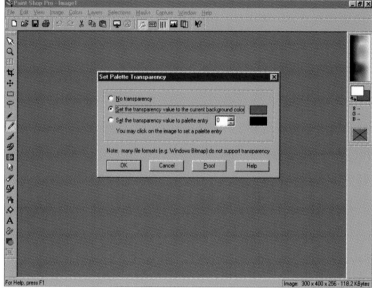

3. Select Set the transparency value to the current background color.

4. If you like, you can proof the result before actually setting the transparent color by clicking the Proof button. To set the transparent color, click OK.

The second method that makes use of the Colors, Set Palette Transparency operation enables you to set transparency by entering the palette index:

1. Choose **C**olors, Set Palette **T**ransparency to open the Set Palette Transparency dialog box, shown in Figure C.4.

Fig. C.4

Set Palette Transparency dialog box set to palette entry.

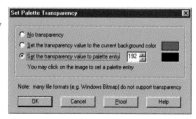

APPENDIXES

2. Select Set the transparency value to palette entry _ and fill in the appropriate palette index.

If you don't already know what the index is, move the cursor to your image. The cursor changes to the Dropper tool, and you can click the color you want for the transparent color. This enters the palette index for you automatically.

Alternatively, you can click the color swatch on the right to call up the image's palette, displayed in a dialog box titled Select Color From Palette. Then click on the background color in your image. The color's tile in the palette will then be highlighted, with the index number displayed at the bottom of the palette (see Figure C.5).

Fig. C.5
Palette index is indicated in the image's palette.

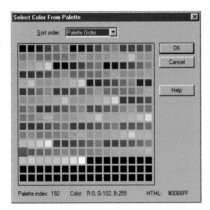

Click OK in the Select Color From Palette dialog box, and the palette index will be inserted in the Set Palette Transparency dialog box.

3. Proof the result, if you like, by clicking the Proof button. Click OK to set the transparent color to the color with the palette index that you specified.

No matter which method you use, you can proof the result after you set the transparent color by choosing **C**olors, **V**iew Palette Transparency. You can toggle off View Palette Transparency by selecting this menu option again. If something looks wrong, you can undo the setting by choosing **E**dit, **U**ndo or by pressing Ctrl+Z. You also can undo the transparency setting at any point (even in a later editing session) by choosing **C**olors, Set Palette **T**ransparency and selecting No transparency.

When you're satisfied that the transparent color has been set correctly, save your image as either a GIF or PNG. Remember that only these file formats support Web transparency.

TIP

Some ghosting almost always appears around the edges of the opaque figure in a transparent GIF or PNG. To lessen this effect, it's best to use as your transparent color a color that matches the color of the Web page on which the image will be displayed.

If there's a possibility that you'll be using the same image on different pages with different background colors, save your image as a PSP file. Place the figure on its own layer, with real transparency surrounding the figure. You can then alter the color of a layer below the figure's layer, as needed, and use Save Copy As to save a GIF or PNG with that background color. Change the lower layer's color whenever you need to, and use Save Copy As again to save another copy with another background color.

Interlaced GIFs and Progressive JPEGs

You should, of course, try to keep the file sizes of your Web graphics as compact as you can (while maintaining acceptable image quality). If you have a relatively large image that you just must use on your site, however, consider saving your image as an interlaced GIF or as a progressive JPEG.

Interlaced GIFs and progressive JPEGs load in stages. Using such an image won't decrease download time—in fact, download time is likely to increase—but many visitors to your site will find that having something to look at makes the wait seem shorter. (Be warned, though, that some folks find the gradual display annoying.)

To save a file as a progressive GIF, click the Options button on the Save As or Save Copy As dialog box, and then select Version 89a and Interlaced. To save a file as an interlaced JPEG, click the Options button on the Save As or Save Copy As dialog box, and then select Progressive Encoding.

NOTE

An interlaced GIF always has a larger file size than its non-interlaced counterpart, but a progressive JPEG almost always has a *smaller* file size than its non-progressive counterpart.

Optimizing Web Graphics

Because server space comes at a premium, and because you want to minimize download times for your visitors, you should do what you can to keep file size as small as possible without losing too much image quality. For JPEGs, you can reduce image size by increasing the compression level. For GIFs, you can reduce image size by reducing color depth or by eliminating dithered areas or other areas of repeated left-to-right color shifts. Be careful, though—overcompression or too severe a reduction in color depth can make image quality unacceptable.

Also keep in mind that you can reduce an image's file size by reducing its actual dimensions. Crop away unnecessary areas of your image or use Image, Resize to make your image smaller.

> **TIP**
>
> Animated GIFs should be optimized, too. You can either optimize each of the individual animation cels before assembling your animation, or optimize the completed animation itself. The second alternative is often the best, since this helps ensure that the individual cels share a common palette.
>
> Some GIF animation programs, including Jasc Software's Animation Shop, include a handy optimization facility.

PSP6's new Transparent GIF and JPEG File export facilities also can be used to optimize your Web graphics. Each of these export facilities is accessed by choosing File, Export on the PSP menubar. (Both export facilities will be discussed in the following sections.)

JPEG Export

JPEG export is great for exporting graphics projects to JPEG and for optimizing existing JPEGs. Try exporting a PSP image, like the one shown in Figure C.6, to JPEG.

Fig. C.6
An image in PSP format ready for JPEG export.

Choose File, Export, JPEG File to open the JPEG Saver dialog box, shown in Figure C.7.

Fig. C.7
Quality tab JPEG Saver dialog box.

The JPEG Saver dialog box has three tabs:

▶ **Quality**—Here, you select the compression level for your JPEG. Notice that when you alter the Compression value, the preview image in the upper-right corner changes to show you how your image will look at the selected compression level. Notice, too, that the file size of the compressed version is displayed below the Preview window.

▶ **Format**—Clicking this tab presents you with a choice of formats: Standard or Progressive (see Figure C.8).

Fig. C.8
Format tab of the JPEG Saver dialog box.

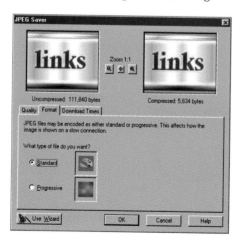

—*Standard.* This is the format you'll normally use, except for very large files. Standard JPEGs are displayed on a Web page only after the entire file is downloaded.

—*Progressive.* Progressive JPEGs are good for very large files. Progressive JPEGs usually have smaller file sizes than their Standard counterparts, and most people find that Progressive JPEGs appear to download faster than they actually do, since they are displayed in stages as they are being downloaded.

▶ **Download Times**—This tab displays the estimated download times of the compressed image at various baud rates (see Figure C.9).

Fig. C.9
Download Times tab of the JPEG Saver dialog box.

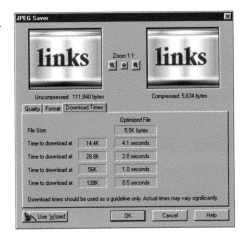

NOTE
There's a JPEG Wizard you can access by clicking the button on the lower left of the JPEG Saver window. You might want to just forgo this wizard, though, since the JPEG Saver itself is very easy to use and provides you with a dynamic preview of the effects of the adjustments you make.

Transparent GIF Export

Transparent GIF export is useful not only for making transparent GIFs, but for optimizing any GIF. Get in the habit of saving your Web graphics projects as PSP files and then using **F**ile, **E**xport, **T**ransparent GIF when you're ready to make the GIF copy. By keeping your Web projects in PSP format and then exporting them at the last minute, you also give yourself an easy way to try the graphic out both as a JPEG and as a GIF to see which results you prefer.

Try exporting the same PSP file just used for the JPEG Saver example. Choose File, Export, Transparent GIF, to open the Transparent GIF Saver dialog box with its five tabs, as shown in Figure C.10.

Fig. C.10
Transparency tab of the Transparent GIF Saver dialog box.

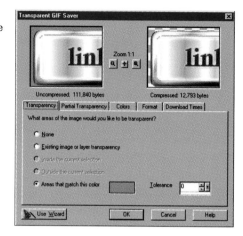

Transparency Tab

You have five options to choose from on the Transparency tab:

▶ **None**—No transparency.

▶ **Existing image or layer transparency**—Maintain whatever GIF transparency has already been assigned to the image, or translate layer transparency (if present) to GIF transparency.

▶ **Inside the current selection**—Areas inside the current selection become transparent. (Available only when the image contains an active selection.)

▶ **Outside the current selection**—Areas outside the current selection become transparent. (Available only when the image contains an active selection.)

▶ **Areas that match this color**—The chosen color becomes transparent. By default, the current background color in the Color Palette is selected and displayed in the color swatch to the right of this option. To change the color, click the color swatch to bring up the Color dialog box, or right-click to bring up the Recent Colors window.

You also can set the Tolerance for the color matching. The higher the Tolerance setting, the less closely pixels must be to the selected color in order for them to be translated to transparency.

Partial Transparency Tab

The second tab of the Transparent GIF Saver dialog box is Partial Transparency (see Figure C.11).

Fig. C.11
Partial Transparency tab
of the Transparent GIF
Saver dialog box.

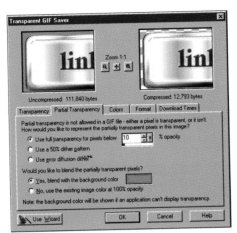

The PSP file format and several other file formats allow semi-transparency, but in GIF format a pixel must be either fully transparent or fully opaque. On the Partial Transparency tab, you tell PSP what to do with any semi-transparent pixels in your image.

There are two sets of options on the Partial Transparency tab. To determine how to represent semi-transparent pixels in your image, select one of these options:

▶ **Use full transparency for pixels below _ % opacity**—If you select this option, then any pixels below the percentage opacity that you specify will be translated to full transparency.

▶ **Use 50% dither pattern**—With this option, semi-transparent pixels are translated to full opacity. The semi-transparent pixels are dithered with the selected blend color or the existing image color, depending on what you select for the blending option.

▶ **Use error diffusion**—As with the previous option, this tells PSP to translate semi-transparent pixels to full opacity. The difference between this option and the previous one is that here error diffusion is the method used for pixel blending.

For the next set of options on the Partial Transparency tab, you're asked to choose whether you want to blend the semi-transparent pixels (if they're translated to full opacity):

▶ **Yes, blend with the background color**—Blends the translated pixel's color with the background color. You can alter the blending background color by clicking the color swatch to call up the Color dialog box or by right-clicking the color swatch to call up the Recent Colors dialog box.

▶ **No, use the existing image color at 100% opacity**—No blending takes place. Instead, all of the semi-transparent pixels keep their original color and are made fully opaque.

Colors Tab

The third tab in the Transparent GIF Saver dialog box is the Colors tab (see Figure C.12).

Fig. C.12
Colors tab of the Transparent GIF Saver dialog box.

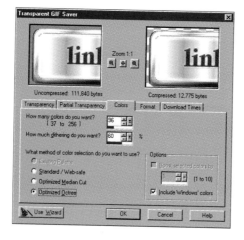

Here, you determine the characteristics of the GIF image's palette, including the number of colors in the palette, the amount of dithering, and the palette creation method.

The fewer colors used, the smaller the image file. If you reduce the colors too much, however, the image quality will suffer. Dithering will increase the file size, at least somewhat, but it can boost image quality by approximating colors that aren't present in the palette. For information on palette creation methods, see Appendix B, "Adjusting Color Depth."

Format Tab

The Format tab of the Transparent GIF Saver dialog box (see Figure C.13) gives you the option of making your image either Non-Interlaced or Interlaced.

Fig. C.13
Format tab of the Transparent GIF Saver dialog box.

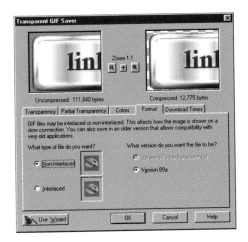

Non-Interlaced files will always be smaller, but you might want to choose Interlaced for large files since the interlacing provides viewers with the illusion that the image is loading faster than it actually is.

The Format tab also gives you the option of saving the GIF in either Version 87a or Version 89a. Since all current Web browsers support Version 89a and that's the only version which supports transparency, there's little reason ever to choose Version 87a.

Download Times Tab

The last tab of the Transparent GIF Saver is Download Times. As with the JPEG Saver, this tab shows estimated download times at various baud rates.

NOTE

The Transparent GIF Saver also offers you a wizard, which you access by clicking the button on the lower left of the dialog box. Creating and optimizing transparent GIFs is not as straightforward as optimizing JPEGs, so you might want to give this wizard a try. The Transparent GIF Saver itself gives you much more control, however, and also offers you a dynamic preview at all times, so try optimizing your GIFs with and without the wizard to see which method you prefer.

Appendix D
Resources

This appendix lists URLs for a number of resources that can help you create graphics with PSP. The list is far from exhaustive, but it's sure to be helpful. Please think of this as just a starting point—you're certain to find many other helpful sites! Remember, though, these links might change periodically, like all things on the Web.

PSP Tips and Tutorials

▶ Lori's Web Graphics at **http://loriweb.pair.com/**

▶ Abstract Dimensions at **http://psptips.com/**

▶ GraphoManiac at **http://hem1.passagen.se/grafoman/**

▶ GraphX Design - PSP Tutorials at **http://www.grafx-design.com/psp_tut.html**

▶ The Hood: Paintshop Pro 5 Digital Art Gallery at **http://bart.northnet.com.au/~robrow/**

▶ Making Graphics at **http://www.interlog.com/~sarahbc/mg/index.html**

▶ Robin's Nest at **http://www.annapolis.net/members/rkirkey/index.html**

▶ State of Entropy: Paint Shop Pro Graphics at **http://www.state-of-entropy.com**

▶ Web Graphics on a Budget at **http://mardiweb.com/web/**

For collections of links to these and other PSP tutorial sites, head over to Jasc Software's Digital Studio at **http://www.jasc.com/studio.html** and to Fritz Wagoner's Paint Shop Pro Tutorials Unlimited at **http://www.kconline.com/fwagoner/indexpsptu.htm** and Renald's PSP Tutorials at **http://www.cablevision.qc.ca/renlev/psp5tut.html**.

APPENDIXES

Tubes and Brushes

▶ Diana's Free Tubes at **http://members.xoom.com/tubes/**

▶ Mousehold Creations – Custom Brushes at
http://www.capecodmouse.com/moushold/psp/t3brush.html

▶ Nikki's Brush Boutique at
http://www.nikkisgallery.com/brushes/brushind.htm

▶ The Page of Blues at
http://members.tripod.com/blueslighthouse/index.html

▶ Tubaholics Anonymous at **http://home.att.net/~skeldalehouse/**

Filters

▶ The Filter Factory Galleries (PC Resources for Photoshop – Plugins),
at **http://www.netins.net/showcase/wolf359/plugins.htm**

▶ The Filter Factory CD at **http://pluginhead.i-us.com/ffcd.htm**

▶ PlugIn Com HQ (home of PlugIn Commander and Edge & Frame
Galaxy) at **http://pico.i-us.com/**

▶ The Plugin Head at **http://pluginhead.i-us.com/**

▶ Alien Skin's Eye Candy and Xenofex at **http://www.alienskin.com/**

▶ AutoF/X's Photo/Graphic Edges and other plugins at
http://www.autofx.com/

▶ Flaming Pear's Blade Pro and other filters at
http://www.flamingpear.com/

▶ MetaCreations Kai's Power Tools at **http://www.metacreations.com/**

▶ Ulead's Web.Plugins and other filters and utilities at
http://www.ulead.com/

Blade Pro Presets

▶ The Cheroke Family's Homepage at
http://www.inland.net/~acheroke/

▶ mypresets at DesignsbyDonna at
http://www.designsbydonna.com/presets1.html

▶ Northlite's Blade Pro Presets at
http://www.northlite.net/bladepro.html

Newsgroups and Discussion Boards

▶ PSP Usenet Newsgroup at **news:comp.graphics.apps.paint-shop-pro**

▶ i/us PSP Discussion Forum at **http://www.i-us.com/share.htm**

▶ PSP Interactive Zone at **http://www.pspiz.com/**

Other PSP and General Graphics Resources

▶ WDVL: Graphics Tools Techniques, Examples, and Resources, at **http://WDVL.com/Authoring/Graphics/**

▶ WebReference.com: Web/Authoring/ Graphics at **http://webreference.com/authoring/graphics/index.html**

▶ Ziff-Davis University at **http://www.zdu.com/**

Scanning and Digital Cameras

▶ Wayne Fulton's Scan Tips at **http://www.scantips.com/**

▶ Microtek at **http://www.microtek.com/**

▶ Kodak at **http://www.kodak.com/**

I listed Microtek and Kodak, the equipment that I personally use, but if you have different equipment, be sure to check out the appropriate manufacturer's site for helpful information and the latest drivers.

Appendix E
PSP Keyboard Shortcuts

Table E.1. PSP Keyboard Shortcuts

Shortcut	Function
A	Freehand Selection tool ("lasso")
B	Paintbrush tool
D	Deform tool
E	Eraser
F	Flood Fill tool
G	Zoom tool ("magnifying glass")
M	Magic Wand
N	Clone Brush
Q	Vector Object Selection tool
R	Crop tool
S	Selection tool
U	Airbrush
V	Mover tool
X	Text tool
Z	Retouch tool
. (period)	Picture Tube
, (comma)	Color Replacer
/ (slash)	Preset Shapes
Spacebar	Step through tools
Del	Clear canvas/layer

Shortcut	Function
C	Hide/Restore Color Palette
H	Hide/Restore Histogram
L	Hide/Restore Layer Palette
O	Hide/Restore Tool Options palette
P	Hide/Restore Tool Palette
T	Hide/Restore Toolbar
Tab	Hide/Restore all floating palettes
Shift+A	Full Screen Edit
Shift+B	Brightness/Contrast Adjust
Shift+C	Start Capture (minimizes PSP to Windows taskbar)
Shift+D	Duplicate Window
Shift+E	Equalize (Histogram function)
Shift+G	Gamma Correction
Shift+H	Hue/Saturation/Lightness
Shift+I	Image Information
Shift+K	Invert Mask
Shift+L	Colorize
Shift+M	Highlight/Midtone/Shadow Adjust
Shift+O	Load Color Palette
Shift+P	Edit Color Palette
Shift+R	Crop to Selection
Shift+S	Resize Image
Shift+T	Stretch (Histogram function)
Shift+U	Red/Green/Blue Adjust
Shift+W	New window
Shift+Y	Hide All (mask)

Shortcut	Function
Shift+Z	Posterize
Shift+right arrow	Nudge selection right
Shift+left arrow	Nudge selection left
Shift+up arrow	Nudge selection up
Shift+down arrow	Nudge selection down
Ctrl+right arrow	Nudge selection right
Ctrl+left arrow	Nudge selection left
Ctrl+up arrow	Nudge selection up
Ctrl+down arrow	Nudge selection down
Ctrl+Shift+right arrow	Nudge selection right 10 pixels
Ctrl+Shift+left arrow	Nudge selection left 10 pixels
Ctrl+Shift+up arrow	Nudge selection up 10 pixels
Ctrl+Shift+down arrow	Nudge selection down 10 pixels
Alt+Ctrl+right arrow	Move a selection and a copy of its contents right 1 pixel
Alt+Ctrl+left arrow	Move a selection and a copy of its contents left 1 pixel
Alt+Ctrl+up arrow	Move a selection and a copy of its contents up 1 pixel
Alt+Ctrl+down arrow	Move a selection and a copy of its contents down 1 pixel
Shift+Alt+Ctrl+right arrow	Move a selection and a copy of its contents right 10 pixels
Shift+Alt+Ctrl+left arrow	Move a selection and a copy of its contents left 10 pixels
Shift+Alt+Ctrl+up arrow	Move a selection and a copy of its contents up 10 pixels
Shift+Alt+Ctrl+down arrow	Move a selection and a copy of its contents down 10 pixels

Shortcut	Function
Ctrl+A	Select All
Ctrl+B	Browse
Ctrl+C	Copy
Ctrl+D	Deselect (select none)
Ctrl+E	Paste as New Selection
Ctrl+F	Float Selection
Ctrl+H	Feather Selection
Ctrl+I	Flip Image
Ctrl+K	Edit Mask
Ctrl+L	Paste as New Layer
Ctrl+M	Mirror
Ctrl+N	New file
Ctrl+O	Open file
Ctrl+P	Print
Ctrl+R	Rotate Image
Ctrl+S	Save file
Ctrl+V	Paste as New Image
Ctrl+W	Fit to Window
Ctrl+X	Cut
Ctrl+Z	Undo
Ctrl+(layer number)	Select as Current Layer
Ctrl+Alt+G	View Grid (toggle)
Ctrl+Alt+N	Normal Viewing
Ctrl+Alt+V	View Mask (toggle)
Ctrl+Del	Delete file
Shift+Ctrl+A	Full Screen Preview

Shortcut	Function
Shift+Ctrl+C	Copy Merged Layers
Shift+Ctrl+E	Paste as Transparent Selection
Shift+Ctrl+F	Defloat Selection
Shift+Ctrl+I	Invert Selection
Shift+Ctrl+L	Paste Into Selection
Shift+Ctrl+M	Hide Selection Marquee
Shift+Ctrl+P	Promote Selection to Layer
Shift+Ctrl+S	Create Selection from Mask
Shift+Ctrl+T	Center Floating Palettes
Shift+Ctrl+V	Transparent Color (Selection)
Shift+Ctrl+1	Decrease Color Depth - 2 Colors
Shift+Ctrl+2	Decrease Color Depth - 16 Colors
Shift+Ctrl+3	Decrease Color Depth - 256 Colors
Shift+Ctrl+4	Decrease Color Depth - 32K Colors
Shift+Ctrl+5	Decrease Color Depth - 64K Colors
Shift+Ctrl+6	Decrease Color Depth - X Colors
Shift+Ctrl+8	Increase Color Depth - 16 Colors
Shift+Ctrl+9	Increase Color Depth - 256 Colors
Shift+Ctrl+0	Increase Color Depth - 16M Colors
F12	Save
Ctrl+F12	Save Copy As

You can use the following shortcuts in Node Edit mode (refer to Chapter 5, "Working with Vectors") to reshape and refine vector objects:

Table E.2. Node Edit Keyboard Shortcuts

Shortcut	Function
Del	Delete
F5	Refresh
Ctrl+A	Select All
Ctrl+B	Line Before (Node Type)
Ctrl+C	Copy
Ctrl+D	Select None
Ctrl+F	Line After (Node Type)
Ctrl+E	Toggle between Edit and Drawing modes
Ctrl+J	Join selected nodes
Ctrl+K	Break the curve
Ctrl+L	Convert to Line (Node Type)
Ctrl+Q	Quit Node Edit
Ctrl+S	Symmetric (Node Type)
Ctrl+T	Smooth/Tangent (Node Type)
Ctrl+V	Paste
Ctrl+X	Cusp (Node Type)
Ctrl+Z	Undo
Ctrl+R	Reverse Contour
Shift+Ctrl+C	Close the curve
Shift+Ctrl+R	Reverse Path
Shift+Ctrl+S	Asymmetric (Node Type)
Ctrl+Alt+Z	Redo
Ctrl+1	Curve Before (Node Type)
Ctrl+2	Curve After (Node Type)

You can use the following shortcuts when the PSP Browser is open and in focus:

Table E.3. Browser Keyboard Shortcuts

Shortcut	Function
Ctrl+A	Select All
Ctrl+B	Go to new folder
Ctrl+D	Select None
Ctrl+F	Find file
Ctrl+M	Move selected image(s)
Ctrl+P	Print
Ctrl+R	Rename selected image
Ctrl+W	Fit window to thumbnails
Ctrl+Y	Copy selected image(s)
Ctrl+Del	Delete selected image(s)
Alt+F3	Find file
F3	Repeat Find
F5	Update Thumbnails
F6	Next pane
Shift+F6	Previous pane
Ctrl+F5	Refresh Tree
* (on numeric keypad)	Expand selected folder
Shift+Tab	Next pane
Shift+I	Image Information
Alt+Enter	Image Information
Enter	Open selected image(s)

You can use the following shortcuts in Animation Shop (refer to Chapter 12, "Animation Shop") to create and modify animations:

Table E.4. Animation Shop Keyboard Shortcuts

Shortcut	Function
F1	Help Topics
F12	Save As
Ctrl+A	Select All
Ctrl+C	Copy
Ctrl+D	Select None
Ctrl+E	Paste Into Selected Frame
Ctrl+L	Paste As New Frames
Ctrl+N	New
Ctrl+O	Open
Ctrl+S	Save
Ctrl+V	Paste As New Animation
Ctrl+X	Cut
Ctrl+Z	Undo
Shift+D	Duplicate Animation

NOTE

For all keyboard shortcuts that use numbers, only the keyboard number keys can be used, not the number keys on the numeric keypad.

NOTE

A keyboard shortcut might be unavailable in PSP if you have another open application and it intercepts the keystroke.

Index

INDEX

INDEX

Order Form

Postal Orders:
  Muska & Lipman Publishing
  2645 Erie Avenue, Suite 41
  Cincinnati, Ohio 45208

On-Line Orders or more information:
  http://www.muskalipman.com
Fax Orders:
  (513) 924-9333

Title/ISBN	Price/Cost

eBay Online Auctions
0-9662889-4-7

Quantity _____

× $14.95

Total Cost _____

MP3 Power! with Winamp
0-9662889-3-9

Quantity _____

× $29.99

Total Cost _____

Paint Shop Pro 6 Power!
0-9662889-2-0

Quantity _____

× $39.99

Total Cost _____

Title/ISBN	Price/Cost

Digital Camera Solutions
0-9662889-6-3

Quantity _____

× $29.95

Total Cost _____

Scanner Solutions
0-9662889-7-1

Quantity _____

× $29.95

Total Cost _____

Subtotal _____

Sales Tax _____
(please add 6% for books
shipped to Ohio addresses)

Shipping _____
($4.00 for the first book,
$2.00 each additional book)

TOTAL PAYMENT ENCLOSED _____

Ship to:

  Company _____

  Name _____

  Address _____

  City _____ State _____ Zip _____ Country _____

Educational facilities, companies, and organizations interested in multiple copies of these books should contact the publisher for quantity discount information. Training manuals, CD-ROMs, electronic versions, and portions of these books are also available individually or can be tailored for specific needs.

Thank you for your order.